The Italian Invert

The Italian Invert

A Gay Man's Intimate Confessions to **Émile Zola**

EDITED BY
Michael Rosenfeld
WITH
William A. Peniston

COLUMBIA UNIVERSITY PRESS
NEW YORK

Columbia University Press
Publishers Since 1893
New York   Chichester, West Sussex
cup.columbia.edu
Copyright © 2022 Columbia University Press
All rights reserved

Library of Congress Cataloging-in-Publication Data
Names: Rosenfeld, Michael, 1976– editor. | Peniston, William A., 1959– editor.
Title: The Italian invert : a gay man's intimate confessions to Émile Zola / edited by Michael Rosenfeld, with William A. Peniston ; translated by Nancy Erber and William A. Peniston.
Other titles: Confessions d'un homosexuel à Émile Zola. English
Description: New York : Columbia University Press, [2021] | "Adapted and translated from Confessions d'un homosexuel à Émile Zola: Première édition non censurée du "Roman d'un inverti," edited by Michael Rosenfeld [copyright] 2017 Nouvelles Éditions Place"—Verso. | Includes bibliographical references and index.
Identifiers: LCCN 2021024752 (print) | LCCN 2021024753 (ebook) | ISBN 9780231204897 (paperback) | ISBN 9780231204880 (hardback) | ISBN 9780231555739 (ebook)
Subjects: LCSH: Zola, Émile, 1840–1902—Correspondence. | Saint-Paul, Georges, 1870-1937—Correspondence. | Homosexuality. | Gay men—Italy—Biography.
Classification: LCC HQ76.2.I8 C6613 2021 (print) | LCC HQ76.2.I8 (ebook) | DDC 306.76/609224 [B]—dc23
LC record available at https://lccn.loc.gov/2021024752
LC ebook record available at https://lccn.loc.gov/2021024753

Adapted and translated from *Confessions d'un homosexuel à Émile Zola: Première édition non censurée du "Roman d'un inverti,"* edited by Michael Rosenfeld. © 2017 Nouvelles Éditions Place.
"The Novel of an Invert": reproduced from *Queer Lives: Men's Autobiographies from Nineteenth-Century France*, edited and translated by William A. Peniston and Nancy Erber, by permission of the University of Nebraska Press. © 2007 The Board of Regents of the University of Nebraska.
"Selected Works by Dr. Saint-Paul," translated by William A. Peniston and Nancy Erber. © 2018 William A. Peniston and Nancy Erber (TXu 2–112–951).
This work received the French Voices Award for excellence in publication and translation. French Voices is a program created and funded by the French Embassy in the United States and the French American Cultural Exchange (FACE) Foundation.

French Voices logo designed by Serge Bloch

Book & cover design: Chang Jae Lee
Cover image: The Metropolitan Museum of Art, Costume Institute

With funding provided by the University of Guelph, Guelph, Ontario, Canada.

Dedicated by Michael Rosenfeld in loving memory of his sister Dania,
October 30, 1972–November 20, 2015

Contents

List of Illustrations ix
Prologue
   Cyrille Zola-Place xi
Foreword to the French Edition
   Alain Pagès xiii
Foreword to the American Edition
   Vernon A. Rosario xvii

Introduction: The *Ménage-à-Trois* of Zola, Saint-Paul, and the Italian "Invert"
   Michael Rosenfeld with Nancy Erber 1

Part I: The Confessions of a Homosexual to Émile Zola 39

Preface by Émile Zola 43

The Novel of an Invert 47

The Sequel to the Novel of an Invert 99

Other Particularities 139

The Italian Man's Family Tree
   Michael Rosenfeld 143

Part II: Selected Works by Dr. Georges Saint-Paul 147

Dr. Georges Saint-Paul, Man of Science
   Clive Thomson 149

First Edition (1896)   169

   Editorial Comment
      Clive Thomson and Michael Rosenfeld   169

   Inquiry Into Sexual Inversion: Questionnaire   170

   Inquiry Into Sexual Inversion: Responses   177

In Memoriam: Émile Zola   187

   Editorial Comment
      Clive Thomson and Michael Rosenfeld   187

   In Memoriam: Émile Zola   188

Second Edition (1910)   205

   Editorial Comment
      Clive Thomson and Michael Rosenfeld   205

   Preface to the Second Edition   206

Third Edition (1930)   215

   Editorial Comment
      Clive Thomson and Michael Rosenfeld   215

   Preface to the Third Edition   215

Acknowledgments   219
Bibliography   223
List of Contributors   231
Index   233

Illustrations

Fig. 1. Émile Zola in his early fifties, photographed by Paul Nadar 42
Fig. 2. Two fragments from the original letter to Zola 46
Fig. 3. First page of recently discovered letter to Dr. Saint-Paul 98
Fig. 4. The Italian man's physical attributes and those of his lover 132
Fig. 5. The Italian man's family tree 142
Fig. 6. Photographic portrait of Dr. Georges Saint-Paul as a medical student 148

Prologue
Cyrille Zola-Place

As the publisher of the original French-language edition of *Confessions d'un homosexuel à Émile Zola*, I am pleased to see this English-language edition, *The Italian Invert: A Gay Man's Intimate Confessions to Émile Zola*. As a descendant of Émile Zola, I am proud of my great-grandfather's role in presenting this remarkable autobiographical account to the public back in 1896. In this restoration, based on the recent discovery of the original manuscript of the September 1896 letter, of passages deleted from the 1889 letters, and of several other documents, the author's words are not only eloquent and fascinating but also revelatory of a unique and optimistic perspective on humanity. The young man refused to accept society's condemnation of homosexuality and questioned the accusations leveled against "inverts." A truly pioneering struggle for the right to be different and the pursuit of happiness, this confession still resonates today, everywhere that freedom is gradually being restricted to a space hemmed in by issues of security and identity.

These *Confessions*, published for the first time in English in their complete and unexpurgated version, have a genuine political power as a message, but they are also poetic as an act. For us at Nouvelles Éditions Place, publishing this book was absolutely necessary. Besides its historical, social, and literary importance, we recognized that we needed to fulfill the mission this young man had chosen for himself in writing his own story for Zola and not holding anything back. His goals were to change the way society regards those who do not belong but who are certainly part of it and to sharpen our senses to combat the sort of cultural uniformity that erases

---

A descendant of Émile Zola, Cyrille Zola-Place is chief editor of Nouvelles Éditions Place and French publisher of *Confessions d'un homosexuel à Émile Zola* (2017). Under the pseudonym Cyrille Comnène, he has written several novels, including *Zola: rêve sans nom: roman* (2014).

all individual differences. This is imperative in order to defend the rights of gays and lesbians, Jews and Muslims, poets and artists, women, and everyone who is different. Publishing the unexpurgated *Confessions* along with their prepublication background, a detailed examination of their reception, and their literary and social history gives us an unparalleled opportunity to send a still urgent message.

Foreword to the French Edition
Alain Pagès

The text of *The Novel of an Invert*—the passionate confessions of a young Italian homosexual—appeared for the first time in 1894–1895 in several successive installments in *Archives d'Anthropologie Criminelle / Archives of Criminal Anthropology*, a journal of psychology and sociology edited by Alexandre Lacassagne. These articles were published under the name of Dr. Laupts. He reissued them in 1896 in his work *Tares et poisons: Perversion et perversité sexuelles / Defects and Poisons: Sexual Perversion and Perversity*, which was published by the publishing house Georges Carré in Paris. The cover announced in bold type a "preface" by Émile Zola. A new edition appeared in bookstores much later, in 1910, which included the initial letters but also a "sequel"—a follow-up letter written to the doctor after the anonymous author discovered his "confessions" in a medical treatise. This time, however, the editor revealed his true identity by appending to it his own name, Georges Saint-Paul; "Laupts" was an anagram—an inversion of his real name. The identity of the author remained unknown.

Therefore, almost fifteen years passed before the sequel of these scandalous confessions saw the light of day. Its publication—and the difficulties arising from it—include a number of concerns. In effect, three obstacles had to be overcome to prevent legal complications or to allay readers' fears: (1) the scientific apparatus had to be situated primarily in a system

---

Alain Pages is the editor of *Les Cahiers Naturalistes*. He has published *La Bataille litteraire* (1989), *Le Naturalisme* (1989), *Émile Zola de "J'accuse" au Pantheon* (2008), *Une journee dans l'affaire Dreyfus* (2011), *Zola et le groupe de Medan* (2014), and *L'affaire Dreyfus: Verites et legendes* (2019). In collaboration with Brigitte Émile-Zola, he has also collected and published Zola's intimate letters to his mistress, *Lettres à Jeanne Rozeot* (2004), and to his wife, *Lettres à Alexandrine* (2015).

of categorization and classification, placing it among "criminal archives" and inserting it into the paradigm of "defects" and "poisons," of "sexual perversion" and "sexual perversity"; (2) a discourse of authority relying on the complexity of psychiatric knowledge and invoking the celebrity of the famous writer Émile Zola introduced a narrative that was presented as a cautionary tale; and (3) authorial anonymity protected Dr. Saint-Paul for a long time and continues, even today, to conceal the identity of the actual author of this story.

The history of this "novel"—of a particular genre—unfolded according to the fragmentary nature of the serial: first, as several installments in the journal *Archives d'Anthropologie Criminelle*, then, as a case study in a medical treatise, and finally, as an autobiography in two parts, composed of a main text and a sequel written several years apart. The long publishing history of these confessions is significant even today because I discovered the manuscript of the author's letter to Dr. Saint-Paul in 2011 during my research in the Zola family archives (thanks to the generosity of Dr. Brigitte Émile-Zola). This discovery clears up an uncertainty: if it does not reveal the author's name, it does, at the very least, attest to the originality of its writing; it provides valuable evidence for the authenticity of this story. Certainly, doubts may persist, but it is difficult to believe that we have here a fictional account, a "novel" that was created out of whole cloth. It is a genuine autobiography, written in the form of a letter, seeking a wider audience by this method.

Inspired by the model of Jean-Jacques Rousseau's work, the author of this story delved into his family origins at length before revealing the details of "an awful illness of the soul" that he described in depth in the course of his narrative. Things that were unclear to him in the first part of these confessions are clarified in the second part. This dramatic story with multiple adventures does not conceal from the reader any of the physical or psychological torments experienced by its protagonist, but it ends on a rather reassuring note.

To understand all its layers, a critical edition that reveals the different versions of these confessions and shows the diversity of the supporting texts is necessary. This is the task that Michael Rosenfeld set for himself in the pages that follow. His attentive and meticulous work allows us to appreciate both *The Novel of an Invert* and its *Sequel* in all their complexity. Complementing this research is the detailed portrayal of Dr. Georges Saint-Paul by Clive Thomson, who explores the fascinating character of this young doctor, the student of the famous professor Dr. Lacassagne, to whom Zola gave this document in 1893.

In this story, Zola played a vital role as an intercessor. He explained it in his letter that Saint-Paul published as the preface to the first edition. As the recipient of a document that had been sent to him several years before, and not knowing what to do with it as a writer, Zola decided to entrust it to a doctor who could make use of it in the interest of science. Ostensibly, he stepped aside, entrusting to another the responsibility of publishing a document that he could not undertake. In reality, he put himself forward by taking action, since his was the only name that appeared on the cover: Saint-Paul had hidden behind the pseudonym Laupts. By doing so, Zola joined the debate. He took a risk by writing a preface in which he defended the interest that the publication of this text offered. It is "a genuine physiological phenomenon," he wrote. "Nothing is more tragic, in my opinion, and nothing calls out more for a cure, if there is one." And he added: "We don't condemn a hunchback because he was born that way. Why despise a man for acting like a woman if he was born half a woman?"

It is probable that the literary quality of The Novel of an Invert counted for much in the decision that Zola made. The human drama that these confessions portrayed in such a clear manner moved him above all else. In November 1897, a year after the publication of Saint-Paul's work, another story caught his attention, motivating him to enter into the great struggle of the last years of his life: "the poignant drama" experienced by an innocent man, Alfred Dreyfus, condemned in an unjust manner for a crime that he had not committed.

"Confronted with these documents of such a tragic beauty that life has put before us, my novelist heart beat with passionate admiration," Zola exclaimed in Le Figaro on November 25, 1897, as he threw himself into the battle over the Dreyfus Affair. For the novelist, there were two kinds of "documents": those that he researched in an active way, and those that he did not invent but that "life" brought to him. The latter were the most destabilizing. Good sense demanded that they be kept at a distance in order to preserve his piece of mind. On the other hand, Zola's greatness had been in determining, during those essential moments in his life, how to use those controversial materials that his contemporaries placed before his eyes. His engagement held fast in his supreme courage: to dare to look when others turned their heads, to dare to speak out against the suffering of the innocents with genuine emotion and in the name of humanity.

Foreword to the American Edition
Vernon A. Rosario

> Don't hide yourself in regret
> Just love yourself and you're set
> I'm on the right track, baby
> I was born this way.
> —Lady Gaga, 2011

The Italian aristocrat who sent his epistolary confession anonymously to the novelist Émile Zola in 1889 was surprised to find it printed in a medical book on "sexual perversion" by a Dr. Laupts under the heading "The Novel of a Born Invert." Although the Italian would have preferred to have been artistically transformed into a fabulous fictional character, he was nevertheless flattered enough that he sent extensive further details of his life directly to the doctor. How much *more* thrilled would he be to see his autobiography republished and translated into English more than a century later! But would he be happy with the multiple reclassifications of his sexual nature? We can never know. Having read his confessions many times over the past three decades, however, I would bet he would simply revel in the attention. Over time he has been labeled an invert, a born invert, a sexual pervert, a feminine-form born invert, a pederast, a homosexual, a gay man. This reclassification over the past century is evidence of the medicalization and the cultural politics of sexuality since the 1880s. It is just

---

An associate clinical professor of psychiatry at the University of California, Los Angeles, Vernon A. Rosario is also a child psychiatrist in the Los Angeles County Department of Mental Health. With a medical degree and doctorate in the history of science, he is the author of The Erotic Imagination: French Histories of Perversion (1997), editor of Homosexuality and Science: A Guide to the Debates (1997), coeditor (with Paula Bennett) of Solitary Pleasures: The Historical Literary and Artistic Discourses of Autoeroticism (1995), and a frequent contributor to The Gay and Lesbian Review.

one of many reasons this text deserves to be republished and reread in the current era of queer sexuality and nonbinary gender. Only by a close reading of the text can we appreciate the author's complex psychosexual development within the context of the medical and social history of his time. His life story challenges easy classification just as much as that of any queer youth today.

The twenty-three-year-old Italian resisted any labels for his sexuality. He never called himself an "invert" or a "born invert." Those were diagnoses applied by Dr. Georges Saint-Paul, who also wrote under the pseudonyms Dr. Laupts and G. Espé de Metz. (He had his own issues in using a single name for himself.) Dr. Saint-Paul entitled the confession "The Novel of an Invert" when it was first published in the *Archives d'Anthropologie Criminelle* (1894–1895).[1] By the second monograph edition of the *Novel* (1910),[2] Saint-Paul was routinely referring to the phenomenon as "homosexuality," and since then, the Italian has routinely found himself inscribed in the genealogical history of "homosexuality," along with the other "contrary sexuals" and "sexual inverts" of the nineteenth century.[3] But were nineteenth-century inverts simply the forebearers of twentieth-century homosexuals? Sigmund Freud's writings certainly support this lineage. His *Three Essays on the Theory of Sexuality* (1905) opens by distinguishing three types of "inversion." By the 1915 edition of the work, however, Freud had switched to using the word "homosexual" for the same phenomenon.[4]

The Italian should have known how to label himself. He was well-educated and claimed to be familiar with the sexological literature. He evidently perused medical books in bookstores often enough to have encountered

---

1. Dr. Laupts [Georges Saint-Paul], "Le Roman d'un inverti," *Archives d'Anthropologie Criminelle* (1894): 211–15, 367–73, 729–31; (1895): 131–38, 228–41, 320–25.

2. Dr. Laupts [Georges Saint-Paul], *L'Homosexualité et les types homosexuels* (Paris: Vigot, 1910).

3. Focusing on literary texts, Benjamin Kahan explores problems with the dating of the emergence of homosexual identity to the late nineteenth century and the simultaneous casting aside of "minor perversions" in the wake of the sexological and cultural focus on a binarized sexuality (homosexual versus heterosexual). Kahan, *The Book of Minor Perverts: Sexology, Etiology, and the Emergences of Sexuality* (Chicago: University of Chicago Press, 2019).

4. Freud's three categories were *absolut invertiert* (absolute invert), *amphigen invertiert* (amphigenic invert), and *okkasionell invertiert* (contingent invert). Sigmund Freud, *Three Essays on the Theory of Sexuality* (1905), trans. James Strachey (London: Imago, 1949).

his own story published in 1896. Therefore, by the time he wrote in the late 1880s, he probably had encountered the terms "*pédéraste*" and "*inverti*" commonly used in the sexological literature of the time. Nevertheless, he emphatically viewed himself as distinct. He refused to be clumped with the "debauched," "common," and "disgusting" men who have sex with men, like Zola's character Baptiste from *La Curée / The Kill*, "because the debauchery in which [Baptiste] engaged has nothing to do with love and is only an absolutely material thing, a question of congenital malformation that doctors have observed and described more than once."[5] No! He saw himself as gorgeous and gifted. Although he often wallowed in self-recrimination for his sexual inclinations, his congenital effeminacy was what made him exquisite: "As a man with a beautiful body, I have the mind, the charm, and all the tastes of the most delightful women. I can therefore profit sometimes from the combined gifts of both sexes even if I sometimes torment myself for being neither a man nor a woman."[6]

Particularly in his first confession to Zola, the Italian emphasized the effeminacy and gender nonconformity in his childhood development. As a child he was "pretty and cute as a little girl," and everyone called him the "Little Madonna." He loved his little dresses, and he had a tantrum when forced to wear boys' clothes at age four: "I experienced a real feeling of shame. . . . It seemed to me that I was being denied something that I was always destined to wear." He secretly continued to engage in cross-dressing: "My love for dresses with trains persisted." He declared: "Other boys' games almost frightened me." He had a fit when someone joked he was sprouting a mustache, and he ran to a mirror. There he was relieved to find not even peach fuzz because "I enjoyed thinking of myself as a woman." After having a chance to stroke a servant's erect penis, the teenage Italian "cursed Heaven that I wasn't born a woman" and had no orifice in which to insert the virile member.[7] After many failed attempts to enjoy anal sex with an older man (the Captain), he declared: "Maybe I will never stop regretting not being a woman."[8]

---

5. *The Novel of an Invert* (hereafter *Novel*), "First Document," in this book.

6. *Novel*, "Third Document." See the introduction to part 1 of this book ("The Confessions") for an explanation of the underlining in this translation.

7. *Novel*, "First Document."

8. *Novel*, "Third Document."

In early adulthood, he still described his body as feminine: "My pelvis is wide like a woman's"; his chin was "smooth and velvety, like that of a woman." Even after joining the military, dressed in his hussar's uniform, he had the "charms of a transvestite."[9] Like many of the "inverts" of the nineteenth century—including the first "Urning," Karl Heinrich Ulrichs— the Italian felt he had a "female soul in a male body" (*anima muliebris virili corpore inclusa*).[10] In addition to his feminine soul, however, the young Italian repeatedly detailed the femaleness of his body. He thus followed the conventions of sexologists who assiduously sought traces of physical hermaphroditism in inverts. Would the Italian and many other adolescent "inverts" of the nineteenth century more comfortably have identified as "transsexual" if the diagnosis had been developed then?

It was only after his first great love affair with a fellow soldier during his military service that the Italian began to enjoy his sexual nature within the constraints of his male sex. "I no longer wanted to be a woman," he asserted. Yet he was happy to report that his lover declared, "You are still my little wife!"[11] He vacillated in his gender identification into adulthood, particularly in his 1896 letter. While this letter is filled with a jumble of conflicting emotions and rationalizations, there are some notable consistencies and shifts. In the initial letters to Zola—tempestuously alternating between narcissism and shame—the Italian found some comfort in the self-defense that he was "born this way" (as we might put it today): "Why should I feel shame for what I have done? Wasn't it nature that made the mistake in the first place and condemned me to eternal sterility?" Had he been born a woman, he would have been perfect; instead, he was a "monstrous being."[12] In the subsequent letter, he continued to rely on a congenitalist view of his sexual nature that became further cloaked in scientific ideas, and yet he had to manage the pathologization that came with these ideas.

At age thirty—having just read Saint-Paul's treatise of 1896—the Italian sent further family history to the doctor, as well as objective, physical data on himself and his beloved sergeant (*The Sequel to the Novel of an Invert*).

---

9. *Novel*, "First Document."

10. Karl Heinrich Ulrichs, *The Riddle of "Man-Manly" Love: The Pioneering Work on Male Homosexuality. 1864–1870*, trans. Michael Lombardi-Nash (Buffalo, N.Y.: Prometheus Books, 1994).

11. *Novel*, "First Document."

12. *Novel*, "Second Document."

This was despite his disappointment at being included as prime evidence of an invert in *Tares et poisons: Perversion et perversité sexuelles*. Like the many people who sent their confessional case histories to Dr. Richard von Krafft-Ebing (swelling each new edition of *Psychopathia sexualis*), the Italian was eager to add his case to the medical database.[13] Given the Italian's narcissism, he probably could not resist sharing more details of his fabulous life. Although voluntarily giving in to the pathologizing data collection, he nevertheless resisted it by continuing to avoid any diagnostic label for himself.

While flattering Dr. Saint-Paul as an "expert," the Italian took a jab at the men of science struggling to understand a condition that he knew "so well through <u>an innate science.</u>" He accepted an implicitly biological, congenitalist view of his condition but did not believe that it required a cure: "Each of us has his tastes inscribed in his brain and heart; whether he fulfills his urges with regret or with joy, <u>he must fulfill them</u>." He still had the same passion for men, but it was not as all-consuming as it had been at age twenty-three, "when even the sight or the thought of an undressed man made me burn with all the flames of Hell." (He was certainly no less dramatic at age thirty.) He finally had discovered the pleasures of receptive anal sex (thanks to good technique and a little cold cream), but he never labeled himself a "sodomite." He still passionately threw himself into sexual situations with attractive men who shared "this vice and this passion": again alluding to older, premedicalization models of the *vice* of "sodomy." He blamed himself for having seduced his sole love (the young sergeant) into the passion for men. This so permanently extinguished the sergeant's potential "normal life" and "ordinary pleasures" that he would have committed suicide had he not been killed in an accident—at least so reasoned the Italian. The beloved, manly sergeant clearly could not have had a congenital passion for men the way the Italian had; he must have been seduced into it.[14]

---

13. Richard von Krafft-Ebing, *Psychopathia sexualis: Eine klinisch-forensische Studie* (Stuttgart: Ferdinand Enke, 1886), translated by F. J. Rebman as *Psychopathia sexualis: with Especial Reference to the Antipathic Sexual Instinct: A Medico-Forensic Study* (Philadelphia: F. A. Davis, 1893).

14. Coincidentally in 1896, Freud espoused his "seduction theory" of the cause of hysteria, before notoriously abandoning it for his theory of infantile sexuality and erotic fantasy. See Jeffrey M. Masson, *The Assault on Truth: Freud's Suppression of the Seduction Theory* (New York: Farrar, Straus and Giroux, 1984).

At times the Italian emphatically rejected the "degenerationist" model of doctors, such as Valentin Magnan and Krafft-Ebing:[15] "I say it again: I have no signs of physical degeneration."[16] Yet he provided his detailed family history in the methodology of Krafft-Ebing's case histories. These case histories highlight the eclectic "defects and poisons" that degeneration theory affirmed and that contributed to progressive illness and hereditary deterioration. The Italian suggested that his mixed racial ancestry (particularly the "Oriental," Jewish, maternal line) had contributed to his passion: "The West and the East with their very different bloods and civilizations are combined in me—could it be that their clash is the cause of my strange personality?" Even his "very handsome" father was not above suspicion as a cause of the Italian's sexuality: "His character had a strange sensitivity; he was high-strung and emotional in a way that was truly effeminate." On the other hand, he concluded the family history with a nod to the cultural (not biological) roots of his passion—a blending of Greek vice, English libertinage, and Italian impetuousness.

In the letter addressed directly to Dr. Saint-Paul (1896), the Italian rejected the gender inversion model he so vividly presented in his earlier letters to Zola. Instead, he evinced what today we could label as internalized homophobia or transphobia: "I am horrified by men disguised as women, and I naturally apply this feeling to myself." He insisted that he was not a "man-girl." He did not explain what triggered this change of attitude concerning effeminacy. He was writing shortly after the Oscar Wilde affair of 1895 (to which he alluded). The Wilde affair had instigated contemptuous distinctions of effeminate inverts versus masculine homosexuals by closeted writers such as Marc-André Raffalovich (whose article on Wilde was included in Saint-Paul's anthology of 1896). Earlier, Raffalovich had even explicitly lambasted the Italian in a review for the *Archives d'Anthropologie Criminelle*: "This autobiography resembles those of all the effeminate uranists who have indulged in self-publicity. Ultramasculine and semimasculine uranists never write their memoirs."[17] The Italian

---

15. Valentin Magnan, "Des anomalies, des aberrations et des perversions sexuelles," Annales médico-psychologiques 7th ser., 1 (1885): 447–74; Krafft-Ebing, Psychopathia sexualis.

16. *The Sequel to the Novel of an Invert* (hereafter *Sequel*), addendum.

17. Marc-André Raffalovich, "À Propos du Roman d'un inverti et de quelques travaux récents sur l'inversion sexuelle," Archives d'anthropologie criminelle 10, no. 57 (1895): 333.

certainly must have read Saint-Paul's own analysis of the autobiography: "The author of this novel is a born invert in the feminine form; he is the classic type of a defective person, of a sick man. This individual is a woman, both physically and morally" (first edition). Despite the Italian's newfound disdain for effeminacy, in a moment of candor a few pages later he admitted to the gendered conflict within: "The most I could wish for is to have the body that suits my soul so that I would stop being an anomaly. Sometimes I also want to masculinize my soul so that it would match my apparent sex: it is an effort that drains me and I abandon it immediately because the realization of my wish seems impossible" (Sequel). He was acutely aware of a discordance between the sex of his soul and that of his body, and he wavered between wishing to resolve that tension by either masculinizing his soul or feminizing his body. If he had been born only a few decades later—after the development of medical interventions for altering the sex of the body—would the Italian have sought these methods through Dr. Magnus Hirschfeld?[18] Or would he have sought psychoanalysis to change the gender of his psyche? Had he been born in the mid-twentieth century, would he have adopted Dr. David O. Cauldwell's 1949 label of "transsexual"?[19] If he were an undergraduate today, would he instead identify himself as "gender nonconforming" or "nonbinary" and choose the pronouns "they, them, their"?

We could also imagine an alternative history—a minor slippage of scientific discovery (say, the discovery of "sex hormones" in 1900)—that leads to a different social history. Invert and intersex identity take precedence over homosexuality. Stonewall, Trans Pride parades start in 1969 and eventually foster Gay Pride in the 1990s. Would TIBLG scholars republish "The Novel of an Invert" as the foundational autobiography of gender fluidity?

But these are completely ahistorical questions. We would do a historical disservice to this person and the text he created by labeling him with either medical terms or contemporary identity labels. As a child psychiatrist, I hear in the Italian's autobiography two interwoven threads of identity evolution: one of personal experiences and psychosexual development; the

---

18. On Hirschfeld's contributions to medical "genital transformation" (Genitalumwandlung) in the 1920s and 1930s, see Joanne Meyerowitz, *How Sex Changed: A History of Transsexuality in the United States* (Cambridge, Mass.: Harvard University Press, 2002), 18–21.

19. David O. Cauldwell, "Psychopathia transexualis," *Sexology* 16 (1949): 274–80.

second, the effects of sociohistorical context (including medical ideology). We can unequivocally admire him for coping with this hostile context and, better yet, enthusiastically embracing his sexual uniqueness: "I will accept what I am: a strange being, neither man nor woman, or, rather, both man and woman at the same time, with strange inclinations, loving men with a woman's passion but also with an impetuousness, an enthusiasm, and an ardor that women don't feel" (*Sequel*). His was a passion beyond the confines of medical labels, innate yet dynamic, tempestuous, and very, very human.

The Italian Invert

Introduction
The *Ménage-à-Trois* of Zola, Saint-Paul, and the Italian "Invert"
Michael Rosenfeld with Nancy Erber

In the Jubilee year 1888 when pilgrims flocked to Rome to pay homage to the Holy Father, an Italian aristocrat spent several evenings in his hotel room writing his life story.[1]

He sent those pages to the French author Émile Zola, calling him "the greatest novelist of our time" and praising the naturalist writer's unflinching approach to "all the oddities, all the infamies, and all the maladies that afflict mankind."[2] Although his exact identity is still unknown, the Italian man, then in his early twenties, filled his letters with descriptions of his family, his artistic tastes, his svelte and handsome appearance, his religious background and conservative politics, and, most important, his adolescent experimentations with other boys, love affairs with men,

---

This introduction is an adaptation of a longer essay, "Dossier génétique des *Confessions*," by Michael Rosenfeld, which appeared in the French edition of this book, *Confessions d'un homosexuel à Émile Zola: Première édition non censurée du "Roman d'un inverti"* (Paris: Nouvelles Éditions Place, 2017), 147–201. We use the term "gay" to describe the Italian's male-to-male desire for lack of a better word. Our choice does not reflect on the Italian's gender identities or sexualities; he himself refused to use "pederast" and "invert" ("homosexual" was not a common word in French at the time) when discussing his feelings. We respect his wish not to use terms that have a pejorative connotation.

1. It is impossible to ascertain the exact date when the Italian man sent his letters to Zola since the original letters and envelopes have never been found. However, there are a few hints in the text itself. The writer mentioned Zola's novel *La Terre/The Earth*, which was published in installments in the daily *Gil Blas* newspaper from May 29 to September 16, 1887, and then as a single volume in November 1887. He also said he was in Rome for the Jubilee of Pope Leo XIII, which was in 1888, possibly extending into 1889. In a subsequent letter, dated September 1896, he recalled: "When I wrote to Mr. Zola, I was about twenty-three years old; I am now thirty." Thus it seems likely that the Italian man's initial letters were written in 1888 or 1889.

2. *Novel*, "First Document."

and occasional, fleeting sexual encounters with strangers. He explained to Zola that he hoped his "confessions" would give the novelist the material he needed for a well-rounded fictional portrait of a man attracted to other men.

"Struck by the great physiological and social interest [these letters] offered," Zola initially did not know what to do with them.[3] He eventually gave them to Georges Saint-Paul, a young medical graduate interested in psychology who was just beginning his career as a military doctor. Saint-Paul published them in a scientific journal in installments in 1894–1895 under the ironic title "The Novel of an Invert" and then included them in a chapter of his book, *Tares et poisons: Perversion et perversité sexuelles* (1896).[4] Saint-Paul condensed, rearranged, and censored parts of the original manuscript; he also rendered some explicit descriptions of sexual activity in Latin when he published it. Our edition, based on recently discovered documents, is the first to present the Italian man's writing in its entirety.

The publication history of the Italian man's story includes more than one lucky accident or fortuitous turn of events. The first incredible coincidence occurred over a hundred years ago, when, strangely enough, "while strolling through the streets" of an unnamed European city, the letter-writer saw Saint-Paul's book *Tares et poisons* displayed in a bookstore window. After noticing its preface by Zola, he bought a copy, saw his "confessions" accompanied by the doctor's analysis, and then wrote directly to Saint-Paul. The second surprising twist occurred in 2011 when the French scholar Alain Pagès came across the original manuscript of this letter, labeled "The Sequel to the Confessions of a Homosexual," in the Zola family archives. And finally, more recently, Michael Rosenfeld discovered additional manuscripts as well as correspondence between the novelist and the doctor in the Saint-Paul family archives. Together, these discoveries encourage us to reexamine this story. They force us to recognize the extent of the doctor's censorship, shed light on the friendship between Zola and Saint-Paul, allow us to analyze the effect these

---

3. "Preface by Émile Zola," in part 1 of this book.

4. Dr. Laupts [Georges Saint-Paul], "Le Roman d'un inverti," *Archives d'Anthropologie Criminelle* (1894): 211–15, 367–73, 729–31; (1895): 131–38, 228–41, 320–25; Dr. Laupts, "Le Roman d'un inverti-né," in *Tares et poisons. Perversion et perversité sexuelles* (Paris: Georges Carré, 1896), 47–95.

"confessions" had on Zola's writing and social conscience, and give us access to the young man's actual words.

The Novel of an Invert and its Sequel are extraordinary documents because they were written by a man who was sexually attracted to other men and unashamed of his preferences at a time when society was not tolerant of them. In addition, the police forces and legal codes of certain countries heavily penalized "homosexual" activity. Despite these risks, he refused to accept any condemnation of his love for men. He discussed his sexual desires and activities in a frank and eloquent manner using clear, everyday language. He was well aware of the social opprobrium he risked if his identity were revealed, but he boldly defended his right to be different. For instance, in his 1896 letter to Saint-Paul, he bluntly explained that he was not asking the doctor for a cure; he was proud of his difference, which, he believed, was innate and incontrovertible: "Each of us has his tastes inscribed in his brain and heart; whether he fulfills his urges with regret or joy, he must fulfill them. He should let others act according to their own nature. It's fate that creates us and guides us throughout our lives: to fight against it would be little more than fruitless, foolish, and reckless!!"

Who was the author of these confessions? We do not know. He claimed in his letters to Zola and Saint-Paul that he belonged to a wealthy, aristocratic Neapolitan family with Spanish and Jewish roots.[5] He was twenty-three years old when he first wrote to Zola, giving a detailed account of his antecedents and his daily life. He also discussed his sexuality: his feelings of alienation and gender dysphoria in early childhood, adolescent episodes of masturbation and sexual experimentation, a few humiliating visits to brothels, his sexual initiation with his first male lover, and his first "true" love affair. By the time he wrote to Dr. Saint-Paul, he was thirty and his life had changed; his parents had died, and he had inherited enough to guarantee financial independence and a life of ease. His first romantic love, "the sergeant," whom he had met during his mandatory military service, had died, and his first lover, "the captain," was also deceased. "Being rich and independent," he declared, "I've been able to arrange my life as I wish—in a manner that is a little strange, like everything I do" (Sequel). Sexual encounters and love affairs now occupied much of his attention and a good

---

5. See "The Italian Man's Family Tree" in part 1 of this volume.

portion of his written "confessions." He found it relatively easy to find willing sexual partners, especially during his travels. He was, as he reminded both his correspondents, slim, well-dressed, and attractive.

The ease with which the writer discussed his sexual experiences may be surprising since modern readers know how risky that must have been. Actually his letter to Saint-Paul was written after Oscar Wilde's well-publicized trial and conviction in England in 1895, when Wilde was condemned to a sentence of two years' hard labor, an event the Italian referred to when he wrote to the doctor. The danger the writer confronted was real, and even if the penalties or threats of prosecution were less severe in his home country, Italy, he still feared social ostracism. By the age of thirty, when he wrote to Saint-Paul, it is clear he had come to terms with his sexuality; looking back on his earlier letters to Zola and his younger self, he wrote: "My mind is the same way. I know now what I <u>am</u> and what I <u>want</u>. I have made up my mind and I look for as much happiness in life as I can, without worrying about the rest" (Sequel).

When he wrote to Zola, he brought up recurrent episodes of emotional highs and lows: feelings of deep depression and despair alternating with periods of euphoria. He even recalled having suicidal thoughts but found that pursuing sexual pleasures helped dispel the dark moods. Seven years later, he still acknowledged periods of depression but seemed to consider sexual activity an antidote; he reveled in providing the doctor with detailed descriptions of his sexual encounters and sensual pleasures: kisses, caresses, and orgasms. A long-running theme in the letters is his quest to experience anal penetration, which, once again, he detailed richly in passages that Saint-Paul censored when he published the text in 1910 and 1930.

Another example of his personal evolution evidenced in the letters is the difference between his self-diagnoses in 1888 and 1896. In 1888 he described himself as a sick man, but by 1896 he displayed a marked sense of self-acceptance. He asserted that nature made him what he was, and that only the tunnel vision of conventional science continued to define men like him as aberrant. In his last pages, the Italian man militantly advocated for nonprocreative sex, arguing that the earth was overcrowded and that "to take and to give a <u>sterile</u> pleasure—<u>one superior to all the others</u>" was entirely natural (Sequel). Far from being ashamed of his sexuality, he was proud of it.

Autobiography or Auto-Fiction?

Zola, as we know, did not accede to the Italian man's request to use his story for inspiration. He hesitated to publish it, he claimed, because it was so well written that "I would have been accused of inventing the story out of whole cloth, out of my own personal corruption." Nevertheless, he was impressed by the young man's fervor and was convinced that it was authentic: "A complete confession, naïve, spontaneous, one that very few men have dared to make, qualities that make it extremely valuable from many points of view."[6] Saint-Paul also acknowledged it as genuine, even though, when he published it, he not only censored it but also gave it a misleading title, *The Novel of an Invert*. "This confession is sincere," he declared, "it is true—derived from a truth that we feel from its emotion and its sadness." "It is the true story of a man with an illustrious name, a very well-respected name in Italy. As accurate as a scientific observation, as interesting as a novel, as sincere as a confession, it is perhaps the most complete and the most engaging narrative of this genre."[7] Nevertheless, he admitted that "a few foreign authors thought that this novel of an invert was really and truly a novel, some of them believed that Zola was the inspiration."[8]

Some modern scholars still consider these confessions to be fictional.[9] Their judgment is based on previous, incomplete editions of the text published before the recent discoveries of manuscripts in the Zola and Saint-Paul family archives. Let us hope that this edition of these letters dispels doubts about their authenticity. If the narrator's sole ambition was to have his testimony included in a medical study, as some have argued, why did he first contact a novelist to tell his life story? If his story were truly fictional, why would he have reacted so forcefully to its publication in *Tares et*

---

6. "Preface by Émile Zola."
7. See "First Edition: Inquiry Into Sexual Inversion: Responses."
8. We are not sure which "foreign authors" Saint-Paul had in mind.
9. See Jean-Louis Cabanès' review of Daniel Grojnowski's edition, "*Confessions d'un inverti-né, preface d'Émile Zola, suivies de Confidences et aveux d'un Parisien par Arthur W*" (Paris: José Corti, 2007), https://serd.hypotheses.org/files/2018/04/CR_20Confessions inverti.pdf; and Jean-Claude Féray, "Des éclairages nouveaux sur Le Roman d'un inverti que Zola et Laupts ont rendu célèbre," a review of *Confessions d'un homosexuel à Émile Zola*, *Bulletin Trimestriel Quintes-Feuilles*, no. 8 (November 2017): 12–14, https://www.quintes-feuilles.com/wp-content/uploads/BTQ-F8.pdf.

poisons, especially when he protested against the doctor's carelessness in masking his identity? It seems reasonable to assume that his stated ambition—to see his story in print as the model for a fictional character—is true.

The French literary scholar Philippe Lejeune included this text in his inventory of eight autobiographies written by men interested in other men and published between 1845 and 1905.[10] There are some distinct differences between these confessions and the other contemporary accounts he chose since most were mediated by prison authorities or doctors. For example, Louis X . . . and Gustave L . . . had been charged with a crime and while in prison were asked to write about their lives and the circumstances leading to their arrest.[11] Dr. Ambroise Tardieu's patient, a classics professor, told his story to a psychiatrist who treated him as a private patient.[12] The cross-dresser Arthur Belorget, known as "The Countess," was also charged with a crime, and he too had his autobiography published by a doctor.[13]

---

10. Philippe Lejeune, "Autobiographie et homosexualité en France au XIXe siècle," Romantisme 56 (1987): 79–100; republished as Philippe Lejeune, Autobiographie et homosexualité en France au XIXe siècle, with a preface by Clive Thomson (Paris: Éditions de la Sorbonne, 2017). These autobiographies were translated into English in Queer Lives: Men's Autobiographies from Nineteenth-Century France, trans. and ed. William A. Peniston and Nancy Erber (Lincoln: University of Nebraska Press, 2007), 165–247, and published in French as Bougres de vies (Queer Lives): Huit homosexuels du XIXe siècle se racontent, ed. William A. Peniston and Nancy Erber, trans. Clément Marie (Paris: ErosOnyx, 2012). Other examples of these kinds of autobiographical texts are reproduced in Philippe Artières, ed., Le Livre des vies coupables: Autobiographies de criminels (1896–1909) (Paris: Albin Michel, 2000).

11. "Notes autobiographiques" by Gustave L . . . , in Paul Garnier, La Folie à Paris: Étude statistique, clinique et medico-légale (Paris: Bailière, 1890), 385–91; reprinted in Paul Garnier, Les Fétishistes: Pervertis et invertis sexuels: Observations medico-légales (Paris: Bailière, 1896), 98–113; "Notes autobiographiques" by Louis X . . . , in Garnier, Les Fétishistes, 113–48. Both are translated in Peniston and Erber, Queer Lives, 95–100 and 101–12, respectively.

12. Anon., "Ma Confession," in Ambroise Tardieu, Étude medico-légale sur les attentats aux moeurs, 5th ed. (Paris: Bailière, 1867), 187–89; translated as "Loves" in Peniston and Erber, Queer Lives, 83–86.

13. "Confidences et aveux d'un Parisien: La Comtesse (Paris, 1850–1861)" by Arthur W . . . [Arthur Belorget], in Henri Legludic, Notes et observations de médicine légale: Attentats aux moeurs (Paris: Masson, 1896), 235–49; translated as "Secret Confessions of a Parisian: The Countess" in Peniston and Erber, Queer Lives, 7–72. The original dates are wrong: they should be 1850–1871. This autobiography is longer and more traditional in its narrative techniques. Given the author's involvement with the theatrical world, it

The Novel of an Invert is exceptional since it was written by a well-educated man for a famous novelist, not for a doctor. *The Sequel* addressed to Dr. Saint-Paul, however, can be more easily compared with the other autobiographical texts written to doctors of the time.

To find analogs to these confessions, we might look to two other contemporary sources: the correspondence sent to Dr. Alexandre Lacassagne and to Dr. Richard von Krafft-Ebing. Georges Apitzsch, a young German, exchanged letters with Lacassagne (Saint-Paul's mentor at the School of Military Medicine in Lyon) from 1903 to 1908. Apitzsch, however, sought medical advice and was not interested primarily in telling his life story.[14] Many other men (and some women) wrote to the Austrian psychiatrist, Krafft-Ebing, and most of them told him that they wanted their stories to be included in his work, *Psychopathia sexualis*, which was first published in German in 1886 and reissued dozens of times.[15] Each new edition was filled with new "confessions" sent from all over Europe and even from the United States.[16] These accounts resemble the Italian man's autobiographical letters; they are personal narratives structured in a similar pattern. For instance, most correspondents recalled recognizing from an early age that their sexual identity was different. In general, most had their initial gay experience in adolescence, usually with someone older and in an authority role, such as a tutor, priest, or doctor. Many of them described a first true love, followed by disappointments and brief sexual encounters. Some of them also recalled, as the Italian man did, an unsuccessful and unsatisfying, even repellent, heterosexual experience or two in a brothel. Feelings of social isolation and loneliness were also common.

---

may have been written for a general audience, not for the doctor who published it. Nevertheless, the doctor stated that the author gave him the text as he was examining him in prison.

14. Georges Apitzsch, *Lettres d'un inverti allemand au Docteur Lacassagne, 1903–1908*, ed. Philippe Artières (Paris: Epel, 2006).

15. Richard von Krafft-Ebing, *Psychopathia sexualis: Eine klinisch-forensische Studie* (Stuttgart: Ferdinand Enke, 1886); translated into English by Charles Gilbert Chaddock as *Psychopathia Sexualis, with Special Reference to Contrary Sexual Instinct: A Medico-Legal Study* (Philadelphia: F. A. Davis, 1893); translated into French as *Psychopathia sexualis. Avec recherches spéciales sur l'inversion sexuelle* (Paris: G. Carré, 1895).

16. Harry Oosterhuis, *Stepchildren of Nature: Krafft-Ebing, Psychiatry, and the Making of Sexual Identity* (Chicago: University of Chicago Press, 2000).

Toward Publication

Zola received the letters in 1888 or 1889, read them with interest, and then put them in a drawer, where they stayed until he met the young medical graduate, Georges Saint-Paul. At the time, Saint-Paul was conducting research for his thesis on interior language—the ways in which human beings formulate ideas.[17] After having interviewed other prominent authors in Paris, he met Zola "without any introduction from anyone or anything to recommend me." The friendship that developed between the two was described by Saint-Paul in his article "In Memoriam: Émile Zola" after the novelist's tragic death.[18] During one of their meetings, the two discussed an unusual subject: "One day I spoke to him about sexual inverts, several of whom I had examined with Lacassagne in Lyon. Already obsessed by the ideas that inspired *Fécondité* [Fecundity], Zola was, I believe, already interested in studies on sexuality." During this conversation, Zola told Saint-Paul about the letters he had received from the Italian man. Shortly after that, Saint-Paul wrote to his mentor, Professor Lacassagne, about the possibility of publishing material from the letters in the scholarly journal

---

17. Zola's responses were included in Georges Saint-Paul's 1892 thesis, *Essais sur le langage intérieur* (Lyon: Storck, 1892), 28–31, and reprinted in Georges Saint-Paul, "Enquête sur le langage intérieur: Réponses: Émile Zola," *Archives d'Anthropologie Criminelle* (1894): 105–8. Some excerpts also appeared in Léon Riotor's articles, "Une enquête sur le cerveau littéraire," *Le Journal, Supplément Littéraire*, no. 5 (October 20, 1892): 3, and "Cerveaux littéraires: Confessions physiologiques," *Le Figaro, Supplément Littéraire du Dimanche*, December 10, 1892, p. 200. Zola spoke about his participation in Saint-Paul's study and about Riotor's articles in a letter to Jacques van Santen Kolff on January 25, 1893; see Émile Zola, *Correspondance*, ed. B. H. Bakker (Montreal: Presses de l'Université de Montréal, 1989) (hereafter cited as Zola, *Correspondance*), 7:358–60. This topic is studied in Clive Thomson's essay "Dr. Georges Saint-Paul, Man of Science," in part 2 of this volume.

18. Georges Saint-Paul, "À la mémoire d'Émile Zola," *Archives d'Anthropologie Criminelle* 22, no. 168 (1907): 825–41. See the translation in part 2 of this volume. Correspondence between Saint-Paul and his wife Yvonne and Zola's wife Alexandrine and his children Denise and Jacques is found in the Saint-Paul family archives (hereafter SPFA) and the Zola family archives. This correspondence indicates that the friendship continued after Zola's death in 1902; it was published in its entirety in Michael Rosenfeld and Clive Thomson's "Lettres inédites de 1893 à 1925 entre Émile Zola, Alexandrine Zola, Georges Saint-Paul et Yvonne Saint-Paul," *Les Cahiers Naturalistes* 95 (2021): 97–126.

that Lacassagne edited.[19] Later, the young military doctor informed Zola: "I saw Dr. Lacassagne. Sometime in the next year, I will publish the confession of the Italian invert that you were so kind to give me, and as soon as possible I will send you the manuscript and the published article."[20]

Zola acknowledged receiving the published article with a card to Saint-Paul on April 1, 1895.[21] Two other letters, dated April 17, 1895, and May 3, 1895, show that the two met to discuss the forthcoming publication of his treatise on sexual perversion, Tares et poisons. Zola confirmed that he would contribute to it discreetly, leaving all the practical details to the young doctor:

> I don't want to profit in any way from the publication of The Novel of an Invert, and on this point, I ask you, and you alone, to deal with this business. Otherwise, for literary reasons, I don't want my name to appear on the book cover; or at the very least, I give my consent only to a note on the cover that states "with a preface by Émile Zola." And this preface will only be a letter that I write to you personally, a rather short one, in which I relate simply the story of the manuscript that I gave you, after analyzing it briefly from my standpoint. Thus, your responsibility will be to write the real introduction, the part that will be, in my mind, strictly scientific.[22]

After this note, the letters dealt with the delay in Zola's promised preface.[23] In an undated letter, Saint-Paul approached the issue delicately, reluctant to pressure the famous author: "At the risk of seeming annoying,

---

19. To Lacassagne, he wrote: "At the same time, if Zola's document is not suitable for the Archives, as I am afraid it might not be, please return the handwritten copy that I sent you. I don't need to tell you that I honestly believed, as I told you, that this document was very interesting, and one that might be relevant to your research." Saint-Paul to Lacassagne, March 21, 1894, found in the copy of Saint-Paul's dissertation in the Fonds Lacassagne in the Bibliothèque Municipale de Lyon.

20. Saint-Paul to Zola, November 1, 1893, in the Collection "Dr. François Émile-Zola." Part of the correspondence between Zola and Saint-Paul has been published previously in Émile Zola, Correspondance: les lettres et les arts (Paris: Charpentier, 1908), 359–67; and Zola, Correspondance, vol. 8.

21. Zola to Saint-Paul, April 1, 1895, SPFA. See also Zola, Correspondance, 8:213.

22. Zola to Saint-Paul, May 3, 1895, SPFA; Zola, Correspondance, 8:216.

23. Zola to Saint Paul, May 16, 1895, and June 8, 1895, SPFA; Zola, Correspondance, 8:216, 221–22.

I'm going to remind you again and distract you from your own work. I'm being deluged with urgent requests, and because of that, I'm forced to act indiscreetly and importune you. Please be assured, dear Master, that I do regret this greatly and I hope you will forgive me."[24] Finally, on June 24, 1895, Zola informed Saint-Paul that he was ready to send the preface, which he mailed the next day.[25] And Saint-Paul immediately replied with thanks for the preface that "<u>gave me such pleasure</u>."[26]

The young doctor negotiated the publication of his book with the Lyon publisher Adrien Storck, whom Professor Lacassagne had recommended. Storck was concerned, however, about the doctor's use of a pen name. (Saint-Paul adopted the pseudonym "Dr. Laupts" for all his writings on sexology.)[27] As he explained: "When an author is anonymous, or publishes under a pseudonym, all the responsibility rests on the publisher. That's me. And so if I do back out of this deal, it's because it's not worth the trouble."[28] At this point Saint-Paul turned to Zola, the experienced author, who counseled caution, replying on July 18, 1895: "I don't think we should ignore the publisher's concerns because if there is any trouble, that would be disastrous. In my opinion, I don't think you should be looking for another publisher because I don't think you will find another publisher, regardless." Zola was frank in expressing his ambivalence about the viability of the project, but, instead of offering help in locating another publisher, he promised, "I would be very glad to safeguard your manuscript, under the conditions you gave me, in the event that it could be used someday."[29] Still, contacts between Saint-Paul and Storck continued throughout the summer, and Saint-Paul kept Zola informed about any glimmers of progress. On July 22 he has some good news: "I received a letter out of the blue from Mr. Storck, asking me to wait a little longer before 'shelving' this deal. Thus, I'm asking you to give me a few more weeks before

24. Saint-Paul to Zola, undated (ca. June 1895), Collection "Dr. François Émile-Zola."
25. Zola to Saint-Paul, June 24, 1895, SPFA; Zola, *Correspondance*, 8:229–32.
26. Saint-Paul to Zola, June 25, 1895, Collection "Dr. François Émile-Zola." Zola wrote: "My dear doctor, please excuse me for having made you wait so long. I cannot always control how I spend my time. I certainly will want to review the proofs of my letter, which I ask you to send to me, and which I will return immediately." Zola's preface appears in part 1 of this volume.
27. Adrien Storck to Saint-Paul, May 18, 1895, SPFA.
28. Storck to Saint-Paul, July 11, 1895, SPFA.
29. Zola to Saint-Paul, July 18, 1895, SPFA.

I return the manuscript to you. I want to make sure that it is completely ready for publishing sometime in the future. I'm very glad to see that you and I agree about this, that the best and most prudent thing to do is to wait."[30]

Saint-Paul also discussed his perceived need for secrecy about the identity of "Dr. Laupts," emphasizing that he wanted Zola's "absolute discretion"—a request that echoed the words of the Italian man. The entire text of the "confessions" would be included in the book, he noted, with certain "obscene parts" translated into Latin.[31] By the end of August, Storck and Saint-Paul embarked on concrete plans for the book, and a detailed chapter outline revealed Saint-Paul's intention of presenting a comprehensive overview of "inversion," including male and female cases, although the final version would be different.[32] Finally, in September, Storck informed Saint-Paul that Georges Carré, a publisher in Paris, would publish the book.[33]

---

30. Saint-Paul to Zola, July 22, 1895, Collection "Dr. François Émile-Zola."

31. Saint-Paul to Zola, July 22, 1895. Saint-Paul wrote: "The reluctance I expressed regarding a future publication by you does not concern your manuscript which belongs to you exclusively. I'm so grateful that you sent it to me so that it could be published in the Archives. (In fact, it is unexpurgated; the obscene parts are translated into Latin.) I'm specifically referring only to the introductory study, which would be integral to any publication. I'm simply asking that if this is published, the real name of the author of the study be kept in the strictest confidence. I'm emphasizing this point in order to convey to you clearly that I don't want any credit or have any rights in this business and that *caution* alone impels me to ask for your absolute discretion regarding the real identity of 'Laupts' in the event that you find his study of sufficient interest to be published sometime in the future, under whatever circumstances."

32. Chapter outline, dated August 24, 1895, SPFA. The outline agreed on was as follows: "The Illness of Sexual Inversion by Dr Laupts, based on the text of The Novel of an Invert (Italy); The Oscar Wilde Affair by Raffalovich; Female Cases of Inversion by [illegible]; Preface by Émile Zola." In the end, the proposed chapter on female inversion was not included.

33. Storck to Saint-Paul, September 27, 1895, SPFA. Carré wrote directly to Saint-Paul on October 2, 1895, setting out the proposed terms of publication. Carré had won a court case in July 1893, after he was accused of disseminating "pornography" when he published the French translation of Dr. Albert Moll's *Les Perversions de l'instinct genital/Perversions of the Sex Instinct*. The French medical establishment strongly and publicly supported the publisher, and the case was dismissed out of hand, which no doubt encouraged Carré to publish Saint-Paul's book.

Defects and Poisons. Sexual Perversion and Perversity

Saint-Paul, a military doctor, was notified of his assignment to a post in the military hospitals of the Nineteenth Division (the Algerian Division) in September, so before leaving France,[34] he spent October 15 to October 18 in Paris, meeting with both Carré and Zola.[35] His contract with Carré was signed on October 15, specifying January 31, 1896 as the deadline for the manuscript, now entitled *Tares et poisons: Perversion et perversité sexuelles / Defects and Poisons. Sexual Perversion and Perversity*.[36] Zola kept his word and sent the corrected proofs of the preface to the publisher in January, and by March Saint-Paul's book was in print. Only 31 copies had been sold by the end of June; by the end of the year, the total was 186.[37] In July Saint-Paul assured Zola that he would receive a copy of his book and apologized to Zola for not being able to write a personal dedication in it.[38] In his "In Memoriam: Émile Zola," he included a lengthy quotation from one of Zola's letters of the period that revealed his reaction to the book and its use of *The Novel of an Invert*:

> Although I have been able only to glance over it while cutting the pages, I had the distinct impression of a serious and powerful work. You placed the documents in an illuminating context and extracted from them a logical and persuasive analysis. I believe that this volume will be significant for this question of sexuality, which is still so obscure. For my part, I am happy to have helped you a little by giving you a curious document, and I thank you for having used it so well, because the question does interest me.

34. Saint-Paul had been an apprentice surgeon (*médecin aide-major de 2ème classe*) in the 91st infantry regiment at Mézières since October 9, 1893, but he was promoted to lieutenant surgeon (*médecin aide-major de 1ère classe*) on October 9, 1895. "État de service," SPFA.

35. Saint-Paul, personal diary, October 15, 16, 17, 1895, SPFA.

36. Contract, October 15, 1895, SPFA. In addition to the deadline, the contract specified the total number of copies to be published (2,200) and the number of complimentary copies for the author (100). The new, sensational title revealed the author's biases; he was clearly making a distinction between "perversion," which denoted a hereditary or acquired defect, and "perversity," which was an instance of temporary "immoral" conduct by people whom the doctor considered "normal."

37. Record of sales, December 31, 1896, SPFA.

38. Saint-Paul to Zola, July 16, 1896, Collection "Dr. François Émile-Zola"; Zola, *Correspondance*, 8:339.

After the publication, the two men's letters came less frequently, probably because both were otherwise occupied: Saint-Paul had his professional responsibilities in the military and Zola became involved in the Dreyfus Affair and went into exile in London. Yet, despite their busy lives, the two men retained a bond of friendship. On September 29, 1902, Saint-Paul noted tersely in his diary: "Zola's death."[39] After that, Alexandrine Zola wrote to Saint-Paul, assuring him of the "heart-felt affection, the interest" that her husband had for him.[40]

THE SEQUEL TO THE NOVEL OF AN INVERT

On January 28, 1897, Saint-Paul informed Zola of a surprising contact with their anonymous correspondent: "Today I am sending . . . the sequel to 'The Novel of an Invert.' Carré sent me the odd document that I am sending on to you, and if it has been a while since I last wrote to you, that is because I have been assigned to a posting in Gafsa, after my tours of duty in half of Algeria and all of Tunisia in one single year. These constant moves are 'killing' my work and my brain."[41] He also admitted that the book they had worked on together was not getting much critical attention, probably because of the difficult subject matter: "My book *Perversion and Perversity* is not doing well. No journal, no publication—not even scientific ones—except for *La Société Nouvelle*—has wanted to review it. *La Revue Scientifique*, the pink journal, has dealt with it discreetly.[42] Yet, I believe it was virtually impossible for me to be more circumspect in my language, and, please excuse the choice of word—'conservative'—in my theory."[43]

After receiving the handwritten *Sequel to the Novel of an Invert*, Saint-Paul immediately thought of publishing it, even though the first edition of *Tares et poisons* was far from being a best seller. Only 500 copies were sold between April 1896 and September 1899, and there were 135 in stock at bookshops.

39. Saint-Paul, personal diary, September 29, 1902, SPFA.
40. Alexandrine Zola to Saint-Paul, February 27, 1907, SPFA; Rosenfeld and Thomson, "Lettres inédites."
41. Saint-Paul to Zola, January 28, 1897, Collection "Dr. François Émile Zola"; Rosenfeld and Thomson, "Lettres inédites."
42. *La Revue Scientifique* was referred to as the "pink journal" because of its pink-colored cover, which distinguished it from *La Revue Politique et Littéraire*, the "blue journal," issued by the same publisher.
43. Saint-Paul to Zola, January 28, 1897, Collection "Dr. François Émile Zola."

On September 7, 1899, Carré, the publisher, told Saint-Paul that he would not consider a second edition, given the slow pace of sales.[44] Five years later, in July 1904, Carré and his partner Naud sold off their business, and the 1,211 copies of Saint-Paul's book that remained unsold (of which 1,000 were unbound) were acquired by the publisher Masson, along with the rights to the work. In May 1909 Masson gave Saint-Paul ominous news about his book: "We still have 1,105 copies in the warehouse. From this point, it seems that they will never be sold. Strictly for practical reasons (lack of space in our warehouse), we plan to pulp 700 copies."[45] Since Saint-Paul wanted to bring out a second edition of the book and include *The Sequel to the Novel of an Invert*, he started looking for another publisher. He succeeded and in July 1910 began negotiating a contract with the publisher Vigot. Now more well established professionally and based in Paris in the War Ministry's division of medical services, Saint-Paul was in a better position to deal with his new publisher.[46] He had also published six books and a dozen articles in medical journals since 1896.

As part of the negotiations, Saint-Paul proposed a plan that would enable Vigot to reuse the remaining copies of the first edition. The contract they signed on July 1, 1910, specified that Saint-Paul would give Vigot 1,083 unbound copies of the 1896 edition and "an addition of approximately eighty pages to be printed at the publisher's expense." This arrangement would "allow the book to be sold as a second edition."[47] Saint-Paul suggested some other changes to the second edition, including a new, more contemporary title, *L'Homosexualité et les types homosexuels / Homosexuality and Types of Homosexuals*. He also agreed to be identified in the book as the author, with his real name in parentheses after his pseudonym "Laupts" on the title page, and another page that listed his other publications.[48] He

---

44. Carré to Saint-Paul, September 7, 1899, SPFA.

45. Masson to Saint-Paul, May 27, 1909, SPFA.

46. He was promoted to the rank of first-class physician-major (*médecin-major de 1ère classe*) in December 1909; this grade was equivalent to major in the army. On December 29, 1910, Saint-Paul was named knight in the Legion of Honor.

47. Contract between Vigot and Saint-Paul, July 1, 1910, SPFA. The 1896 and 1910 editions are identical up until page 337; then they diverge slightly until the end of chapter 5. The 1896 edition has 370 pages in five chapters; the 1910 edition has 446 pages in six chapters. The sixth chapter includes the censored version of *The Sequel to the Novel of an Invert*.

48. Contract between Vigot and Saint-Paul, July 1, 1910. Other changes included removing the original dedication to Théodore-Armaud Ribot, adding a two-page

highlighted what was new and different about this edition that was "already a classic" in a press release he drafted, noting that it "includes the end of 'The Novel of an Invert,' the autobiography sent to Zola, and whose author, after having read *Tares et poisons*, decided to write a sequel."[49]

The third and final edition of the book was published in 1930 with yet another new title, *Invertis et homosexuels / Inverts and Homosexuals*, in Vigot's "Psychological Themes" collection. Saint-Paul oversaw this edition as well, adding a few previously unpublished paragraphs from the letter he had received from the Italian in September 1896, but certain passages that he had judged too explicit for the earlier editions were also not included in this edition.[50] Saint-Paul summarized some of the deleted material in a note to readers: "The original document relates at great length details that I will not reproduce. It is with acute precision that the author describes the preliminary acts, the first attempt that almost succeeded, the second attempt that succeeded completely, and the following nights, etc." In fact, this type of heavy-handed editing was a common practice in the nineteenth century for doctors cognizant of their position as educators and moral leaders.[51] Enhanced by a sense of nationalism, this ideology outweighed concerns about scientific objectivity.[52]

Saint-Paul's Censorship

Although some of the changes that Saint-Paul made to these letters were purely stylistic, others altered the work's original meaning so that it would more accurately reflect his theories, and this censorship persisted through

---

preface, removing the last sixteen pages of the original book, and adding a new final chapter "focused on recent work in 1908."

49. Draft of a press notice, undated, SPFA.

50. The manuscript of the letter sent to Saint-Paul is 15,585 words long. Saint-Paul published approximately one-fourth of it in 1910 (3,585 words) and one-third in 1930 (6,000 words).

51. Oosterhuis, *Stepchildren of Nature*, 19.

52. The interaction of ideology and medicine in Saint-Paul's work is more obvious in his stage play, *Plus fort que le mal. Essai sur le mal innommable* (Paris: Maloine, 1907), published under his literary pen name, G. Espé de Metz. In this play, the power and privilege of an aristocrat suffering from hereditary syphilis is confronted by the prejudices of a renowned military doctor.

the decades in every edition. Saint-Paul kept a notebook with "observations about inversion" that reveal some common biases and prevalent stereotypes about "homosexuality."[53] The observations show a typical concern with classification and definition—for instance: "Every man whose desire is aroused by someone of the same sex is an invert." Among the types are "the passive invert (the woman)" and "the active invert (the man)." There is also "the indifferent type" who is "a cousin of . . . [the active invert]." The same schema recurs in Saint-Paul's analysis of the Italian man's psychology in Tares et poisons, but the language is harshly negative: "The author of this novel is a born invert in the feminine form; he is the classic type of a defective person, of a sick man. This individual is a woman, both physically and morally."[54] He argued that the Italian man's personality, character, and behavior were feminine and went so far as to invent a few colorful details about this effeminacy and insert them in the Italian's narrative. For example, when the author recalled his love affair with the sergeant, Saint-Paul added some lilac scent to the lovers' perfumed bathwater, emphasizing their feminity. He also altered the text to bolster readers' impression of hetero-normative relations between the two men, as the sergeant took the man's role and the Italian the woman's. The Italian angrily disputed this depiction of him as effeminate in his letters to the doctor. "Sir," he wrote, "you are wrong when you insinuate that I must like to dress in women's clothing. . . . I am <u>horrified</u> by men disguised as women, and I naturally apply this feeling to myself. I like the most <u>serious</u>, the most <u>correct</u>, the most <u>masculine</u> kind of elegance—<u>English chic</u>, in fact" (Sequel).

Another stereotype concerned the danger gay men pose to society: the belief that same-sex attraction was contagious or could be acquired, infecting "normal" men. According to Saint-Paul, "He does not hesitate to seduce a young man, a very masculine and very handsome one, probably a normal man up to that point, and one who succumbs to an attraction to him as if he were attracted by a woman, yielding to an almost normal love, yielding also, perhaps, as he hints in one of his postscripts, because of

---

53. Notebook, "observations about inversion," SPFA. The notebook jottings probably predate the first publication of his book in 1896 since the notebook he used was supplied by the School of Military Medicine in Lyon, where he obtained his medical degree in 1892.

54. "First Edition."

certain financial considerations."⁵⁵ In contrast to Saint-Paul's interpretation, in which the young sergeant was the victim of the Italian man's seduction and his "innate cunning," the Italian man's account emphasized that the two men's feelings were reciprocal and that the sergeant "showed me an equally ardent passion." Saint-Paul prescribed heterosexual marriage as the cure for the sergeant's temporary aberration,⁵⁶ even if he risked passing on to his children "a troubling predisposition, a tendency toward inversion."

The 1910 edition of the book was revised even more extensively. Saint-Paul believed that the sections that defended "homosexuality" exaggerated its importance, explaining in the preface that gay writers were not always credible sources.

> The reader must be forewarned that some of [the contributions] betray the homosexual nature of their authors. As interesting and important as they may be, these works have too often inflated or exaggerated the importance of homosexuality. In that way, the homosexual writer reveals more than he realizes, more than he would like to reveal about what we still do not know about the psychology of the invert.⁵⁷

---

55. "First Edition."
56. The belief that male homosexuality could be cured by heterosexual intercourse and marriage was widespread at the end of the nineteenth century (see, for example, Pierre Garnier, *Hygiène de la génération. Anomalies sexuelles, apparentes et cachées*, 2nd ed. [Paris: Garnier Frères, 1891], 506), although some experts, such as Marc-André Raffalovich, dismissed it as ineffective and dangerous. Raffalovich, *Uranisme et unisexualité: Une étude des manifestations différentes de l'instinct sexuel* (Lyon: Storck, 1896); translated by Nancy Erber and William A. Peniston as *Marc-André Raffalovich's Uranism and Unisexuality: A Study of Different Manifestations of the Sexual Instinct* (London: Palgrave Macmillan, 2016), 49–50 and passim. In his autobiography, André Gide recalled a consultation with a doctor before his marriage in October 1895: "Shortly before becoming engaged I had therefore made up my mind to unbosom myself to a doctor, a specialist of considerable renown, whom I was rash enough to consult. He smiled as he listened to the confession, which I made as cynically complete as possible; then: 'You say, however, that you are in love with a girl and that you are hesitating to marry her, knowing your tastes on the other hand. . . . Get married. Get married without fear. And you will soon see that all the rest exists only in your imagination. You remind me of a starving man who has been trying until now to live on pickles.'" André Gide, *Et nunc manet in te* (Paris: Ides et Calendes, 1947), 29; translated by Justin O'Brien as *Madeleine (Et nunc manet in te)* (New York: Knopf, 1952; reprint, Chicago: Elephant Paperbacks, 1989), 21.
57. Preface to the second edition.

One of the most striking omissions is the long section at the end of the manuscript where the narrator described feelings of sexual attraction and sensual pleasure, and in particular, the urgency of mutually shared desire. This memorable sentence was excluded: "When <u>we</u> are ensconced in a cozy, safe bedroom, we forget <u>everything</u> else and only one idea, or rather, <u>one feeling</u> remains: a desire that <u>nothing</u> can stop and that must be satisfied, no matter the cost." The entire conclusion, which contains an eloquent apologia for gay individual pleasure, was jettisoned. Saint-Paul substituted the following, less dramatic, passage: "I've told you the <u>causes</u> and the <u>effects</u>; now you must study them for the benefit of science and humanity. It's a beautiful thing to make the world better or at least want to do so. As for me, such as I was born, I will live, and as such, I will die" (Sequel).

As we have argued, the doctor's nationalist and moralistic ideology motivated him to alter the original text and, without acknowledging the interventions, publish a "confession" that better conformed to his own biases. His preface to the third edition described it as "a summary of my essential ideas regarding homosexuality." Although this version of these confessions was longer than the previous one by approximately 2,500 words, it promulgated the same beliefs. For instance, he eliminated passages that he found too pornographic, such as the detailed account of the narrator's affair with the man from Milan, but he did include the Italian man's joyful inventory of male partners (the sergeant, the captain, the Spaniard, etc.); this reinforced a common stereotype about the promiscuity of gay men.

Although the narrator directly disputed the doctor's presentation of him as physically degenerate and visibly effeminate, Saint-Paul eliminated much of the evidence he offered, such as the measurements and descriptions copied from his army personnel file. In their place was a terse footnote: "The author of the document gives details about his anatomy and sexual physiology that indicate that they are completely normal."

Reactions to the Italian's Confessions

The Novel of an Invert did not provoke the controversy that its initial publisher, Storck, once feared. Press reaction at first was slow in coming, and Saint-Paul wrote in disappointment to Zola on January 28, 1897: "No journal, no magazine—not even a scientific one—except for *La Société*

Nouvelle—has deigned to review it."[58] During the following months and years, however, notices, reviews, and reactions—cautious, laudatory, or critical—did appear.[59] Some reviews in medical journals took note of the significance of the topic but, at the same time, endorsed popular theories of degeneration that purported to explain "homosexuality" and marked it as aberrant. A review in *La Tribune Médicale*, for instance, acknowledged the book's contribution to the growing field of sexology by shedding light on "this social evil":

> *The bibliography on sexual perversion is growing day by day. Yesterday it was Mr. Raffalovich's book, and today it is Mr. Laupts'. The source is inexhaustible and the effort increases every day. Would that this social evil lose its grip! Mr. Laupts' book, which begins with a preface by Mr. Zola, also includes the confession of a born invert, which the latter author had provided. These kinds of documents are extremely valuable and must be studied carefully. In the past few years, in fact, a great many autobiographies of this sort have been made public.*[60]

Another doctor, Dr. Dumas, writing in *La Revue Philosophique*, published a favorable review but demurred to give a more precise discussion of the book's contents because of the "nature of the topic." He characterized the Italian author as "a sick man." In contrast, *La Société Nouvelle*, a "rational socialist" journal, was one of the first to review the book and criticized Saint-Paul's views on "homosexuality."[61]

---

58. Saint-Paul to Zola, January 28, 1897, Collection "Dr. François Émile Zola." See also Rosenfeld and Thomson, "Lettres inédites."

59. The Saint-Paul family archives contain a number of press clippings about the book, testifying to Saint-Paul's interest in its critical reception.

60. Review in the February 24, 1897, issue of *La Tribune Médicale*—*Revue Française de Médicine*, a weekly journal specializing in medical science.

61. Augustin Hamon, "Revue des livres," *La Société Nouvelle* (September 1896): 428–29, https://gallica.bnf.fr/ark:/12148/bpt6k1083192/f427.item. *La Société Nouvelle* was founded in 1884 by Fernand Brouez, who edited the journal with a pluralistic left perspective, known as "rational socialism." The Belgian writer Georges Eekhoud, who was himself attracted to men, became a key contributor to it. Hamon (1862–1945), a French writer, philosopher, and editor of political journals, also wrote a review of Edward Carpenter's book on homosexuality, *Homogenic Love*, which appeared in the same issue. Hamon is considered one of the forerunners of the field of social psychology. In 1894 he published *La Psychologie sociale du militaire professionnel*. He and his wife were the official French translators of the works of George Bernard Shaw. The

Not surprisingly, one of the most detailed analyses of the book was by Marc-André Raffalovich, who was himself a contributor to the book that he was reviewing; he had written the third chapter, characterizing Oscar Wilde as a "pervert" rather than an "invert." An "expert" on "unisexuality," as he called homosexuality, Raffalovich was a frequent contributor to the Archives d'Anthropologie Criminelle, in which the review appeared.[62] He gingerly approached areas of disagreement with Saint-Paul, explaining that he felt "awkward trying to find a way to characterize Dr. Laupts' book."

> [It] will be useful, but it could have been much more useful, and I do not know whether I should congratulate him or quarrel with him. . . . His own contributions are interesting even if we do not agree with them, even if we feel compelled to argue against them. It seems to me that, if I had to identify the basic error in his work, it would be that he has focused too much on studying inversion through books than through impartial and penetrating observations of life, and more than once, personal beliefs substitute for professional research.[63]

In addition to his differences with Saint-Paul's analyses, Raffalovich reiterated his ideological opposition to effeminacy, using The Novel of an Invert as an example:

> Mr. Zola graciously submitted the autobiography of an innate effeminate homosexual. . . . I am not as tolerant of Mr. Zola's innate homosexual as Laupts is because that effeminacy, that self-love, that limitless vanity, is disgusting to me in all senses, and because the amateurishness, the pseudo-artistic pose of this poor Narcissus, is rather unconvincing, except as a piece of psychological evidence.[64]

Saint-Paul family archives contains a robust correspondence between Saint-Paul and Hamon. For anarchist writers of the period, such as Hamon, see Caroline Granier, Les Briseurs des formules. Les écrivains anarchistes en France à la fin du XIXe siècle (Coeuvres-et-Valery: Ressouvenances, 2008).

62. Marc-André Raffalovich, "Annales de l'unisexualité," Archives d'Anthropologie Criminelle (1897): 198–202.

63. Raffalovich, "Annales de l'unisexualité," 198–99.

64. Raffalovich, "Annales de l'unisexualité," 199. Writing about Zola's preface, he noted that he would have preferred seeing the "confessions" incarnated in a fictional character in a Zola novel: "This statement by the conquering hero [Zola], proclaimed in this way, serves as a challenge to science, history, and society. It seems odd as the introduction to a scientific study. We would have preferred to see [this document]

In 1911 Dr. Éric Simac published an article entitled "Des types sexuels intermédiaires" / "Intermediate Sexual Types" in the journal *Biologica: Revue Scientifique du Médecin*, which mentioned the recent new edition of Saint-Paul's book, *Invertis et homosexuels*. Although the updated title included more modern terminology, Simac pointed to limitations in the author's understanding of sexuality, which he attributed to a lack of familiarity with more recent German studies. Referring specifically to these confessions, he wrote: "The expanded Chapter V is slightly revised with an addition to *The Novel of an Invert* (entertaining because of its exaggerated and genuine cynicism, which is elegant, nevertheless)."[65]

Letters from Gay Men to Saint-Paul

The publication of Saint-Paul's book prompted gay men in France and elsewhere in Europe to write directly to him. The author of *The Novel of an Invert* was one of these correspondents. Other readers responded to the doctor's survey about "homosexuality" or explained that they hoped to end their isolation through contact with him. Their references to other books, such as contemporary fiction with gay male characters and other studies of sexuality, reveal that the written word was an important point of contact for men struggling with a marginalized sexual identity.

William Robertson was a twenty-four-year-old man living in London. He sent a long letter to Saint-Paul in French on January 19, 1897, proudly proclaiming on the first page: "I am a boy-lover!"[66] He explained that

---

treated as a very meaningful psychological text; we would have preferred to read it coming from the mouth of one of Mr. Zola's characters, a foot soldier in his powerful army that marches toward the conquest of a city, an idea, or a world" (199). He further proposed: "Something that could help effeminate inverts, like this Italian man, would be for them to give up their vanity and repent in their hearts. I do not see any cure for them except one achieved through suffering and faith. Their vanity, their egoism, and their pettiness provide a solid foundation for their lechery" (199).

65. As both a medical doctor and a homosexual, Simac was perhaps doubly qualified as a reviewer. See the new book by Kevin Dubout, *Éric Simac (1874–1913). Un oublié du 'mouvement de libération' homosexuel de la Belle Époque* (Paris: Quintes-Feuilles, 2014), 109.

66. "Je suis païdophile." If Robertson was using Saint-Paul's terminology in his self-diagnosis, a "pedophile" was a male homosexual who preferred effeminate partners, categorized there as the "innate feminiform invert" type.

reading the book motivated him to write and share his own frustrating attempts to find a lover. He boldly asked the doctor to serve as a go-between, arguing:

> In London, there must be many other boys who are suffering greatly, so why don't you enable us to get in touch with each other?... I would be eternally grateful if you could tell me where and how I could find another poor fellow and make him happy, so that both of us would be better equipped to keep working and to destroy the evil within us, along with the lack of tolerance that is everywhere in society.

Demonstrating that he was well-read on the topic, Robertson proposed an intermediary located in London: "Your friend, Mr. Raffalovich, seems to be an extremely enlightened man, free of common prejudices." Perhaps he could help him find a kindred soul. "Wouldn't it be possible," he asked, "to give me one name, and in the process, to make two awfully damaged souls happy, two beings who are not responsible for their malady?"[67]

Another correspondent took greater precautions, and in his letter of May 13, 1903, he used what is most likely a pseudonym, "Gabriel Le Most, traveler." He asked Saint-Paul to reply via the publisher Carré or by sending an answer to the train station at Dreux. Like Robertson, this man said that reading the book prompted his letter. He wanted to participate in Saint-Paul's survey of "homosexuality" and admitted that he too felt isolated. He self-diagnosed himself as follows:

> I feel a feminiform tendency inside me that has gotten stronger in recent years. After a very specific personal situation . . . , I got into the habit of dressing in women's clothes from head to toe, privately, with my wife's consent. . . . Now I have a burning desire to meet another man around my own age, about forty years old, give or take a few years, who would, like me, want to maintain his good reputation. . . . I would like us, as men, to be two lady friends, on occasion two tribades, perhaps even two lesbians.[68]

---

67. William Robertson to Saint-Paul, January 19, 1897, SPFA.

68. "Tribade" was a contemporary term for a female same-sex lover, originating in a term for "rubbing" and the idea that women would stroke each other's genitals to achieve orgasm. It was often used interchangeably with "lesbian" and other, more slangy epithets. It is unclear why this man used both terms in this sentence.

Demonstrating that he was an educated man who understood the conventions of writing about sexuality, he translated the names of sexual acts that attracted and repulsed him into Latin. As a Frenchman, "Le Most" suggested meeting with the doctor in person to discuss these issues.[69]

Another man, Athan Lechmitzky, was a twenty-six-year-old Polish law student in Kiev, who explained that he was a homosexual and an avid student of human psychology. He had clearly read widely, citing Magnus Hirschfeld's advocacy for homosexuals as well as an array of contemporary French novels with gay content: Catulle Mendès's *La Maison de la vieille* / *The Old Lady's House*, Abel Hermant's *Le Disciple aimé* / *The Beloved Disciple*, and Achille Essebac's *Dédé*. Unlike some of the other correspondents, he sounded a militant note, calling same-sex attraction "this love which is the most superior of all of mankind's loves," ending his letter with a phrase from Oscar Wilde, and encouraging Saint-Paul to continue his research: "This science of love, 'the love that dares not speak its name and which our century does not understand' as Oscar Wilde put it, ah, it must be understood."[70]

A man named Ettinger sent seven letters to Saint-Paul between January 1910 and September 1913. A twenty-five-year-old Parisian, he wanted to end the social isolation he felt and asked the doctor for a list of the homosexuals who had written to him, explaining: "I would like to start an association of serious-minded inverts whom I could get to know. The association's goal would be to look into everything that might improve a man's moral well-being, which is so important because of the isolation imposed on us that is often the cause of so many personal traumas."[71]

---

69. "Gabriel Le Most" to Saint-Paul, May 13, 1903, SPFA. We do not know if the meeting ever took place. The writer explained: "I've owned your book *Sexual Perversion and Perversity* for a few years now, the 1896 edition, and I see that, at that time, you asked your readers to submit any psychological documents about sexual inversion. Is there still time for me to send you information on this topic?" He continued his account, writing that he was forty years old, married, and had "a very respectable position, which is very dignified," but he admitted that "I'm a lonely man."

70. Athan Lechmitzky to Saint-Paul, September 29 and October 20, 1905, SPFA.

71. Ettinger to Saint-Paul, January 26, 1910, SPFA. Ettinger also praised Saint-Paul's work highly: "I like your book a lot because it isn't simply a jumble of unfounded observations yielding more or less fanciful conclusions. . . . *The Novel of an Invert*, which you

Saint-Paul noted in pencil on Ettinger's February 4, 1910, letter "probably advanced stage tuberculosis," suggesting that Ettinger had consulted him in person.[72]

Georges Hérelle, an accomplished ethnographer and philosophy teacher, wrote to Saint-Paul on April 30, 1897. Like Lechmitzky, he rejected the contemporary belief that homosexuals were sick men and also disputed the efficacy of any purported "cure": "I have no faith in your preventive measures, nor in your treatment; I don't expect to be cured by you; I don't consider myself to be sick in the ordinary and accepted sense of the word." He accused Saint-Paul of lacking scientific objectivity, which blinded him to his correspondents' real motives: "This, I think, is the actual state of mind of most of the men who are sending you their 'novel.' Consider the results. You are making a grave error, I believe, if, by being overly credulous about their confessions and their complaints, you claim without reservations that they are all begging you for a cure."[73]

Although not all the letter-writers were as assertive as Hérelle or Lechmitzky, a striking number of them were very frank. Often well-versed in contemporary medical theories, the men diagnosed themselves, were not ashamed of their sexuality, and often advocated for changes in society rather than a personal cure.

---

published in your work, is an authentic masterpiece of sincerity and truth. It is rare to find confessions that are so free of bragging and lies." Ettinger to Saint-Paul, February 4, 1910, SPFA. Ettinger's reaction suggests that in 1910 the Italian man's confession was still a compelling personal story whose authenticity he did not question.

72. Notation on Ettinger to Saint-Paul, February 4, 1910. In a letter dated March 7, 1912, Ettinger thanked Saint-Paul for having written to the medical officer of his regiment, where Ettinger was fulfilling his reserve duty, so clearly some kind of professional relationship had been established. Ettinger to Saint-Paul, March 7, 1912, SPFA.

73. Georges Hérelle to Saint-Paul, April 30, 1897. We do not know if Hérelle sent this letter to Saint-Paul or if it was merely an idea. The rough draft is located in the Fonds Hérelle in the Médiathèque Grand Troyes, Ms. 3257. The letter was published in full for the first time in 1987 by Philippe Lejeune in "Autobiographie et homosexualité." Hérelle's groundbreaking research into the history of homosexuality is also significant, but it remained unpublished during his lifetime; see Clive Thomson, *Georges Hérelle: Archéologue de l'inversion sexuelle 'fin de siècle'* (Paris: Le Félin, 2014).

Zola and the Italian's Confessions

Émile Zola played a crucial role in publishing The Novel of an Invert, and Saint-Paul repeatedly acknowledged the importance of his contributions. Without Zola's support and the powerful preface that he wrote, the autobiography might not ever have been published, or if it had, it would not have garnered the same amount of attention. What motivated Zola? Reconstructing the stages in the process will help clarify the connections between the famous novelist and these autobiographical letters.

At the time that Zola received the letters in 1888, he was working on his novel La Bête humaine, and a short paragraph in Zola's preparatory notes for the novel suggests that he may have read The Novel of an Invert then, since they show him considering, then rejecting, gay love as an element in the plot.[74]

> Put a rotten tale of money and love underneath the crime. Of pederasty, no doubt. If the man dies with no heirs. The woman is sure to profit from his death: she knows he is a pederast; she doesn't love him; he disgusts her; it's a real relief for her to be rid of him; but she is implicated, and doesn't want the truth to come out. . . . No, I'll rethink that, no pederasty; that's a detour, sends me into trite and despicable territory.[75]

In his letter, the Italian man drew parallels between his own life and that of Zola's characters, especially the effeminate Maxime in La Curée / The Kill: "The book that I like the most is La Curée, where I find characters with similar feelings to my own and who live in a society in which I've lived almost my entire life, the upper class in which I was born and still live."[76] He emphasized their resemblance with more details from the novel: "I enjoy women's company a great deal. It really affects me the same way the ladies in La Curée do for your Maxime, whom I resemble a little. But, being

---

74. Henri Mitterand, Zola, vol. 2: L'Homme de Germinal, 1871–1893 (Paris: Fayard, 2001), 941–84.

75. The manuscripts of the preparatory notes are preserved at the Bibliothèque Nationale de France, NAF, 10274, ff. 346–47. We thank Clive Thomson for giving us this reference.

76. Novel, "Third Document."

more unhappy than he, my nature will not allow me to love, and it leaves me only with cold <u>debauchery</u>, which I end up finding repulsive."⁷⁷ In fact, the fictional Maxime was endowed with some personality traits presumed to be typical of gay men of the time; Zola's notebooks for La Curée include a description of him as "virtually pederastic."⁷⁸ Maxime, however, engages in relationships only with women. Another character, the valet Baptiste, is revealed to be gay by the novel's end; the Italian man categorically rejected any identification with him and tried to draw distinctions between them:⁷⁹

> You yourself, Sir, in your admirable La Curée have only touched on one of the most frightful vices that dishonors mankind in the character of your Baptiste. That man is despicable because the debauchery in which he engaged has nothing to do with love and is only an absolutely material thing, a question of congenital malformation that doctors have observed and described more than once.⁸⁰

Like the Italian author, another anonymous correspondent wrote to Zola from Venice, on April 8, 1890, to ask Zola: "Before you reach the end of your great novel cycle, The Rougon-Macquart, why don't you describe the aberration of the reproductive instinct?"⁸¹ He went on to explain: "A male by

---

77. Novel, "Second Document."
78. Émile Zola, La Fabrique des Rougon-Macquart. Édition des dossiers préparatores, ed. Colette Becker and Véronique Lavielle, 7 vols. (Paris: Honoré Champion, 2003–2017), 1:492, 494.
79. We can propose several reasons that the letter writer would not identify with Baptiste, the valet of Maxime's father, Aristide Saccard, in the novel. In the first place, he seems to exploit his position as a domestic servant in order to have sexual relations with stable hands. His desires are strictly physical and not tempered with any emotion. Even so, this character's actions resemble the Italian man's recollections of his relations with servants during his adolescence, except the letter writer was of a different class and age than Baptiste. It may be that as a member of the Neapolitan aristocracy, a certain snobbery prevented him from identifying with a fictional servant. For an in-depth analysis, see Michael Rosenfeld, "Zola et l'homosexualité, un nouveau regard," Les Cahiers Naturalistes 89 (2015): 213–28.
80. Novel, "First Document."
81. René Ternois, "Mélanges—ce que Zola n'avait pas osé dire," Les Cahiers Naturalistes 35 (1968): 59–160. The original letter sent to Zola has not been found in the Zola family archives, even though René Ternois reproduced it in his article, thus indicating it was in the archives in 1968. The term "aberration of the reproductive instinct"

birth, brave, intelligent, but condemned from a young age, from birth, in fact, to love only members of the same sex? This type of hereditary nervous disease is your kind of story. It might not be as tragic as Jacques Lantier's fate, but it's a thousand times more common than the murderous mania that destroys the lives and happiness of his miserable victims."[82]

Saint-Paul also wondered why Zola had never addressed homosexuality. "The first time we discussed inversion," he wrote in 1907, "a very natural question came to my lips: 'Why haven't you dealt with inversion? Why haven't you devoted one of your novels to this subject? Isn't it worth the trouble?' Zola never gave me a precise answer. No doubt, he told me he did not dare, and later on, he wrote the same thing to me." At that point, Saint-Paul was immersed in his medical studies with Lacassagne and his research study about inversion; he had read only one or two of Zola's novels: "L'Assommoir and another one whose title I had forgotten. 'The one that takes place on the railroad,' I told him (La Bête humaine). He smiled. A few days later, I received The Debacle with a cordial, hand-written dedication."[83]

Zola's choice of a novel to give Saint-Paul was surely not accidental.[84] The Debacle was written in 1891–1892, published in installments from February 21 to July 21, 1892, and brought out in one volume in June 1892

---

was, like "inversion," "unnatural love," and "uranism," a contemporary term for queerness.

82. Ternois, "Mélanges." Jacques Lantier was the main character in Zola's novel La Bête humaine, published serially from November 14, 1889, to March 2, 1890; it appeared as a single volume in March 1890, published by Charpentier. Lantier was obsessed by homicidal impulses. The English poet and critic John Addington Symonds (1843–1893) mentioned to his friend Edmund Gosse that he wanted to send a letter to Zola about the character Lantier: "I, too, felt deeply moved by the analysis of Jacques Lantier in La Bête humaine. On my way from Milan, I wrote a letter to Zola, suggesting that he should make a study of sexual inversion. I think I am going to send it. But I do not suppose he will follow my suggestion." The similarities between the contents described by Symonds and the letter found by Ternois suggest that it could be attributed to the English poet. If so, however, the letter was not found in the Zola family archives. See also John G. Younger, "Ten Unpublished Letters by John Addington Symonds at Duke University," Victorian Newsletter 95 (spring 1999): 1–10. We thank Giovanni Dall'Orto for bringing this article to our attention.

83. "In Memoriam: Émile Zola."

84. The copy Zola gave Saint-Paul is in the Saint-Paul family archives. It is an 1894 edition with a dedication: "To Dr. Saint-Paul, your sincere and faithful friend, Émile Zola."

by Charpentier-Fasquelle.[85] The gay relationship between the two main characters, Jean and Maurice, has very strong parallels to one described in The Novel of an Invert—the affair between the narrator and his sergeant during their military service.[86] For example, in The Debacle, Zola wrote:

> Maurice was crying like a child, and tears rolled slowly down Jean's cheeks. It was the reaction after their long torment, the joy of telling themselves that suffering might take pity on them at last. They hugged each other in a passionate embrace, made brothers by all they had gone through together, and the kiss they exchanged seemed the gentlest yet the strongest in their lives, a kiss the like of which they would never have received from a woman, undying friendship and absolute certainty that their two hearts were henceforth one forever.[87]

In The Novel of an Invert, the anonymous letter-writer wrote:

> Our tongues joined in our mouths. We held each other so tightly we could barely breathe. I stroked this beautiful body, so ardently desired, with my feverish hands, and the lovely, serious, virile head that made such a pleasing contrast with mine. At last, our pleasure reached its climax, and we had the joy of reaching orgasm at the same time. We held each other for a long time, caressing each other, and

---

85. Émile Zola, La Débâcle, Les Rougon-Macquart (1892) (Paris: Gallimard, 1960), 5:1361, translated by Leonard Tancock as The Debacle (New York: Penguin Books, 1972).

86. Researchers view the nature of the relationship between Jean and Maurice in this novel differently. Brian Joseph Martin also noted the similarities between the two stories in his work, Napoleonic Friendship: Military Fraternity, Intimacy, and Sexuality in Nineteenth-Century France (Durham: University of New Hampshire Press, 2011), 262, but he views the bond between them as homosocial. Nicholas White adopts a nuanced approach in a variety of articles, underlining the homosocial bond between Jean and Maurice in "L'homos et l'heteros des Rougon-Macquart" and "Zola's 'champ limité de la réalisation': La Débâcle and the Commune." He also emphasizes the homoeroticism between the two men in " 'L'enclume toujours chaude': Émile Zola's Newspaper Trilogy" (340) and in "Style Wars: The Uniform and the Polymorphous in La Débâcle." We see the relationship between Jean and Maurice as queer, as shown by the two passionate kisses they exchange in the novel, and we attribute this interpretation to the influence of the Italian's text on Zola. An in-depth analysis of this relationship is found in Rosenfeld, "Zola et l'homosexualité."

87. Zola, La Débâcle, 785; Zola, The Debacle, trans. Tancock, 388.

exchanging sweet words. "Never have I had such pleasure with a woman," he said. "Their kisses and their caresses are neither as warm nor as passionate."

In both narratives, where the comrades share final words before parting, there are also striking similarities. The Debacle has a dramatic, heartfelt farewell:

"Kiss me, boy." They kissed each other, and as in the woods the day before there was in this kiss a brotherly love born of dangers shared, of these few weeks of heroic life in common which had united them more intimately than years of ordinary friendship could have done. . . . Can two hearts ever take themselves back again when a mutual gift has thus welded them to each other? But the kiss exchanged in the darkness among the trees had been full of new hope opened up by escape, whereas this one now was full of the anguish of parting.[88]

The Novel of an Invert describes the wrenching pain that the author and the sergeant faced at their separation:

My year of military service was almost at an end, and I thought about my approaching departure with real terror—something that I would have believed was impossible a year before. The idea that I would have to be separated for a long time, if not forever, from my friend was unbearable, and at night we would often cry together. He still had several years to serve, and he was pained to see the time coming when he would be left alone and lonely, now that he had a friend who was so passionately attached to him. . . . Finally, the terrible day arrived. We said our good-byes in the little room where so many happy hours had been spent, and I delayed my departure in order to enjoy my dear and beloved friend one last time.

In addition, we can see the intimacy between the men developing along the same lines. At first there is distrust, then the men become closer emotionally, and finally they share a physical bond. In The Novel of an Invert, the men repeatedly have sexual relations, whereas in Zola's novel they exchange two passionate kisses. In each story, one comrade dies. Perhaps not surprisingly, since it provides a more moralistic ending, in The Debacle, one man kills the other (by mistake during the Paris Commune). In the Italian man's account, his sergeant-lover died six months after their last kiss, murdered

---

88. Zola, La Débâcle, 793; Zola, The Debacle, trans. Tancock, 396.

by a drunken comrade. The anonymous author even remarked on the novelistic overtones of the circumstances of his lover's death, while insisting that all the details were accurate. It seems likely that, given the similarities between the two stories of doomed lovers, Zola gave Saint-Paul a copy of The Debacle as a partial answer to his question about inversion in fiction, subtly pointing out his own inspiration by The Novel of an Invert.

When he received The Sequel to the Novel of an Invert in January 1897, Zola was working on another novel, Paris. This novel first appeared in installments from September 1897 to March 1898 and then was published in one volume in March 1898 by Charpentier-Fasquelle.[89] In it, the character Hyacinthe is identified as a "sodomite."[90] Zola's preparatory notes describe him as "a degenerate sort but very elegant. Very stylish, very well-dressed and well-groomed. Long blond hair, curly. . . . Goes to all the extremes: Ibsen, Nietzsche, individualism, sodomy. He's a braggart of vice, and especially of pederasty, Douglas-style. Women disgust him."[91] Although this sketch of Hyacinthe seems to draw on contemporary stereotypes of modern, effete young men, and Zola even cites Lord Alfred Douglas as a model, there are a number of similarities, too, with the self-presentation of the Italian man. We will cite only a few examples.[92] The name Hyacinthe itself appears to be borrowed from these confessions; he is mentioned a number of times, and the Italian compared himself to him: "My body resembles the most charming Greek statues: but I'm more like the statuette of Hyacinth in the Naples Museum . . . than the statue of Hermaphrodite" (Sequel).

---

89. Émile Zola, Paris, vol. 7 of Oeuvres complètes (Paris: Cercle du Livre Précieux, 1968), 1578, translated by Ernest A. Vizetelly as Paris (New York: Macmillan, 1897), reprinted in The Three Cities Trilogy (2015). Henri Mitterand followed the work on the writing of this novel from the end of 1896 to the first half of 1897: see Zola, Paris, 1598.

90. Zola, Paris, 1198. Zola's English-language translator, Vizetelly, removed the word "sodomite" from his translation.

91. "Douglas-style" is a reference to Lord Alfred Douglas, Oscar Wilde's lover. In Zola's novel, Hyacinthe pursues the young English Lord Elson, "a languid and pale ephebe with girlish locks." Zola's preparatory notes to this novel are preserved in the Bibliothèque Méjanes in Aix-en-Provence, Ms.1471, ff. 120, 271.

92. In his dissertation from 1977, Clive Thomson detected some of these similarities in the text. See Clive Thomson, "Critical Edition of Paris by Émile Zola, with Historical Introduction, Genetic Study, and Literary Analysis," Ph.D. diss., University of Toronto, 1977. We arrived at the same conclusions forty years later without knowing about his discoveries.

The narrator's family and that of Hyacinthe also resemble each other. In *Paris*, Baroness Duvillard, Hyacinthe's mother, is described as an exotically beautiful woman: "Her Jewish origins were revealed by her somewhat long and strangely charming face, with blue and softly voluptuous eyes. As indolent as an Oriental slave, disliking to have to move, walk, or even speak, she seemed intended for a harem life, especially as she was forever tending her person."[93] The Italian man's mother was also Jewish, from "a European country that was still quite <u>Oriental</u>," and a striking beauty: "Her <u>beautiful</u> blue-green eyes, her delicately chiseled features, her rosy complexion, and her golden brown hair never hinted at her race, which acquaintances would have suspected only because of her slightly hooked nose and something odd about her light-colored eyes" (Sequel).

Hyacinthe and the Italian man share other traits. In *Paris*, Zola described Hyacinthe as an attractive, though affected and degenerate, young man:

> He was twenty and had inherited his mother's pale blond hair and her long face full of Oriental languor; while from his father he had derived his gray eyes and thick lips, expressive of unscrupulous appetites. He took some interest in poetry and music, and lived in an extraordinary circle of artists, low women, madmen and bandits, boasting himself of all sorts of crimes and vices, [affecting a horror of women].[94]

In *The Novel of an Invert*, we learn that the narrator was also blond and handsome:

> My head is pretty, and at eighteen, it was even more so. Its oval shape is perfect and everyone is struck by its childlike form. . . . My forehead isn't handsome; it is receding slightly with deep-set temples; luckily, it is half covered with curly, sandy-blond hair that is naturally frizzy. . . . My eyes are wide and bluish gray with long dark eyelashes and thick arched eyebrows. . . . My mouth is rather large with big red lips; my lower lip hangs down a little.

Furthermore, the Italian man explained that he did not care for women: "I have an aversion—the most <u>absolute</u> kind—to women, but I do consider

93. Zola, *Paris*, 1194; Zola, *Paris*, trans. Vizetelly, 37–38.
94. Zola, *Paris*, 1198; Zola, *Paris*, trans. Vizetelly, 45–46. The last phrase, "affecting a horror of women," is in the original, but Vizetelly cut it from his translation.

women to be most like me." Like Hyacinthe, however, in *The Sequel*, he did love art, literature and music: "Literature still interests me a great deal. I have journals in many languages everywhere. I devour a large number of books. Paintings (by other artists) please me immensely. But the art that thrills me the most is music." It seems clear that in this novel Zola not only drew on the Italian man's autobiography to construct this character but also adopted Saint-Paul's approach to the "treatment" of "homosexuality". Here the plot of the novel diverges from the Italian man's autobiography: Hyacinthe marries a woman as a "cure" for his malady, although the letter-writer never considered this option.[95]

The Influence of the Italian's Confessions on Zola's Opinions

Did reading the Italian man's letters influence Zola's attitude toward gay love in any way? There is little direct evidence since the preface he wrote for Saint-Paul's *Tares et poisons* is one of the few examples of his engaging with the question.[96] There he condemned love between men with epithets such as "repulsive instincts," "abominable loves," and "the human and social disease of sexual perversion," concluding with nationalistic fervor: "Everything related to sex is related to society itself. An invert is a disruptor of the family, the nation, and humanity. Man and Woman are surely here on earth only in order to have children, and they destroy life the day when they no longer do what they must."

Some scholars have concluded, on the basis of this text, that Zola's reluctance to discuss gay love indicates a deep personal disgust with it.[97] We can, however, also read his statements in the contemporary

---

95. On the influence of Saint-Paul on Zola's novel *Fécondité* (1899), see Michael Rosenfeld, "Zola à la pointe des savoirs. Théories scientifiques et personnages de médecins dans Fécondité," *Les Cahiers Naturalistes* 95 (2021): 65–80.

96. For a more detailed analysis, see Michael Rosenfeld, "Genèse d'une pensée sur l'homosexualité: La préface de Zola au Roman d'un inverti," *Genesis* 44 (2017): 213–17.

97. Philippe Ariès, "Réflexions sur l'histoire de l'homosexualité," *Communications* 35 (1982): 56–67; Lejeune, "Autobiographie et homosexualité"; Rudi Bleys, *The Geography of Perversion* (New York: New York University Press, 1995), 211–12; Patrick Cardon, *Discours littéraires et scientifiques fin-de-siècle, autour de Marc-André Raffalovich* (Paris: Éditions Orizons, 2008), 71–73; Stéphane Gougelmann, "Le Naturaliste, l'homosexuel et

context of French nationalism and Zola's strident advocacy for pronatalist policies. As a member of the National Alliance for Population Growth, he called for increasing the French birth rate; it was a patriotic duty.[98] In fact, he published an open letter, "To Young People," in *Le Figaro* in 1896 with many of the same themes. Like his preface, the letter cautioned against selfishness and individualism "that can so easily be diverted into the worst perversions, the most serious and fatal social dangers. You are already caught up in it, in mysticism, satanism, occultism, a religion that thrives on the devil, on love that doesn't make babies."[99]

Zola addressed the same arguments to French women later that year in another article in *Le Figaro*, linking France's birth rate to women's love of country: "O French mothers, make babies so that France will keep its place in the world, its strength, and its prosperity, because, to save the world, France must live. She is the source of human emancipation; she is the wellspring of all truth and all justice!"[100] Clearly, Zola was condemning practices and beliefs, including same-sex love, that jeopardized France and sapped its powers from within. Yet he also expressed profound sympathy in his preface to Saint-Paul's book for "an unhappy man [who] sent me the most poignant cry of human suffering that I have ever heard." We need to recognize that the same polemicist who urged his fellow citizens to "make babies" in order to "save the world" also penned one of the most compelling defenses of queer love at the turn of the century. He based his appeal on science, arguing:

> *Are we not witnessing a genuine physiological phenomenon, a hesitation, a partial error of nature? Nothing is more tragic, in my opinion, and nothing calls out more for a cure, if there is one. In the mystery of conception, which is so poorly*

---

l'éloquence de la vérité," in *Le Réalisme et ses paradoxes (1850–1900)*, ed. Gabrielle Chamarat and Pierre-Jean Dufief (Paris: Classiques Garnier, 2014), 471–79. Saint-Paul definitely influenced this interpretation, writing in "In Memoriam: Émile Zola": "The sight of and, above all, contact with inverts were disagreeable for Zola. 'I have met them in society,' he told me one day, 'and I feel an instinctive revulsion when shaking their hands—a revulsion that I have trouble controlling'" (see part 2 of this volume).

98. Andrew J. Counter, "Zola's Fin-de-Siècle Reproductive Politics," *French Studies* 68 (2014): 193–208.

99. The open letter appeared on February 7, 1896. See also Émile Zola, *Chroniques et Polémiques II*, vol. 12 of *Oeuvres complètes* (Paris: Cercle du Livre Précieux, 1968), 723–28.

100. "Dépopulation," *Le Figaro*, May 23, 1896, 785–90.

understood, can this be considered possible? A child is born: Why a boy? Why a girl? We do not know. But what complications of darkness and torment are there if nature has a moment of uncertainty, and a boy is born partly a girl, or a girl is born partly a boy? The evidence is there—every day. The uncertainty can start simply with merely their physical appearance or with certain aspects of their temperament: a man is effeminate, delicate, and cowardly; a woman is masculine, aggressive, and unfeeling. And it can go so far as verifiable monstrosity: hermaphroditic organs or unnatural feelings and passions. Certainly, morality and justice are right to intervene because they must uphold public order. But by what right when one's willpower has been partially eliminated? We don't condemn a hunchback because he was born that way. Why despise a man for acting like a woman if he was born half a woman?[101]

Zola was well-known for championing medical theories about heredity and using them to great effect in his popular novels.[102] If an "error of nature" was responsible for the existence of "homosexuals," as he argued, they should not be condemned for their aberrant behavior—a position contrary to one held by contemporary leaders in politics and the criminal justice system.[103] Zola had already publicly expressed compassion for pariahs and other vulnerable members of society, a role that he would enact even more prominently during the Dreyfus Affair. In a letter to the author Marc-André Raffalovich, he explained that, although he did not understand "homosexuality," he wanted to learn more about this aspect of human nature. Drawing a distinction between sympathy and empathy, he wrote:

> I'm reading your book, Sir. It's quite interesting for me, but I don't understand the topic very well. Even though I'm overwhelmed with pity for the men you call "uranists," I don't empathize with them at all, no doubt because I'm different. Man

---

101. "Preface by Émile Zola."

102. Christopher Rivers, "Improbable Prescience: Émile Zola and the Origins of Homosexuality," *Excavatio* 14 (2001): 41–62. Zola's ideas about human conception, reproduction, and sexuality were directly inspired by Dr. Julien Chevalier's book, *Une maladie de la personnalité. L'Inversion sexuelle* (Lyon: Storck; Paris: Masson, 1893).

103. Richard M. Berrong, "A French Reaction to the Wilde Affair and Increasing Homophobia in Late Nineteenth-Century France: Pierre Loti's Judith Renaudin," *Neophilologus* 95 (2011): 177–89; Henri Mitterand, Zola, vol. 3: *L'Honneur, 1893–1902* (Paris: Fayard, 2002), 155–57.

and woman—I can't visualize any other kind of couple that is possible in nature, unless it is due to a physical or psychic perversion. Perhaps I'm simply uninformed; and if circumstances permit, I would enjoy discussing this with you. During the winter, I'm always at home for visitors at 6:00 p.m.[104]

After Zola's death, Saint-Paul made a point of recognizing Zola's defiance of convention when he expressed compassion for gay men and decried their treatment in society, but the doctor credited personal contacts and an open heart, rather than advances in medical knowledge, for this attitude:

> For a Frenchman, it was not an easy task to study the problem of homosexuality when the translation of Krafft-Ebing's work was unknown to everyone except a few psychologists or when a publisher was dragged before the courts for having published Moll's work. . . . Zola had not read any studies on inversion. He was unfamiliar with Krafft-Ebing, Moll, Chevalier, or Lacassagne, but he had received documents and confessions from unfortunate individuals who painfully described their torment, and since he was immensely kind and had an extraordinarily lucid mind, he understood and was moved.[105]

Zola had other social contacts with gay men, mostly fellow writers. He helped the poet Paul Verlaine when he was down on his luck,[106] and he met Oscar Wilde several times.[107] When Wilde came to Paris in 1891, trailed by an entourage of journalists, Zola received him, along with Robert Sherard and Carlos Blacker, calling the visit "a great honor."[108] In 1893 Zola and Wilde met again in London, where Zola praised him as a "very

---

104. Zola to Raffalovich, April 16, 1896, in Zola, Correspondance, 8:315–16.
105. "In Memoriam: Émile Zola."
106. Zola sent Verlaine some money in 1888. Verlaine led an erratic life, had a tumultuous affair with the young poet Arthur Rimbaud, and fell in love with one of his students, Lucien Létinois, who died young. Zola to Verlaine, July 5 and August 8, 1888, in Zola, Correspondance, 6:310–11, 317, 324.
107. Hugues Le Roux, "Oscar Wilde," Le Figaro, December 2, 1891, 3; Jacques Daurelle, "Un poète anglais à Paris," Écho de Paris, December 6, 1891, 2; Oscar Wilde, "À propos du Journal des Goncourts," Écho de Paris, December 19, 1891, p.2.
108. J. Robert Maguire, Ceremonies of Bravery: Oscar Wilde, Carlos Blacker and the Dreyfus Affair (Oxford: Oxford University Press, 2013), 125. Sherard was Wilde's first biographer; Blacker was Wilde's close friend in the 1880s and 1890s.

charming and remarkable poet."[109] Nevertheless, a few years later, in 1895, in a blow to French and Belgian artists' defense of Wilde, he publicly refused to sign their petition calling for leniency.[110]

Despite this very public rejection, Wilde did play a part in Zola's advocacy for Dreyfus a few years later, as J. Robert Maguire has found, by giving him information about the actual traitor, Ferdinand Walsin-Esterhazy.[111] Wilde communicated through an intermediary, Chris Healy, a young poet who was the lover and "secretary" of an English journalist named Rowland Strong. Healy recalled that Zola wanted to meet Wilde in person to find out more, even though Wilde was a social pariah after being released from prison.[112] Surely, this is a testament to the novelist's pragmatism.[113]

A few years later, Zola defended the Belgian writer Georges Eekhoud, signing a letter of support in October 1900 and joining many other prominent French authors in an open letter published by the literary journal *Le Mercure de France*.[114] Eekhoud was accused of violating the laws on pornography in his 1899 novel *Escal-Vigor*, which depicted queer love in a

---

109. Colin Burns, "Le Voyage de Zola à Londres en 1893. 'Notes sur Londres,' texte inédit d'Émile Zola," *Les Cahiers Naturalistes* 60 (1986): 65.

110. "Petition for Wilde a Failure," *New York Times*, November 27, 1895; Stuart Merill, "Pour Oscar Wilde—epilogue," *La Plume*, no. 161 (January 1, 1896): 8. See also Nancy Erber, "The French Trials of Oscar Wilde," *Journal of the History of Sexuality* 6, (1996): 549–88.

111. Maguire, *Ceremonies of Bravery*. See also J. Robert Maguire, "Chronique dreyfusienne," *Les Cahiers Naturalistes* 67 (1993): 326–34. Ferdinand Walsin-Esterhazy's role as a spy, along with other information, was revealed in an article entitled "La Vérité sur Esterhazy" in *Le Siècle* on April 4, 1898.

112. Chris Healy also published a book on the role of Wilde and Zola in the Dreyfus Affair: *Confessions of a Journalist* (London: Chatto & Windus, 1904).

113. In this case, Wilde refused to meet Zola. For more on Wilde's role, see Erin G. Carlston, *Double Agents: Espionage, Literature and Liminal Citizens* (New York: Columbia University Press, 2013), 84–86.

114. "Les procès Georges Eekhoud et Camille Lemonnier," *Mercure de France* 36 (October–December 1900): 573–74. The original petition with the signatures of Zola, Maurice Montégut, and Paul Brulat is preserved in the Archives et Musée de la Littérature (Brussels): MLA 2967. Among the other French writers who signed on were Jean Lorrain, René Maizeroy, Catulle Mendès, Octave Mirbeau, Abel Hermant, Rachilde, Anatole France, Léon Blum, and Alfred Jarry.

positive light. The author was acquitted at his trial in October 1900.[115] Finally, Magnus Hirschfeld noted in his *Jahrbuch für Sexuelle Zwischenstufen / Yearbook of Sexual Intermediates* in 1902 that he had sent his petition calling for the abolition of Germany's Paragraph 175, the section criminalizing sodomy, to Zola and other European luminaries, such as Leo Tolstoy, Georg Brandes, and Bjørnstjerne Martinus Bjørnson.[116] Zola has long been credited with signing this petition, but in fact, only the Norwegian Bjørnson supported the campaign. Since only citizens of the German Reich could legally sign a petition sent to the Reichstag, and since we cannot find any trace of Zola's name on supporters' lists kept by the Magnus Hirschfeld Center in Berlin, we can conclude that Zola never replied to this request.[117] We think that Zola was thought to be one of the signers for so long because of his image as a man who defended the defenseless.[118]

---

115. Jacques Detemmerman, "Le procès d'Escal-Vigor," in *Le Naturalisme et les lettres françaises de Belgique*, ed. Paul Delsemme and Raymond Trousson, *Revue de l'Université de Bruxelles* 4–5 (1984): 168–69; and Michael Rosenfeld, "Gay Taboos in 1900 Brussels: The Literary, Journalistic and Private Debate Surrounding Georges Eekhoud's Novel Escal-Vigor," *Dix-Neuf* 22 (2018): 98–114.

116. Magnus Hirschfeld, "Jahresbericht 1901 von Dr. med. M. Hirschfeld-Charlottenburg," *Jahrbuch für Sexuelle Zwischenstufen* (1902), 971.

117. This information comes from Ralf Dose, a researcher at the Magnus-Hirschfeld-Gesellschaft in Berlin, in an e-mail to Michael Rosenfeld dated November 13, 2013.

118. The pioneering researchers on the modern homosexual rights movement, John Lauritsen and David Thorstad, stated that Zola had signed the petition. John Lauritsen and David Thorstad, *The Early Homosexual Rights Movement (1864–1935)* (New York: Times Change Press, 1974), 14–15. In November 2013, in an exchange of letters, they admitted that their interpretation of the publication in the *Jahrbuch für Sexuelle Zwischenstufen* could be contested. This error has been repeated in a long list of publications: Dominique Fernandez, *Le Rapt de Ganymède* (Paris: Grasset & Fasquelle, 1989), 73–74, 81; Florence Tamagne, *Histoire de l'homosexualité en Europe: Berlin, Londres, Paris, 1919–1939* (Paris: Seuil, 2000), translated as *A History of Homosexuality in Europe: Berlin, London, Paris, 1919–1939* (New York: Algora, 2004); Rivers, "Improbable Prescience"; "Hirschfeld, Magnus," in *Dictionnaire des cultures gays et lesbiennes*, ed. Didier Eribon (Paris: Larousse, 2003), 286; Nicholas Matte, "International Sexual Reform and Sexology in Europe, 1897–1933," *Canadian Bulletin of Medical History* 22 (2005): 253–70; and dozens of others. The page on Magnus Hirschfeld in the French version of Wikipedia (http://fr.wikipedia.org/wiki/Magnus_Hirschfeld, consulted March 5, 2022,) perpetuates this error, but the one in the English version does not (https://en.wikipedia.org/wiki/Magnus_Hirschfeld).

How should we evaluate this contradictory evidence of Zola's attitudes toward queer love? Zola, as a novelist and an advocate, was concerned with the vagaries of human sexuality. He admitted that he could not understand same-sex attraction or empathize with gay behavior, which he saw as a threat to society, but he did call for compassion for the men whose heredity made them that way. Zola's collaboration with Saint-Paul on his book is a sign of his goodwill toward the young doctor who risked his early career and reputation with studies of inversion. Zola's contribution to the book, his preface, is proof of his own courage. The fact that love between men became a thematic element in two of the novels he wrote after 1888 suggests that reading these confessions had deepened his engagement. It seems clear that Hyacinthe, in Zola's novel *Paris*, is the Italian man's alter ego. We do not know if the author of these letters ever read this novel, and if so, we do not know how he reacted to it. Did he recognize himself in it? Did he finally have the satisfaction of knowing that he had become a character in a novel by Zola?

PART I
The Confessions of a Homosexual to Émile Zola

The letters that the young man addressed to Émile Zola in 1888 or 1889 were published in installments in the *Archives d'Anthropologie Criminelle* in 1894–1895 under the title "Le Roman d'un inverti" / "The Novel of an Invert." They were published entirely in French, with a few editorial changes made by the doctor. We have indicated those changes in footnotes. In 1896, when they were published in Saint-Paul's book *Tares et poisons. Perversion et perversité sexuelles* / *Defects and Poisons: Sexual Perversion and Perversity*, the title was changed to "Le Roman d'un inverti-né" / "The Novel of a Born Invert," and several passages were translated into Latin. We have put these passages in *italics*. Some, but not all, of these passages were copied from the original manuscript into another, entitled "Passages qui ont dû être supprimés" / "Passages to be suppressed." We have enclosed these passages in curly brackets { }. Notes provide additional information if it is available.

The 1910 and 1930 editions of the letters to Zola were identical to the 1896 edition. Although the title of the 1910 edition was still "Le Roman d'un inverti-né," the text included a letter from the Italian to Saint-Paul as an addendum with the title "Suite du roman d'un invert-né" / "Sequel to the Novel of a Born Invert." In the 1930 edition, both were published together under the title "Portrait d'inverti. Silhouettes de bisexuels" / "Portrait of an Invert. Profiles of Bisexuals." Alain Pagès found this letter to Dr. Saint-Paul in the Zola family archives in 2011 under the title "Lettre au Dr Laupts. Suite des confessions d'un homosexuel" / "Letter to Dr. Laupts. Sequel to the Confessions of a Homosexual." It is forty pages long (ten double folio sheets), written on high-quality paper of a small format, with very few corrections or crossed out words, which indicate that the author probably wrote a draft beforehand. The addition of notes at the bottom of some of the pages suggests that he added information at certain points during the writing of the text. We have included these notes in this book. The handwriting becomes increasingly smaller toward the final page, as he struggled to write everything he wished. The letter contains nearly sixteen thousand words. The entire manuscript was reproduced in facsimile in the French edition, *Confessions d'un homosexual à Émile Zola* / *Confessions of a Homosexual to Émile Zola*. We have reproduced only a few of these pages throughout the text.

Both the 1910 and 1930 editions of the "Sequel" reveal that Saint-Paul expunged large sections of the autobiographical letter. In fact, he published only about one-third of it. Some passages were deleted from the 1910 edition but added back into the one published in 1930. In these cases, we have used square brackets [ ] to indicate the various editorial changes that Saint-Paul made, and footnotes provide further information if it is available. Likewise, the portions of "The Sequel to the Confessions of a Homosexual" that did not appear in the 1910 and 1930 editions appear in this distinct sans serif font, and footnotes provide further information if it is available.

<u>Underlined words</u> or <u>double-underlined</u> words were first published in italics in the published versions, but they are underlined in the original manuscripts that have recently been found in the Saint-Paul family archives and the Zola family archives, and so we have underlined them or double-underlined them according to how the Italian author emphasized them.

We have corrected misspelled words and punctuation errors, and we have used standard paragraphing, adhering to modern English-language usage. The anonymous letter writer often used very short paragraphs or very long paragraphs. We have either combined the short paragraphs or broken up the long paragraphs wherever appropriate. At the syntactical and morphological level, in order to render the author's expression faithfully, only the clumsiest phrases have been adapted so that the text can be read easily.

In this way, we have tried to present *The Novel of an Invert* and its *Sequel* in their entirety and to make the censored sections and the changes in various editions visible to all.

Fig. 1 Émile Zola in his early fifties, photographed by Paul Nadar. Médiatèque de l'Architecture et du Patrimone, Charenton-le-Pont, France. © Ministère de la Culture/Médiathèque du Patrimone, Dist. RMN-Grand Palais/Art Resource, NY.

Preface by Émile Zola

To Dr. Georges Saint-Paul[1]

My dear doctor,

I see no problem with your publishing *The Novel of an Invert*; on the contrary, I am very happy that you, in your capacity as an expert, may be able to do something with it that a mere writer like me did not dare to.

When I received this very curious document several years ago, I was struck by the great physiological and social interest it offered. It touched me with its absolute sincerity, because one feels the passion, I will almost say, the eloquence of truth, throughout the text. Just think: the young man who is making this confession is writing in a language that isn't his own; and tell me whether in certain passages he doesn't attain a style marked by feelings that are truly[2] felt and expressed. It is a complete confession, naïve, spontaneous, one that very few men have dared to make, qualities that make it extremely valuable from many points of view. Also, thinking its publication might be useful, at first I wanted to use the manuscript, to give it to the public in some form for which I searched in vain and which finally made me abandon that plan.

[At that time, I was in the midst of an extremely difficult literary battle. Critics treated me daily as if I were a criminal, capable of all vices and all debaucheries. Do you really see me, at that time, as the principal editor of *The Novel of an Invert*? First, I would have been accused of inventing the story out of whole cloth, out of my own personal corruption. And then I would have been condemned for having considered the whole business only as a vulgar speculation on the most repugnant instincts. And what an outcry

---

1. "To Dr. Laupts in Lyon" in the 1896 and 1910 editions; "To Dr. Laupts (Dr. G. Saint-Paul)" in the 1930 edition.

2. "Profoundly," not "truly," in the 1896, 1910, and 1930 editions.

would have been heard if I had said that no subject is more serious or sadder than this one, that there isn't an affliction more common or more profound than this one—one that we pretend not to believe exists—and that the best thing to do to cure these ills is to study them, to expose them, and to treat them!

But, my dear doctor, chance had it that, in chatting together one evening, we began to discuss the human and social disease of sexual perversions. And I entrusted to you this document that had lain dormant in one of my drawers. And that is how it came to see the light of day, in the hands of a doctor, an expert, who would not be accused of trying to cause a scandal.][3] I do hope that you are going to make a decisive contribution to the question of born inverts, which is so misunderstood and so serious.

[In another confidential letter that I received around the same time and that I have unfortunately been unable to find again,[4] an unhappy man sent me the most poignant cry of human suffering that I have ever heard. He did not yield to these abominable loves, but he asked: Why, if he felt in the core of his being an aversion to women and a passion for men, was there such universal contempt for it? Why was the justice system ready to punish him? Never has someone possessed by a devil, never has a poor human being subject to the unknown destinies of desire, screamed so horrifically in pain! This letter, I remember, troubled me greatly, and don't we see the same thing in *The Novel of an Invert*, but with a more felicitous lack of awareness? Are we not witnessing a genuine physiological phenomenon, a hesitation, a partial error of nature? Nothing is more tragic, in my opinion, and nothing calls out more for a cure, if there is one.][5]

In the mystery of conception, which is so poorly understood, can this be considered possible? A child is born: Why a boy? Why a girl? We do not know. But what complications of darkness and torment are there if nature has a moment of uncertainty, and a boy is born partly a girl, or a girl is born partly a boy? The evidence is there—every day. The uncertainty can start simply with their physical appearance or with certain aspects of their

---

3. Later republished in "In Memoriam: Émile Zola," included in part 2 of this volume.

4. René Ternois reproduced this letter, the manuscript of which has not been found, in "Mélanges (suite) III. Ce que Zola n'avait pas osé dire," *Les Cahiers Naturalistes* 36 (1968): 156–60. The letter is dated "Venice, April 8, 1890."

5. Later republished in "In Memoriam: Émile Zola."

temperament: a man is effeminate, delicate, and cowardly; a woman is masculine, aggressive, and unfeeling. And it can go so far as verifiable monstrosity: hermaphroditic organs or unnatural feelings and passions. [Certainly, morality and justice are right to intervene because they must uphold public order. But by what right when one's willpower has been partially eliminated? We don't condemn a hunchback because he was born that way. Why despise a man for acting like a woman if he was born half a woman?][6]

Certainly,[7] my dear doctor, I am not even sure how to present the problem. I am only explaining[8] the reasons that made me support your publishing The Novel of an Invert. Perhaps it will inspire a little pity or a little fairness for certain unfortunate beings. And then, everything related to sex is related to society itself. An invert is a disruptor of the family, the nation, and humanity. Man and Woman are surely here on earth only in order to have children, and they destroy life the day when they no longer do what they must.

Cordially yours,

Émile Zola, Médan, June 25, 1895

---

6. Later republished in "In Memoriam: Émile Zola."
7. "Naturally," not "certainly," in the 1896, 1910, and 1930 editions.
8. "I merely explain," in the 1896, 1910, and 1930 editions.

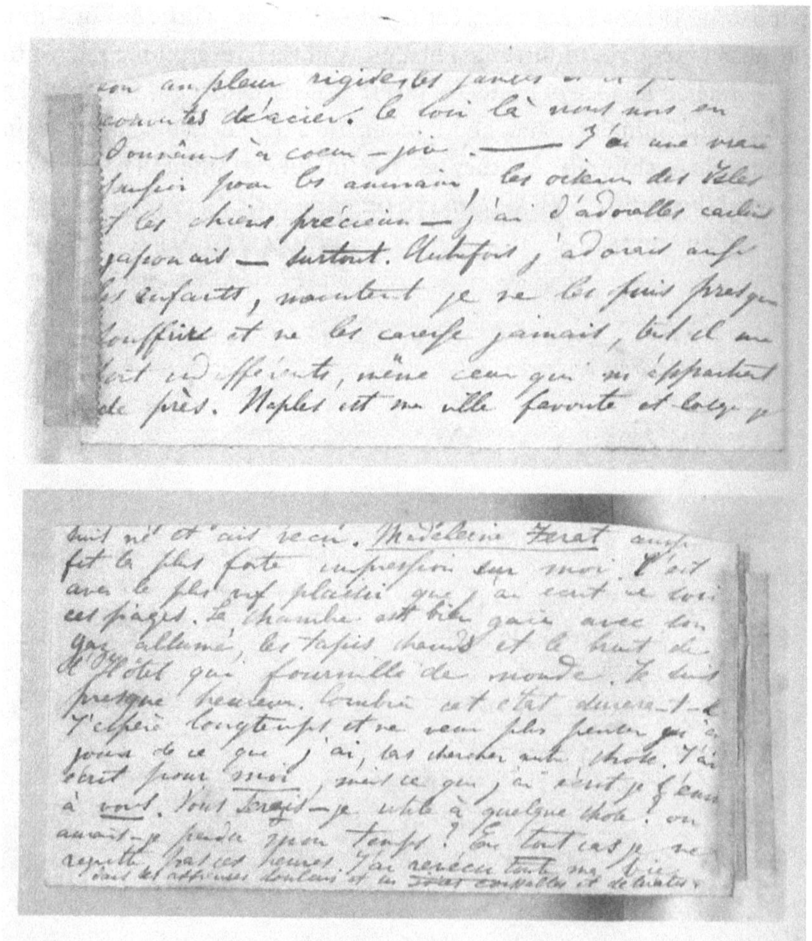

Fig. 2 Two fragments from the original letter to Zola. Georges Saint-Paul family archives © Nouvelles Éditions Place.

The Novel of an Invert

First Document (1888 or 1889)

To Mr. Émile Zola in Paris:
It is to you, Sir, the greatest novelist of our time, who, with the eye of a scientist and an artist, perceives and paints so powerfully <u>all</u> the oddities, <u>all</u> the infamies, and <u>all</u> the maladies that afflict mankind, that I send these <u>human documents</u> so sought after by the learned men of our time.[1]

This confession, which no spiritual director has ever heard from my mouth, will reveal to you a frightful illness of the soul, a rare case—if not a unique case, unfortunately—which has been studied by psychological experts, but which, until now, no novelist has dared to dramatize in a literary work. Balzac wrote *La Belle aux yeux d'or*, but he only touched on the awful vice that is a <u>counterpoint</u> to the story.[2] Sarrasine truly loved Zambinella, believing he was a woman, and stopped loving him after he discovered the truth.[3] It is not, therefore, like the even more horrifying situation that I want to tell you about today.

---

1. The title "The Novel of an Invert" was given to these letters by Dr. Georges Saint-Paul in 1894–1895. In his 1896 book, he used "The Novel of a Born Invert." The term "invert" was commonly used in scientific discourse at the time to designate men who were sexually involved with other men. The letters were written in the Jubilee Year of Pope Leo XIII (1810–1903, pope 1878–1903), which began in 1888 and ended in 1889.

2. The actual title of Balzac's novella is *La Fille aux yeux d'or / The Girl with the Golden Eyes* (1834–1835). It is about the rivalry between a young man, Henri de Marsay, and his half sister, Mme. de San-Réal, over a seductive young woman, Paquita Valdès. The "counterpoint" refers to the novella's themes of lesbianism and cross-dressing.

3. Another early work by Balzac (1830), the novella *Sarrasine* concerns a French sculptor, Ernest-Jean Sarrasine, who fell in love with a Roman castrato, "La Zambinella," not realizing he was a man.

You yourself, Sir, in your admirable *La Curée* have only touched on one of the most frightful vices that dishonors mankind in the character of your Baptiste.⁴ That man is despicable because the debauchery in which he engaged has nothing to do with love and is only an absolutely material thing, a question of congenital malformation that doctors have observed and described more than once. All of this is very <u>common</u> and very <u>disgusting</u> and has nothing to do with the confession that I am sending you and that could perhaps be useful to you.

I am not French—even though I know the most important cities of France and have even lived in Paris for a while. So, no doubt I am writing to you in a very incorrect manner. It has been a long time since I have spoken or written in this language: Would you please excuse the improprieties and the mistakes that undoubtedly mar these pages?

I don't know if you know Italian. If I could write you in that language, I would certainly express myself better. I am not concerned with style here, but I will simply say what could be of interest to you. Through these poorly written lines, you will discover, with your eagle eye and your artistic heart, the plight of a soul who seems to be pursued by a horrible fatality, who is ashamed of himself, and who will certainly find peace and happiness only when he is sleeping in this *Earth* that you have described so marvelously.⁵

[ANTECEDENTS AND FIRST YEARS OF CHILDHOOD]

I am twenty-three years old, Sir, and I was born into a family of rather affluent and independent means.⁶ In this sense, I lack nothing. My father is Catholic; he calls himself a deist, but his religion is more like a kind of pantheism, which he doesn't want to acknowledge. My mother is a Jew who has converted, but she remains faithful to her religion, even though she observes only its most important rituals. I am the <u>fourth son</u> of this marriage.

---

4. *La Curée/The Kill* (1872) is the second novel in Zola's series *Les Rougon-Macquart*. Baptiste, the butler, is a minor character, who was dismissed because of sexual improprieties with a stable hand at the very end of the novel.

5. *La Terre/The Earth* (1887), the fifteenth novel in Zola's *Rougon-Macquart* series, is about peasant life in France.

6. We have retained the section headings that Saint-Paul used in his published versions, and we have added a few of our own.

My father is one of the handsomest old men that you could imagine. His head with the profile of a patriarch attracts attention even in the street. He was incredibly handsome in his youth and still is at such an advanced age.

Our family is originally from Spain but has been living in Italy for centuries. My father was married at nineteen; my mother was eighteen, and she was far richer than my father. They were very much in love and still love each other. My father has a very impressionable and nervous temperament, artistic right down to his fingertips; he has had a rather adventurous life with notable highs and lows, but even at times when he was down on his luck, he didn't let himself get discouraged, and he always knew how to recoup his fortune. He has always earned a lot and spent a lot. Several years ago he made a great sum in the stock market, but he lost it all again. Without being rich, he is well-to-do now and can enjoy the sort of luxury that he has always admired. He has traveled to several European capitals, and his family has almost always followed him. He cares little for society and seldom mingles in it, except for business contacts.

He loves the arts with a passion and surrounds himself voluntarily with beautiful things—lovely statuettes and beautiful paintings. Even during those times when luck rarely smiled upon him, he did without necessities in order to buy a beautiful book or an attractive print—something that exasperated my mother a great deal. She was much more prudent owing to the instincts of her race. My father loves his family passionately and makes all possible sacrifices in order to see us happy and contented, but he has his days of ill humor, and then whoever approaches him had better watch out! He always makes drastic decisions without much reflection and has thus gotten embroiled in many touchy situations. He has seen a lot, traveled a lot, earned a lot, and spent a lot. He has a passionate love of reading, and since we have settled down, he has collected a fine library. His intelligence is very well developed; his forehead is magnificent; he is only of medium height, but he looks very tall. Monsieur Desbarolles, whom he consulted a number of years ago in Paris, told my father that he was born under the influence of Jupiter and Venus and that he would make a fortune again—something that has since come to pass.[7]

---

7. Adrien-Adolphe Desbarolles (1801–1886) was a painter and student of the occult who lived and practiced in Paris. He published a number of books on his methods of divination, such as *Les Mystères de la main / The Secrets of the Hand* (1859) on palm-reading

He is fairly musical and plays the piano rather well. He is best at rendering the <u>melody</u> but balks at the <u>harmony</u>. In the past he also took up painting in oils and watercolors, but he no longer does that because he <u>says</u> that as soon as he picked up his pencils and brushes, his business affairs would go badly. He is very proud of his good looks and takes great care of his big beard and beautiful silver hair. He fondly recalls his own father, who, according to everyone who knew him, was one of the handsomest men of the time and was loved and respected by all. He died fairly young from an illness.

My mother was very pretty in her youth, even though she came from a <u>very ugly and vulgar</u> family.[8] She has always had very <u>little</u> intelligence, and I have always reproached my father for marrying into a family that was so unattractive and undistinguished. He tells me that he was very young then and didn't understand how important marriage was.

When I look at my mother, who at fifty-five still has a good figure even though her face is ravaged by age, I always think of your <u>Angèle</u> in *La Curée*.[9] She has the same softness, the same lack of energy, an astonishing weakness of character; she can't read a short romantic story without crying, she has a poor memory, and her only good point is her great kindness. She is stubborn about certain things, however, and nobody can get out of her head what she has put there. I always think this is one of the qualities or defects inherent in the race from which she is descended and for which I feel no sympathy, and even a secret aversion. Nevertheless, I love my mother, but in my imagination, I would like her to be different—a feeling I regret greatly and criticize in myself.

I was born ten years after my last brother, when the oldest son was fourteen. My birth was a disappointment to my mother who had hoped, after three boys, to have a girl. I was, however, as pretty and cute as a little girl,

---

and *Les Mystères de l'écriture / The Secrets of Handwriting* (1872) on graphology. He became known as the "Father of Modern Palmistry."

8. The author had an ambiguous view of his mother's, and his own, Jewish ancestry, which is reflected throughout the text, a topic we study in "The Italian Man's Family Tree" in this volume.

9. Angèle, the first wife of the main character, Aristide Saccard, in the novel *La Curée*, was depicted as a submissive wife. She discovered the secret of her husband's schemes when he revealed Baron Haussmann's plans. On her deathbed, after a terrible illness, she realized that Saccard planned to remarry but seemed to forgive his cruelty.

and I often hear that people who saw me in my mother's arms—with my beautiful golden curls and my pretty blue eyes—always said: "But it's impossible that this is a boy!"

Whenever she sees me, my wet nurse always reminds me that the women she knew nicknamed me the <u>Little Madonna</u>, since I was such a cute and delicate child. I have a portrait of myself at the age of two, and I can swear to you that no one has ever seen a more beautiful child.

The entire family was very proud of me, my mother above all. My intelligence revealed itself very early on, and I was considered a little prodigy.

I was at that time the only child at home, since my brothers were away at boarding school in a neighboring town. I was very proud of my charm, and even though I was a young child, I would blush with pleasure at hearing my beauty praised. I still recall the thrill of joy and pleasure that coursed through my little body when I went out in my little dress of flouncy blue piqué decorated with blue bows, and a big Italian straw hat. When I was four years old, my little dresses were taken away and I was dressed in trousers and a little jacket. When I was dressed as a boy, I experienced a real feeling of shame—I recall it as if it were yesterday—and I quickly ran to hide and cry in my maid's room. To console me, she had to dress me as a girl again. People still laugh when they remember the cries of despair I made as I watched those little white dresses, which were my sole source of happiness, being taken away from me. It seemed to me that I was being denied something that I was always destined to wear. This was my first great unhappiness.

[CHILDHOOD—FIRST DEVIATIONS]

I was sent to school at the age of five, but I stayed only a few weeks since the school doctor noticed that I was becoming pale and sickly from sitting on the school benches for too long.

When I was seven years old, we moved to Florence. My father's business affairs went magnificently, and we had a splendid coach, footmen, and a beautiful house where my father collected everything imaginable that is beautiful and elegant. A governess was hired for me, and I quickly felt an intense and emotional friendship for this lady, who was very distinguished and cared for me a great deal.[10] I even preferred her to my mother, who was

---

10. The Italian consistently used the French word *amitié*, friendship, to denote different kinds of relationships, usually using qualifying terms such as "intense and

very jealous of her and tried as much as possible to separate us, something at which she didn't succeed. At seven, I was also as charming a little boy as I had been a beautiful child, with an intelligence that surprised everyone who met me. I had the greatest admiration for all that was beautiful and grand, and I developed a real passion for all the beautiful ladies and queens whom I read about with my governess.

I had an intense admiration for the French Revolution, and one day, having found a summary of Lamartine's *History of the Girondins*, I devoured it in a few hours.[11] At night, I dreamed about it, and I couldn't stop wanting to talk about this grand epoch in French history. Marie-Antoinette, Madame Élisabeth, and the Princess de Lamballe were my greatest passions.[12] I didn't like the popular heroes and heroines as much, but I have always had a limitless admiration for these heroines and unfortunate women, dressed in velvet and trailing their ermine coats. I made rapid progress in my little studies, and the speed with which I learned and understood everything astonished my teachers.

At that time I was completely <u>innocent</u> and I didn't know anything about anything. I often visited museums with my governess, where, even at such a young age, I took a lively interest in the arts, for which I still have a great affection. The sight of a work of art moved me deeply, and the study of mythology, which I pursued in the company of these historic masterpieces, enthralled me. I dreamed only about heroes, gods, and goddesses. The Trojan War made the greatest impression on me, but the strange thing—and one to which I paid attention only later on—was that all my thoughts, all my enthusiasm, were for the <u>heroes</u> more than the <u>heroines</u>. I admired Helen, Venus, and Andromache a great deal; however, my great love, my great admiration, was for <u>Hector</u>, <u>Achilles</u>, and <u>Paris</u>, but for the first one

---

emotional," "tender," or "passionate" to differentiate between them, and we have adopted the same emphasis, while keeping the word "friendship" throughout the text.

11. Alphonse-Marie-Louis de Prat de Lamartine (1790–1869), one of the leading Romantic poets of the era, also wrote a sensational polemic about the French Revolution in 1847, in which he detailed the excesses of the Terror.

12. Known as Madame Élisabeth, Élisabeth-Philippine-Marie-Hélène of France (1764–1794), the sister of Louis XVI, was executed during the Terror. Marie-Thérèse-Louise de Savoy-Carignano, Princess de Lamballe (1749–1792), a friend and confidante of Marie Antoinette, was killed by the mob during the September Massacres.

above all.[13] I had a real passion for him, and I used to enjoy imagining myself as Andromache in order to be able to hold him in my arms. This hero, dressed in armor, with a handsome, athletic body, beautiful naked arms, and magnificent helmet made me daydream for long hours at a time. I still recall the sweet emotions of those hours spent in the long corridors of the museums where I saw so many handsome heroes and naked gods that populated my imagination as they took on an imaginary life of their own. I spent hours thinking about the happiness of this whole world of marble, so perfect, so far above reality, that I couldn't even explain to myself all that I felt.

I already loved solitude, and other boys' games almost frightened me. My brothers were too big to pay any attention to me, and besides, they spent very little time at home. I never had much affection for them. My oldest brother was very handsome, but the other two were less attractive, especially my third brother, who, with his short legs and long arms, resembles my mother's family in every respect, a family, which, thank God, lived far from us and which I didn't like at all. My brothers are all very well established in life; they all have families and are very happy, especially the first two. I am the only one who is still living at home with our parents, something that I don't regret at all.

So, I continued my studies, but in a very irregular fashion. I learned several languages and devoured all sorts of literature, enjoying everything that was beautiful and, above all, poetic. Poetry had a great influence on me. Its cadences gave me real <u>thrills</u>, and I learned long monologues and entire scenes from my favorite tragedies by heart. Music also enchanted me infinitely. I was carried away by beautiful verses as much as by beautiful music. I truly lived in an ideal world, as perhaps a ten-year-old child could do only in his own dreams. I was always fascinated with the beautiful heroines of history and poetry, and I loved them like friends, because women seemed to me to be exquisite and charming beings, so far from the earth that I almost made them into divine beings.

At that time I had the greatest fervor for the Virgin Mary, whom I considered the ideal type and model for all women. I was tempted to

---

13. Hector was the Trojan hero of Homer's *The Iliad*. He was the son of King Priam and Queen Hecuba, the brother of Paris who had abducted Helen, the wife of Menelaus, and the husband of Andromache. He was killed by Achilles, the Greek hero, who wanted to avenge the death of his friend and lover Patroculus.

participate in the cult of her Divine Nature, and I spent several months in the most outrageous devotion, all the more extraordinary since in our house all religious practices had been abolished and nobody took any notice of them. From her former religion, my mother retained a hatred of churches and of all religious pomp, but it was the pomp, above all else, that charmed me. So, I changed my tastes and, instead of Helen of Troy and the goddesses and heroes of mythology, I took pleasure in the company of saints, virgins, and martyrs. The walls of my bedroom were covered with little images of saints and angels before whom I said my prayers at almost any time of the day or night. I would ask to leave in the middle of my lessons for some reason, and I used to run to my bedroom to say my prayers to the charming Madonna, whom I considered a sister and a friend.

This devoutness lasted a short time and disappeared all of a sudden. I don't know why. I always blame it on the little image of Saint Mary Magdalene of Pazzi, which my mother's maid had, and which I found so horrible that I couldn't keep a straight face before this little monster.[14]

After that, my admiration for virgins and saints ended and I fell back on mythology. I almost became an idol-worshiper, and I even bought a statuette of Venus to honor with burning incense and bouquets of flowers every morning.

For some time I felt a whole new life stirring inside me. I could no longer keep still, and the most beautiful images appeared in my imagination, keeping me awake at night. I read everything that fell into my hands, and I devoured the illustrated novels in my father's library. This excited me so much that I became so passionate, so nervous, that everyone was amazed. I always spoke out of turn, and in the ebullient outbursts of precocious youth. I had the most audacious thoughts and veered from the heights of enthusiasm to the depths of sadness and dejection for no obvious reason. I often cried when I was alone and would take refuge in an imaginary world to console myself.

---

14. Saint Mary Magdalene of Pazzi (1566–1607), a member of the prominent Pazzi family in Florence, was a Carmelite nun known for her austerity and her ecstatic visions during which she exhibited the stigmata. Canonized by Pope Clement IX in 1699, she is honored as one of the patron saints of Florence.

My love for dresses with trains persisted, and when I was alone, I would go to my mother's mirror and walk up and down trailing behind me sheets and old shawls. Their long folds caressing my body, and the rustling sound they made on the carpet had me shivering with joy. I always wanted to swathe myself in long veils, and this desire that, since my childhood, has never entirely left me now tormented me more and more.

One day a friend of my mother's jokingly told me that she was beginning to see my mustache sprouting. I nearly strangled her, since this remark seemed so insulting and the news made me very sad. I quickly ran to my mirror and was very happy to see my beautiful red lips entirely free of the horrible peach fuzz that I feared so greatly. I enjoyed thinking of myself as a woman, and this was easy with the imagination and beauty with which I was endowed. The adventures that played out in my mind made me shudder with pleasure.

I was still very innocent at the age of thirteen, which I was then, and I had no idea about relations between the sexes or the differences between them. This will seem odd in a child so advanced for his age, but it is the simple truth. I lived too much in my heart and in my imagination. I loved everything that was <u>ideal</u> far too much to be able to see things that were right in front of me.

A groom about fifteen years old soon put an end to my innocence on this subject. It was during a stay in a resort town where all our servants had come along with us. I often went to the stables to look at our horses, and I enjoyed playing and speaking with a boy of my own age with whom I was sometimes allowed to run in the large garden. I was soon enlightened by this lad, who told me everything he knew. When I learned how children were made, I was so indignant that I felt a profound disgust for my parents, who were not ashamed of having made me in such an awful manner. These conversations ended up upsetting me terribly, because, if I was very gifted in intelligence—too well, alas!—I was far from mature physically, and at thirteen, I wasn't yet a <u>man</u>.

This young man corrupted himself in front of me several times, and although I was dying to imitate him and my blood throbbed in my veins, I couldn't manage to do it when I was alone.

Soon this boy was sent away, and if I didn't forget his lessons, I no longer thought of them much. However, what really surprised me was that he was always talking about sleeping with naked women and doing to them what one usually does, whereas I experienced no desire to do this at all and would have found it much more natural to sleep with a man. I seemed to be too weak, too pretty, too delicate to sleep with a woman, whom I resembled too closely, and besides, I would never have had the courage.

Man seemed to me, since that time in my life, much more attractive than woman because I admired a man's strength, his dynamic capacity, which seemed impossible for me to ever have. I always thought of myself as a woman, and all my desires were, from then on, those of a woman.

At that time I had a few friends, and without being conscious of it, I felt an exaggerated feeling of friendship for them. I was jealous of them, and when they casually draped an arm around my shoulders, I would tremble all over. I envied them, and my greatest joy was to give them proof of my affection and to make small sacrifices for them. I was tormented by their indifference and their boisterous tastes, which were so different from my own, but I would have preferred it if they had spent all their time with me.

But what attracted me most were mature men, men of thirty to forty years of age. I admired their well-built bodies and their deep voices, which contrasted strikingly with our own still childish ones. I still didn't understand what I was feeling, but I would have given anything in the world to be held in their arms and to press my whole body against theirs.

I spent entire nights dreaming of these things and trying to give them a semblance of reality. I didn't yet know where the awful vice that I unwittingly harbored inside me would lead and which has since made me so unhappy.

A servant, who was in our service for a short time and who had a striking figure, a black mustache, and sideburns, attracted all my attention. Using the petty subterfuges of a young boy, I tried to get him to speak to me about indecent things, and he gave in to it with all his heart. I liked him a lot and always wanted to have him at my side whenever I went anywhere. In the evenings, he came with me into my bedroom on the second floor and stayed near me until I was almost asleep. I made him tell me about his mistresses, about the bad places where he went, and I got so much pleasure from it that I stayed up for hours and hours afterward, completely awake and filled with desires that I could barely understand. I would have liked to have him sleep next to me, to feel his blond and sleek body. I would have liked to have kissed him and to have him next to me in order to take pleasure and to give him some. My desires didn't go any farther than that, and I couldn't imagine anything else.

One night, after long conversations on our favorite theme, when I was questioning him about the most indecent things, I was seized suddenly with the desire to know him entirely and without any shame, and as a joke,[15] *I asked him to show me his virile member so that I could judge if it was as big and as beautiful as he said. At first he refused, but after having made me promise not to say anything to anyone, he opened his pants and showed it to me, completely erect since he had been aroused by my words. He approached the little bed where I was panting with desire and shame. Never had I seen the virile member of an adult male, and I was so overwhelmed that I couldn't utter a word. Prompted by some sort of impulse, by some innate desire, I seized it with my right hand and stroked it, stuttering: "It's so beautiful! It's so beautiful!" I had an overwhelming desire to do something with this virile member that filled my whole hand, and I so desperately wanted an orifice in my body to put it in—this thing that was the object of all my desires.*

Hearing a noise, the servant adjusted his clothing quickly and left, leaving me burning with desires I had never had before and that I thought were impossible. In the back of my mind, there was already a sort of hopelessness, as if I knew that I would never enjoy what I would have loved so much.

The following night I wanted to relive the events of that horrible evening, but the man apparently feared some indiscretion and no longer wanted to show me anything. I writhed in anger. One evening my father harshly scolded the servant and nearly threw him out of the house, after noticing that the man had been bringing one of his mistresses into our house almost every night. When I heard about this—that there was someone close by who enjoyed so much pleasure, the pleasure I so desired, with him—I sobbed with rage and cursed Heaven that I wasn't born a woman. This man left our house soon afterward, but that barely affected me. I was then still very young, and my emotions, though strong, didn't last very long.

[YOUTH—FIRST ACTS]

I developed a strong affection for a magnificent young man who had been working as a groom in our stable for some time. He was truly superb, young with a little brown mustache. He was of medium height, robust, and

---

15. Saint-Paul placed the following note here in his 1896 edition: "Readers will understand why I am obligated to put into Latin certain sentences that were written in French in the original document." We have indicated these passages by placing them in italics.

very well built. I used to secretly bring him cigars that I took from my father's smoking room, and I also deprived myself of cakes and sweets to take to him. He was a very honest boy, who loved to talk very freely, but who didn't allow himself any liberties. One day while joking with him, I asked him to show me his naked body; he scolded me and didn't want to indulge me in my desire. I liked him even more than ever, and the desire to see him, to be near him, and to touch his face became a real obsession.

Since I could not expect anything from him, I tried to imagine I was a woman, and at night I put my pillow by my side and kissed it and bit it as if it was a living person. I thought of the handsome young man, so robust and so fresh, and I tried to give myself the illusion of sleeping with him by making some movements. *In doing this, and almost without wanting to, I corrupted myself and experienced my first ejaculation.*

I was terribly frightened by this, and despite the pleasure that I felt, I promised myself that I would no longer commit such an error. I hardly kept my promise, and soon I adopted one of the most degrading vices possible. My lively imagination provided the most stimulating images, and I enjoyed this awful pleasure by evoking the sight of men who attracted me and with whom I would have liked to be. Although I looked delicate, my constitution was very strong, and there were no ill effects from something that might have undoubtedly killed anyone else.

At this time, my father's business was going badly, and we had to leave Italy for France in order to start over. For several months, we lived in Paris—a city I had already visited many years earlier. Our luxurious style of life was replaced by a very simple one, and I can assure you that it was the most miserable time of my life. My father grew more and more bitter; even in Paris, his business affairs went from bad to worse. My governess left us at this time, and I enrolled as a day student in one of the Parisian boarding schools. I couldn't stand my school lessons, and in order to have more time to myself and not to follow the regular curriculum, I said that I had no desire to become an engineer, which is what my father wanted me to do, and instead I wanted to study painting since I had a bit of natural talent for drawing.

With my charm and my persuasive abilities, I succeeded in convincing my father that I needed to leave the school to study with a painter. Actually I went to his studio very rarely, and preferred strolling around Paris, visiting galleries and museums. I used to go to the painter's studio in the morning, since he lived very far from my parents, and I would spend the afternoon reading and drawing. That time was very pleasant for me, but the desire to be with a man still plagued me, and I felt terribly unhappy belonging to a sex to which my soul didn't also belong. I continued with my solitary vice, which soon no longer appealed to me, and which I therefore abandoned, because it began to tire me, both body and soul, and hardly gave me any pleasure.

After several months in Paris, we returned to Italy, where business had summoned my father again. I then entered an academy of fine arts, but I no longer had any interest in it, and I only went there in order not to be forced to do something else that would particularly repulse me in my present state of mind. The boys who attended the school of fine arts with me seemed to be horribly common and vile; they had frightful hands, while mine were the most beautiful and the most well-taken-care-of ones that anyone could find. In addition, I was very proud of my birth, my travels, and my superior education, and I had no desire to mix with such low-class people, most of whom were the sons of butchers and merchants. Nowadays several of them are gifted artists, while I haven't made any progress at all in the art that I had chosen—on a whim, it is true.

I was usually free during the day because I only rarely went to school, and I spent my time thinking and reading. It was during this time that several of my friends and cousins who were my own age took me to a brothel for the first time. I left it feeling disgusted and sad. The women didn't attract me at all, and I felt nothing but repugnance for them.

One of them kissed me and I felt such a violent disgust for this frightful person that I turned away from her as quickly as I could and left as quickly as possible, to the great astonishment of the young men who had brought me there. I went back several times hoping to overcome my aversion and to do what all the others did, but I never succeeded. I remained absolutely frigid under the most passionate caresses and I felt only the most horrible disgust. One day, one of my friends, a young libertine, wanted me to watch one of his love-making sessions with one of those women, but I couldn't get over my innate aversion and that scene of debauchery left me cold. Nevertheless, those places of ill-repute provoked a sort of mysterious attraction in me, and many times I envied not the men who went there, but the women who lived there.

I began to think of myself as an exceptional and fantastic being in which nature had made a mistake—and as one who, while recognizing the horror of his existence, couldn't do anything to change it. I lost my taste for everything. My sad and gloomy soul abandoned itself to a profound feeling of discouragement, and I fell into a deep depression.

I spent my mornings and afternoons walking in the gardens and along the promenades all alone, tormented by a great sadness, doubting everything from nature to God. I wondered why I was born into such a miserable condition and what crime I had committed before my birth to be punished in such a frightful manner.

No one around me noticed anything, and they attributed my silence and my sadness to a bad temperament and natural eccentricity. My father was too absorbed with his business affairs and with rebuilding his fortune, which preoccupied him a great deal, and my mother thought about the house and her visits and wasn't, in any case, the type of person to worry about the afflictions of a soul. My brothers were far away, so I lived all alone, prey to my sorrows and my sad thoughts. I saw before me an entire life destroyed by a horrible passion that blind nature had inspired in me. I felt treasures within me that nobody would ever want, that would stay forever locked in my soul and would end by quickly killing me.

I began to long for death and to summon it up in my awful solitude. I could never describe the horrible tortures that afflicted me then. I sometimes emerged from these long painful moments with incredible optimism, unfounded joys, and unattainable dreams. I tried to change my nature through serious reading and religious devotion. Everything was useless, and each new attempt left me more discouraged than ever.

I wanted to feel affection for women, young girls, even children, but I couldn't. To me, women were lovely and sweet friends. They could have slept next to me undisturbed; I wouldn't have felt the slightest desire for them.

Men struck me as charming and handsome because of their strength and vigor, and I felt attracted to them by an unknown force, an irresistible attraction. I used to like to watch handsome young men pass by in the street, and when someone pleased me, I would retrace my steps to see him again. Thus, I had <u>spiritual lovers</u>, whom I loved and followed in silence, without anyone suspecting a thing. I had no social life, for fear of betraying my awful secret, which terrified me and made me feel ashamed. I will not tell you how I suffered then or the frightful thoughts that suddenly popped into my head. You can imagine them easily enough. Thus, I reached my eighteenth birthday without any of these moral torments having noticeably affected my constitution or my health.

I was then what I am now with only slight differences. I am taller than normal (1 m., 65 cm. [5 ft., 5 in.]), well proportioned, with a slender but not too thin frame. My torso is superb; a sculptor wouldn't have found anything to criticize about it and wouldn't have found any great difference between it and that of <u>Antinous</u>.[16] I have very broad shoulders, perhaps too broad, and my hips are well developed. My pelvis is wide like a woman's;[17] my knees are slightly bent inward, and my feet are very small. My hands are superb, and my fingers are finely modeled with shiny, pink, polished fingernails that are carefully manicured, like those of antique statues. My neck is long and rounded, and the nape of my neck is charming, covered with down. My head is pretty, and at eighteen, it was even more so. Its oval shape is perfect, and everyone is struck by its childlike form. At twenty-three, people still take me for seventeen at the most. My complexion is white and pink and becomes crimson at the least sign of emotion. My forehead isn't handsome; it is receding slightly with deep-set temples; luckily, it is half covered with curly, sandy-blond hair that is naturally frizzy. The shape of my head is perfect because of my frizzy hair, but up close, it reveals an enormous bulge at the back of my skull. My eyes are wide and bluish gray with long, dark eyelashes and thick, arched eyebrows. My gaze is liquid, but my eyes are almost always dark with circles under them; they are also subject to swelling, which passes rapidly. My mouth is rather large with big red lips; my lower lip hangs down a little; people say that I have an Austrian mouth. My teeth are dazzling, and even though I have three badly discolored teeth, luckily nobody ever sees them. My ears are small with colored lobes. My chin is round, and even at eighteen, it was smooth

---

16. Antinous was the youthful lover of Emperor Hadrian (76–138), who deified him upon his death in 130. His cult was quite popular in the latter part of the Roman Empire. Sculptures of Antinous depicted him as a muscular, handsome, often nude, youth. Recognized as classical examples of male beauty, many of these sculptures have been displayed in European museums, including the Louvre, the Vatican, and the Gardens of Versailles.

17. In the 1910 edition, Saint-Paul added the following note at the very end of his version: "A word about an error that I was unable to clarify in the original document: in 'The Novel of an Invert' (chap. II, p. 61), it is necessary to delete the reference to the exaggeration of the man's hips and pelvis. After checking, I discovered that a line was added that was not part of the original manuscript. This error can only be by a copyist or a typesetter." We have placed this footnote here since it refers to this passage about his hips and pelvis.

and velvety, like that of a woman; at present, a light beard, closely shaved, hides it a little. There are two black and velvety <u>beauty spots</u> on my left cheek, contrasting with my blue eyes. My nose is thin and straight, slightly but imperceptibly curved, with soft nostrils. My voice is sweet, and people always regret that I didn't learn to sing.

This is my portrait. Perhaps it could serve you to reconstruct the strange being that it pleased nature to make, to my great despair.

[MILITARY SERVICE]

I was to join the army at the age of twenty, the normal age for military service, but my father, having rebuilt his fortune once again, made it possible for me to enter as a volunteer earlier than the deadline established by law. My father chose the cavalry for me, which cost much more and was, consequently, much more <u>chic</u>. Besides, he was told that the strains of military service were much more bearable in this branch of service. Therefore, before I turned nineteen, I joined a garrison regiment in a small town, far from the eyes of the General Command. The officers, we were assured, were very well brought up and very polite. They treated their volunteers well.

I had always had a real <u>horror</u> of military life. Its physical toll, its constraints, its terrible discipline frightened me a great deal, and I would have given anything to be spared the horrible boredom of spending a year in such an unpleasant way. The first few months seemed really quite hard, but little by little I grew used to this life. Besides, there were distractions. I had several companions, young gentlemen, infatuated with their own nobility and wealth, with whom I quickly became quite friendly. Everyone soon befriended me because my pretty childlike face contrasted attractively with the hussar's uniform that I wore, giving me the charms of a transvestite. The various duties, the riding lessons and the open-air life, all had a very positive effect on my health and my spirits. The holidays, the long rides on horseback, the suppers and the dinners, all ended up by reconciling me to military life and, in addition, the officers' indulgence made it somewhat bearable. What we enjoyed most of all was to play <u>the prince</u> with ordinary soldiers and demonstrate our superiority over these poor folks.

We all slept together with our platoon in large upper rooms. We would have liked to have a separate room, but it was impossible and I haven't regretted it since. The petty officer who slept with us was an old grump, very sullen and annoying. We had very little influence over him, and he didn't want to accept anything from us, for fear of compromising himself or of not being able to scold us at his leisure. The other petty officers were, on the other hand, very friendly to us and never refused what we offered or the dinners to which we invited them.

In this exciting and busy life, my senses calmed down and the incessant hallucinations that had tormented me for such a long time became less frequent and almost disappeared entirely. We were too tired to dream about anything except our duty. The men who slept side by side with us didn't tempt me at all. They were too rough, too ugly, too stupid to inspire in me any desire for them. They were, in addition, very dirty, and they never tempted me in any way.

Six months went by and spring arrived. Part of the regiment changed its billet, and other platoons came to take the place of the ones who left. In our room, there was a real revolution the day the new troops arrived. I took advantage of the situation to change places and put my cot in the most comfortable and most remote corner of the room. My bed was across from the sergeant's, who commanded the platoon that had just arrived.

This man was young (twenty-five or twenty-six years of age), and he had a very handsome face. At first I didn't pay a great deal of attention to him; I didn't even think about him. He was very quiet and modest, rarely mistreating the soldiers and not speaking much when off duty. He led the platoon with a lot of grace and energy, and later I admired the charming and chivalrous manner in which he handled his horse. He made it jump over the ditches and other dangerous obstacles on the parade ground that I was terribly afraid of.

The first feelings that I had for him were jealousy and envy. He seemed too tall compared to my small and slender self. He seemed too courageous and too skillful compared to all the rest of us. He had a way of commanding that I envied and that I would never achieve.

Ordinarily he went to bed very early, whereas my friends and I didn't. We would go to the theater or spend the whole evening in the regimental canteen, playing music and having a late dinner. One evening, on a whim, I left my group of friends and returned to our dormitory. Many soldiers were already asleep and their sergeant was in the middle of undressing.

I did the same and lay down to sleep without missing a single gesture by my neighbor. He was already stripped down to his shirt and soon, seated on his bed, he took off his last article of clothing and climbed into bed wearing only his nightshirt.

I was struck by the beauty and the perfection of his body, which in the dim light of the lamp hanging from the ceiling seemed to possess a marvelous beauty, surpassing the masterpieces of antiquity that had enthralled me previously. But those were made of marble and this lovely body was full of strength and youth. His legs impressed me especially; they were perfectly shaped, wiry, thin, and supple all at the same time. His entire handsome body suggested an extraordinary strength joined to the most graceful form. The next day I watched him closely, and I was struck by his handsome face, the elegance of his manners, his well-kept hands, and his carefully trimmed nails. I felt overcome with friendship for this young man, who did his duty so sadly, was so sober, and went out so little. However, I didn't have any desire for him. I admired him as if he were a handsome statue, and I didn't think that he would ever be able to understand me. Often, in the evenings, I sat next to him and enjoyed having him tell me something about his origins, his hometown, or his family. He didn't have a mother, and his father had several children with another wife. This is why he stayed in the military. His father was a petty clerk who had given him some education; he wrote very well, and in his free time he read books translated from French, especially those by Dumas the elder.[18]

I began to enjoy his company more and more, and soon I developed the most tender friendship for him. Several times I invited him to come to the theater with us, and this didn't seem to disturb my friends, who were also friendly toward this young man. He also came to dinner with us a couple of times, but he was always very cold and reserved. He had a great many duties, and so often in the evenings he was so tired that he preferred not to leave the barracks. I would have offered him money, but I was afraid that he wouldn't accept it. Soon I couldn't do without him, and I looked for every excuse to please him. I was content to take his hand and sometimes stroke his fine, sleek, dark brown hair and his head, which was so charming and serious. I noticed and admired the beauty of his teeth and his handsome mouth, which was adorned but not hidden by a little brown mustache. I saw in him my favorite heroes, and when he rode by in his handsome black

---

18. Alexandre Dumas the elder (1802–1870), a novelist and dramatist who specialized in historical fiction, was the author of *The Count of Monte Cristo*, *The Three Musketeers*, and *The Man in the Iron Mask*, among many other works. He was also the father of Alexandre Dumas the younger (1824–1895), the author of *La Dame aux camélias / The Lady of the Camellias* and several other novels and plays.

and yellow uniform on a beautiful horse, I compared him to Hector or Achilles.

I was jealous of him, but I enjoyed having him tell me about his military adventures and his passing love affairs. Even though he had a remarkable physique, he sought out women only twice a month at the most because they were too expensive and he had so little money.

Besides, he had scant experience with women and love affairs, having been in the military since the age of seventeen and not having opportunities to indulge his senses. I fiercely envied all the women who, even if only once, held this young man in their arms and made him happy since I looked on him as a god! I would have given an entire lifetime of joy to be able to have had that satisfaction at least once. I was definitely very unhappy! And never would I have the immense pleasure, compared to which all others pale.

And yet I would never have dared to say a word to him about all this. I would have died of shame before finishing what I had to say. But what had to happen happened. One evening we all dined together and our friend was part of the party. Everyone drank too much. Coming back to our barracks, several of us were dreadfully ill. The soldiers were no longer sleeping with us but were in a neighboring room. Our eight or ten beds were hard to see in the shadows of the darkened room, lit only by a very small lamp that went out in the middle of the night.

We were more or less excited, and our escapades continued well into the night. The quartermaster, who slept in the little room next to ours, was dead drunk and snored horribly. My bed was in the darkest corner of the room, just opposite that of the young petty officer who was himself in very high spirits, thanks to the generous amount of wine that he had drunk, which he wasn't accustomed to for all sorts of reasons.

My companions had fallen asleep a long while ago and we hadn't even undressed. Finally I decided to do so, and, taking off my uniform, I curled up in my finest linen shirt and got into my little bed. I had my young friend sit on my bed, and in our excitement and in the intoxication caused by the wine and the noise that we had just made, I lavished upon him the sweetest caresses and the most flattering words as if in jest. I was half lying down on the cushion that we were allowed to keep in our bed.

He was half undressed, *sitting on the bed, touching my legs*. I was speaking to him as if I were hypnotized or half-drunk from the drowsiness and the warmth of the bed that was beginning to overwhelm me, when he stretched out on top of me. He took me in his arms, gave me a lengthy kiss on the cheek, all the while slipping his hands under the covers and grasping my manhood in a tight grip. I felt as if I had died of an immense joy that had suddenly swept over me. We stayed like that for several moments, our heads pressed together, our burning red cheeks touching, my mouth pressed against his mouth in the warmth of the pillow. I had never been so happy!

The lamp standing on the floor sent flickering rays of light into the immense dormitory where my companions slept in beds far away and left the corner where we were in ecstasy in the deepest shadows. I was afraid, however, that someone would see us, and, wanting to enjoy completely my friend's lack of restraint, I whispered in his ear while kissing it: "Go and turn out the light and then come back, but do it quickly." He got up, stumbling, and went to drink from the pitcher that was resting on the floor next to the lamp; he very quietly put out the small flame that was on the verge of going out. The dormitory was no longer illuminated by anything but the lamp in the neighboring dormitory. As a result, you could see only a little in the center of the room; everywhere else was in deep darkness. I saw him in the shadows, coming back to his bed, which was in front of mine. I heard him undressing himself very quickly and coming toward me, holding his breath.

These few seconds seemed to last for a century, and when I felt him next to me under the warm sheets, I held him around the waist and caressed him and gave him very passionate kisses {stifling the cries of joy and pleasure ready to escape from my lips. He showed me an equally ardent passion. In an instant, we were naked and seemed to form one single body, so closely were we intertwined. Never would I have believed such ecstasy to be possible. Our tongues joined in our mouths. We held each other so tightly we could barely breathe. I stroked this beautiful body, so ardently desired, with my feverish hands, and the lovely, serious, virile head that made such a pleasing contrast with mine. At last, our pleasure reached its climax, and we had the joy of reaching orgasm at the same time. We held each other for a long time, caressing each other, and exchanging sweet words.}[19] <u>"Never have I had such pleasure with a woman," he said. "Their kisses and their caresses are neither as warm nor as passionate."</u>

19. This passage in curly brackets { } was copied from the original manuscript by Saint-Paul into another one entitled "Passages qui ont dû être supprimés" / "Passages to be suppressed." The manuscript was recently found in the Saint-Paul family archives. A facsimile of this manuscript was published in *Confessions d'un homosexuel à Émile Zola: première édition non censurée du "Roman d'un Inverti*, ed. Michael Rosenfeld (Paris: Nouvelles Éditions Place, 2017), Ms. (1), 232.

These words filled me with joy and pride. I was holding him at last, this man whom I had desired so much. And what a charming man! Any woman would have envied me. Finally, we separated, promising to love each other forever and to do whatever was possible to stay together.

The next morning when we got up, we didn't dare look at each other even once, shame having momentarily overtaken our mad passion, and the fresh morning air made us completely sober. Throughout the morning we exchanged only a few words, but that night as soon as we were in bed and alone in total darkness, my desire for him was rekindled and I got up, holding my breath, and went to him. {He was awake and waiting for me, he said.

It was a wonderful night that we made last as long as possible, and I don't believe that there has ever been a more loving and passionate couple. We writhed in lustful spasms touched by madness, and the passion that my caresses awakened in him led him to grab hold of my foot and cover it with kisses.

Since that night, we shed all restraint and spent nearly every night together in my bed or his, kissing and caressing each other. "What pretty cheeks you have," he told me.}[20] "They are softer than a woman's, and your feet, they are like those of a child." His words filled me with joy. I no longer wanted to be a woman, because I found this awful passion so much more delectable and enjoyable, superior to what ordinary love could offer, which, in any case, didn't attract me at all. I felt so much affection for this handsome young man that I ended up loving him more than anyone else in the whole world, and I thought of nothing but him. I wanted to see him handsome and well dressed; I ordered and paid for a new and elegant uniform for him; I wanted to see him beautiful, perfumed, and nicely turned-out. Money meant nothing to me, and I spent it on him liberally without regret. At first he didn't want to take anything from me, but I soon convinced him to accept my gifts. He never asked for anything, but I knew what he needed and could anticipate his desires. I wanted him to eat with us, but he didn't want to embarrass my companions or to let some gossip raise suspicions about our too passionate friendship. I withdrew from my companions as much as possible, finding many pretexts to excuse myself from joining in their amusements. I cut myself off from them completely when they went for walks or went to the theater. I stayed alone in the furnished room I had

---

20. Copied from the original manuscript into "Passages to be suppressed" and partly translated into Latin. See *Confessions*, Ms. (2), 232.

rented in town, where my friend came to join me on Sundays and holidays. There we indulged ourselves with fine dinners and lovely late, intimate suppers, and they almost always ended in the same way.

I thought of my friend constantly and never stopped. I would have sacrificed everything for him. And nevertheless, we took our pleasure in the most innocent of ways; that is to say, in the least criminal of ways.[21]

He wasn't used to the sweet perfumes or scented colognes in my bath, and even though he was extremely clean, he knew nothing about these sorts of refinements that charmed him nevertheless. Following the fashion of the time, I wore silk nightshirts with drawstrings that felt good and were so soft to the touch! The good food and the fine wines that I gave him acted powerfully on this person who wasn't used to such a refined and easy lifestyle, though he appreciated its sensual charms.

When he came to my room, I was almost always in bed. He would kiss me, saying: "God, what a lovely spouse you would make! But that does not matter! You are still my little wife!" {*And in the darkness of the bedroom, there were endless whispers and caresses and burning kisses in the big bed covered with fine white sheets I had brought from my father's house, a stark contrast with the rough gray bedding in the barracks. But our greatest pleasure was the warm bath that we took together on Sundays and holidays in the bathhouse of this charming little town; we often climbed into the same bathtub and kissed for a long time in the warm perfumed water.*}[22]

My friend grew so used to me that he couldn't do without me, no less than I could do without him. He had never been so loved, and he had never enjoyed all the luxuries I offered him. We even took carriage rides into the

---

21. After the Italian unification in 1861, "sodomy" was a crime only in Northern Italy; it was not a crime in the former Kingdom of the Two Sicilies, of which Naples was the capital city. The crime of "sodomy" was abolished in 1889 when the whole of unified Italy adopted the new penal code (Codice Zanardelli), indicating that the Italian was keenly aware of the distinct legal issues in his country when he wrote to Zola. For a more detailed analysis, see Lorenzo Benadusi, *The Enemy of the New Man: Homosexuality in Fascist Italy* (Madison: University of Wisconsin Press, 2012), 87–95.

22. These last few sentences were published in French in the 1894–1895 edition but translated into Latin in the 1896 edition. They were also slightly modified: "But our greatest pleasure was the warm baths that we took together on Sundays and holidays. There were two bathtubs in the same cubicle and we scented the bathhouse water with lilac perfume that I had brought." They were also copied from the original manuscript into "Passages to be suppressed," with the following note: "I beg you not to communicate this document to anyone; I ask you on your word of honor." See *Confessions*, Ms. (3) and Ms. (4), 232–33.

countryside surrounding the town, drove across moonlit fields, and felt a perfect happiness. He also wanted to show his friendship for me and to demonstrate that he thought of me as much as he thought of himself. One day, on one of our regimental marches, he jumped over an enormous ditch in order to get me a bunch of grapes that I had wanted. In the end, never were there truer lovers than we were, who were as happy as we were, who had greater passion in their hearts. The horrible and accursed passion that had burned inside me ever since my childhood had at last found its way and had taken flight and had entangled with it a being that was innocent of its faults. Only an accursed passion could have ensnared and poisoned such an innocent soul. I have often reproached myself for having corrupted and demoralized such a young man through my example and my influence. He had probably never imagined such abominable passions. However, at that time, I didn't think of such things and I didn't find anything reprehensible in my conduct. It was only later that I was struck by remorse, and I bitterly regretted my fault and his.

My year of military service was almost at an end, and I thought about my approaching departure with real terror—something that I would have believed was impossible a year before. The idea that I would have to be separated for a long time, if not forever, from my friend was unbearable, and at night we would often cry together. He still had several years to serve, and he was pained to see the time coming when he would be left alone and lonely, now that he had a friend who was so passionately attached to him. I will not tell you everything we felt then and during the days before our final farewell. I had neglected my comrades a lot in those last few weeks, and although they didn't suspect a thing, they noted with displeasure that I preferred a young man whom they didn't consider their equal in rank.

Finally, the terrible day arrived. We said our good-byes in the little room where so many happy hours had been spent, and I delayed my departure in order to enjoy my dear and beloved friend one last time. I left him all the money I had and gave him several mementos, asking him to write to me as often as possible. He promised me to do so, and at last I left.

When I returned to my father's house, I felt a frightful void, and my family's habits seemed unbearable. Everyone gave me the warmest of welcomes, and they pampered me in the nicest way. My nerves were worn out, and an insurmountable melancholy took hold of me, gripping me in a vise. I had such intense nervous crises and fevers that I was advised to seek a change of climate and spend some time in the south of Italy. This was all in vain, however, and my only consolation was in the letters that I received from time to time.

Yet, three months later I had regained my health completely, and I again took up painting and literature, which had so interested me before. My friend's image soon faded in my memory and lost all its charm and vivacity. He still wrote to me sometimes, but I responded only after long delays and with colder and colder letters. Soon he stopped writing to me, and I wasn't too upset about it.

Six months after I left, his regiment had been deployed to a different garrison and he was shot to death by one of his drunken companions with whom he had quarreled about his duties. He died right away on the road lined by fir trees that led from the town to the fort. His murderer was given a life sentence of hard labor. I didn't regret his death, which I first learned about through the newspapers. Later, a petty officer whom I had met afterward gave me more details. The passionate friendship that I had for him had burned itself out and there was nothing left, not even ashes. I would have had no pleasure in seeing him again, and I would have been ashamed for both of us. The earth will keep this secret and only these pages will reveal it to you. I have told you only the pure and simple truth; you are free to believe it or not. Its dénouement may read like a novel to you, but it is, nonetheless, very real.

I now live alone as a virgin, having no taste for a life from which I get no pleasure. The desire for men still torments me, but no longer having any opportunity to give in to it, I will surely not revert to the horrible error of my senses. I won't have a family; I'll never have children. Everyone is surprised to see me so sad and gloomy, especially at my age, with my looks and in my position. If you knew me, Sir, would you also be surprised? I don't believe so. Everyone is wracking their brains to find the cause of my sadness and distress. I have virtually withdrawn from the world, and I live in almost complete solitude, to everyone's amazement. My health is deteriorating, a condition that pleases me; even though I am afraid to die, I would rather be dead already.

Forgive me, Sir, if these pages are so badly written, but I won't even reread them because if I did, I wouldn't send them. Doesn't such a terrible illness of the soul deserve to be described? Or at least known by the greatest collector of human documents of our time? I don't know whether you can do something with the terrible passion I have confessed to you; in any case, I am glad to have revealed it to you. If, in the sublime descriptions of human miseries, the misery that afflicts me can find a place in your work, please, Sir, don't make me too odious. With death in my soul, I no longer have any joy waiting here below. I feel guilty and afflicted by a frightful destiny that I can't escape from. Have I not already been punished enough?

It has been five hours since I began to write, and now the pen is falling from my exhausted hand. If these pages of mine helped you with anything, then I don't regret the time I have spent writing to you, if it weren't for the awful motive that made me take up a pen.

Second Document (1888 or 1889)

[NEW CONFESSIONS]
This morning I just reread the pages that I finished last night. I only glanced at them, but I was tempted to throw them into the fire. I didn't do that, sure that I would have regretted it afterward. These pages may have some interest for you. For this reason, I'm going to fill in a gap that I deliberately left out, from a false sense of shame, but which will certainly not escape your clairvoyant eye. Since I have confessed so many horrors, I can't help confessing others and reveal myself completely. I would have liked to spare myself this rather filthy tale, but then you certainly wouldn't understand how a young man of nineteen, completely virginal, could have corrupted a man of twenty-five so easily, especially a man who had already known several women. That is something that was and still is absolutely unknown to me and something that I don't even want to know. However deeply corrupted my morals are, and even though I have dreamed since a very young age of the most exquisite depravities, I didn't lose what could be called my innocence until the age of sixteen. Until then, I was content with imaginary debaucheries and solitary pleasures.

My first tutor was a friend of the family, who had been a friend of my father's since his youth. He was an ex-captain in the Piedmont cavalry, having served in all the Italian wars where, as they said, he had brutally cut down many Austrians. He seemed to be completely dissolute, and it was whispered that he had lived for a long time with a young man whom he had helped squander three-fourths of his inheritance. This captain lived off his pension and the numerous horse deals that he made. He had traveled a lot, and he had been in Hungary for a long time. Even though he was from the lower classes, he frequented the best houses. Ladies could barely tolerate him because of the lack of respect he showed them in both actions and words. Men, on the other hand, especially <u>sportsmen</u>, welcomed him with open arms.

He came to see us sometimes but at first paid no attention to me. However, I felt attracted to him and showed him my friendly feelings. His skin was dark; he was very tall with a frame that seemed indestructible with bulging muscles, as firm as steel, that seemed to take the place of any flesh. For me, he was the archetype of the old <u>baron</u> in a suit of armor, and I never saw him without thinking about one of the characters in *Ivanhoe*.[23] His head was superb, thin, brown like that of a mulatto, with a great hooked nose that slanted slightly to the left; his black, deep-set eyes shone forth with an extraordinary clarity; his long black mustache revealed a curved mouth, a mouth that mocked everyone, with thick brown lips and strong, white teeth. His enormous head was almost entirely bald and covered with a down of short black bristles at the back and sides. His hands matched the rest of his body; his voice was harsh and deep; and his entire athletic body had a Herculean force about it. He could bend horseshoes with his bare hands. He had a way of looking at you that made you lower your eyes, and he didn't spare anyone anything.

He took the greatest of liberties with me, tickling me under the chin, and when he met me in the corridor or when I walked him to the door, he pinched and caressed me for a long time, even in front of my father, who didn't see anything wrong in it.

As I have already told you, I knew nothing at the time except through hearsay. I trembled with desire to finally experience something, and when this man touched me, my blood rushed through my whole body. One day, when he was talking to my father about the wounds that he had received during the war, he wanted to show us a scar that he had on his thigh. He had avenged himself by splitting the head of the German soldier who had given it to him. He unbuttoned his pants and to my great joy, he showed us his enormous thigh, gleaming and brown, covered with coarse black hairs, split by a large pink gash that seemed to me to be quite handsome in the midst of the dark flesh and the hair that gave it a brown border.

---

23. *Ivanhoe*, written by Sir Walter Scott in 1819, was set in the time of King Richard I, the Lionheart, who reigned over England from 1189 to 1199.

I tried to see {what he was hiding under his shirt, but I saw nothing except a dense, black bush that made me tremble violently.}[24]

Still, I didn't have any affection for this man,[25] but he seemed so <u>masculine</u> to me that I very much wanted to belong to him, even if only for a few moments. Ever since that day, whenever he looked at me, I was always very excited; I would blush, and when he touched me, I shuddered with pleasure. Even today, in writing these lines, I feel an emotion that I would rather suppress welling up inside me again, and I feel that, if he were here now, I would give myself to him completely. As a man accustomed to these kinds of encounters, he understood what he could get out of my youth and my charm—the charm of a young girl disguised as a boy. He invited me to come and see the horses in his stables which, I believe, he was soon sending away to I-don't-know-what country. I went there full of desire for an experience where I could at last learn something and indulge my own longings. These desires, since they had not yet been satisfied, had become so overwhelming that they left me no peace. After the visit to the horses, which I admired a great deal without understanding anything, he showed me his apartment. It consisted of a living room off the landing, a bedroom, and a toilet. For servants, he had a groom and an old porter.

When I entered this furnished room, which was all smoky, smelling of cigars and the stables, and where everything was lying about, I was dumbfounded, and my desire gave me such violent palpitations that I could barely breathe. I felt my extremities freeze. Even now I still often have this cruel and delicious feeling at times.

He sat me on his sofa next to him, caressed me, laughed in a very forced manner, and gave me such strange looks that I was afraid, while at the same time I was charmed. I didn't know what to say; I was ashamed, and I was as red as a peony. He took hold of my hands, seated me on his knees, and began to kiss my ear, whispering things so quietly that I couldn't hear him. We were both silent; I remained immobile on his knees while he continued to kiss my head, my cheeks, and my neck. I felt I was dying of pleasure because I had never experienced such lust. At last he got up, saying: "Do

---

24. Copied from the original manuscript into "Passages to be suppressed" and translated into Latin. See *Confessions*, Ms. (5), 233.

25. Saint-Paul changed "I didn't have" to "I didn't feel" in the first published version in the *Archives d'Anthropologie Criminelle* in 1894–1895.

you want to . . . ? Do you want to . . . ?" with a husky voice that nearly frightened me. I didn't answer because I was so excited!

He got up abruptly, locked the door, and closed the shutters on the window. Then he came toward me. I was panting with desire, shame, and fear. He undressed me in the blink of an eye, all the while running his hands over my body, removing everything, including my socks and shoes, throwing off my shirt, and carrying me, like a little child, to his bed. Just as quickly he was himself completely naked and lying next to me, where I felt I was in a dream, no longer aware of my actions and my thoughts.

{*He stretched out on top of me, panting and sighing strongly, pressing me so violently in his arms like a vise that he cut off my breath, and he began to writhe on my body. He had an enormous penis that I felt rubbing against me, a sensation that aroused me most delightfully. Meanwhile, he licked my ears and slipped his tongue in my mouth and caressed my whole body with his hands. In a voice choking with emotion, he murmured the sweetest and most irrational words. When he ejaculated, he unleashed a flood on me but did not stop moving and bellowed like a raging bull. Meanwhile, I had a copious orgasm, and we lay there for a long time, exhausted in each other's arms, as though we were glued together. In fact, we had to struggle to untangle ourselves.*}[26]

At that moment I no longer had any shame, and he himself seemed completely happy. He let out a long sigh of pleasure and satisfaction. After we got up and dressed with care,[27] I looked at myself in the mirror. I was struck by the strange and almost frightening beauty that I had at that moment. My face was flushed; my lips were as red as blood; my eyes sparkled with all their most beautiful radiance. I was proud of myself, of the pleasure that I had given and received. I almost felt grateful to the captain and felt as if I belonged exclusively to him. He made me promise to come and see him often, which I did with all my heart. I never had such bright and happy days, and it seemed to me that I began to live only from that day on.

From that time on, we saw each other often and always at his place. We used to eat lunch at a café; then we would spend hours together in his room. {*That man was a real satyr! I don't think a decadent Roman ever knew about or devised the sensuous variations in his repertoire. He would say that all our limbs must contribute to our pleasure and he would make it happen. He also dreamed up the strangest positions,*

---

26. Copied from the original manuscript into "Passages to be suppressed" and translated into Latin. See *Confessions*, Ms. (6), 233.

27. Saint-Paul changed "After we got up" to "Afterward we washed up" in the 1894–1895 edition.

back-and-forth rhythmic motions, the most extraordinary leaps and twists. I can't begin to describe everything he taught me.

When I got to know all of his repertoire, he said to me one day: "Now you must belong to me completely, and I must possess you entirely."}[28] I couldn't ask for anything better; my nature urged me to it; and I panted with desire to know new and secret pleasures. I soon understood what he wanted; this seemed quite natural to me, and I didn't refuse. He didn't expect me to abandon myself so completely, and it made him burst with joy. He told me that I was his treasure, that he loved me a great deal, and that he would give me the greatest pleasure that I would ever know.

{Yet I felt a bit alarmed, watching his penis swell to an enormous size and stand fully erect as he anointed it with cold cream.[29] I didn't think that it would be possible to put this enormous thing in my soft and delicate body. He smeared me with the cold cream, and I let him do it all the while anxiously awaiting the result of these preparations, which made me pant with expectation and, almost, impatience. He stretched me out on the bed as usual, raised my legs and put them on his shoulders, slid in between my thighs until his penis made contact with my body. At the same time he took hold of my shoulders and drove home the first stroke.}[30] I felt such sharp pain that I pushed him away, and despite the effort that he made to hold me, I was able to get out from under him. I jumped off the bed, telling him I no longer wanted to do it.

He ground his teeth, cursed at me, begged me, but I held my ground. Since I am confessing to you, it was the physical pain that made me withdraw from the violent act; it wasn't shame or any other feeling. I only yielded to my nature that wanted me to do so.

He had to content himself with the liberties that he had already taken with me, because I never wanted to satisfy him in the manner that I found so painful. I preferred more delicate pleasures, which wouldn't leave any traces. I wanted to try this means of love-making with my <u>friend</u>, but that time the pain was also too intense and I had to give up, though I did so with regret.

{Otherwise, I dearly loved the captain, who certainly felt very manly compared to me, who was so delicate and charming. He often asked me with tears in his eyes to

---

28. Copied from the original manuscript into "Passages to be suppressed" and translated into Latin. See *Confessions*, Ms. (7), 233.

29. "Cold cream" is in English in the original manuscript.

30. Copied from the original manuscript into "Passages to be suppressed" and translated into Latin. See *Confessions*, Ms. (8), 233–34.

satisfy him completely, but I never would. In any case he took the greatest pleasure with me, and he often said he preferred me to the most beautiful girls he had had. When he took me in his arms, he would kiss me, suck me, and bite my flesh. One day, when he ejaculated, he bit me on the right shoulder so violently that the marks remained for days. Never did I love him as much as I did then!

I didn't think it was possible for a man to be so robust. I often marveled at the striking sight of him naked. His skin was, and still is, the color of polished bronze, scarred by three or four saber wounds. His whole body radiates the strength of Hercules, despite being fifty-two or fifty-three years old (which he doesn't admit!). He says he is forty-eight, which is false. He is extremely virile. He told me that when he was young, he would have intercourse three or four times a day, but now he is content to have intercourse five or six times a week. His ejaculations are copious, and he feels so much pleasure at these moments that he huffs and roars like a lion. He never needs to get ready because he is always ready for pleasure. I was very jealous of him, but not as much as I envied my other lover, who was even more charming, more graceful, and more youthful.

He was my teacher, and if I had had others like him, I wouldn't have complained at all. My departure for military service, and, after a few months, my new, more tender, passion, separated me from him; but I saw him again recently, and although he is far away, I hope to see him again and often in the future.}[31]

I then had an adventure with a young Spaniard, who was for me what I had been for others. He followed me around everywhere for a long time, waiting under my balcony for hours on end, and walking along the riverbank when I was there. When I met him, he showed me the most passionate friendship. I had him come to my place several times, but he had the same character as I had: he was very shy, and, being used to powerful men, I quickly developed an aversion to him. I took leave of him in a way that really wasn't decent, and I haven't seen him since. I believe that he returned to Spain with his family.

One day, while in town, a man followed me. My captain was traveling; my Spaniard bored me; and I was in need of distraction. We understood each other very well very quickly. I agreed to meet him in the captain's apartment, to which I had the key. I was disgusted with this man, who had the same vice as your Baptiste. He was cold and slimy, a bitter and

---

31. Copied from the original manuscript into "Passages to be suppressed" and translated into Latin for the most part. See *Confessions*, Ms. (9), 234–35.

disagreeable blond; I could do nothing with him, because I was so disgusted with him. He went away as quickly as he came, and I never saw him again.

Here, Sir, is the confession that I wanted to make to you; it has reached the end. Maybe you will feel compassion for me, with the gift that great intellects have: to know and understand both good and evil. In the society where I live and where I spend my days alone, even abandoned by my thoughts, I feel deeply sad and thoroughly disgusted. I shake off this lassitude only at those moments when I can lose myself in a foolish passion, and these moments are rare because I don't want to let anyone in on my sad secret. Ladies make a big fuss over me, and more than one of them has made very gallant advances toward me, advances that I have always refused with a smile but feeling genuine despair and great regret. I enjoy women's company a great deal. It really affects me the same way the ladies in La Curée do for your Maxime, whom I resemble a little.[32] But, being more unhappy than he, my nature will not allow me to love, and it leaves me only with cold debauchery, which I end up finding repulsive.

People often joke about my melancholy and my pose as Werther, but if they could read my heart, then they would pity me, or maybe they would just laugh at me.[33] As I have already told you, I don't have any hope here on earth, and everyone else's joy seems to be an insult to my existence. I will remain always what I am—a pretty, cute, perfumed, irreproachably elegant, frivolous, and secretly debauched being. I say "secretly," because nobody knows what I am and what I do. When I say "nobody," I mean that I do make exceptions for three or four people, who truly have understood me, but since they have shared my weaknesses and my shame, I don't need to blush when I'm with them, or at least we will blush together.

And why should I feel shame for what I have done? Wasn't it nature that made the mistake in the first place and condemned me to eternal sterility?

I could have been an adorable and adoring woman, an irreproachable mother and wife, but I am only an incomplete being, a monstrous being,

---

32. Maxime was the son of the main character, Aristide Saccard, in the novel La Curée/The Kill (1872). He was depicted as an indolent young man, rather effeminate at times. In his preparatory notes, Zola used the term "virtually pederastic" to describe him.

33. Werther was the hero of Johann Wolfgang von Goethe's novel The Sorrows of Young Werther (1774). He committed suicide because of his unrequited love for a married woman.

desiring only what is not allowed and desired by women who could be regarded only as friends, not mistresses. Do you know of a more terrible torture? But our sins, aren't they forgivable?

I am sure, Sir, that you will keep this confession as one of those human documents that is the least understood and that you'll appreciate my sending it to you.

I'll tell you more about something that might interest you about my entourage and the environment in which I live. . . .[34] {As I have already had the pleasure of telling you, my ancestors are Spanish, having come to Italy at the time when the Spanish ruled over Naples. The senior branch of the family holds the title of <u>duke</u>, but it is separated from us by several degrees; we hold the title of <u>count</u>. In fact, claiming ties to the Neapolitan or Spanish nobility is insignificant because almost everyone here has blue blood}, and if it weren't for my mother's dowry and some lucky investments, we would be pretty poor examples of the nobility. My father's marriage will explain both our decline and the source of our wealth. My brothers are all well established and have beautiful families. I always pray to God that none of my nieces or nephews take after me either physically or morally.

I feel that as I get older, I will become more and more devout, since it offers me the only possible consolation, but my most ardent desire isn't to grow old at all but to die in the flower of my youth and beauty. If I did grow old, I would despise and hate myself too much.

I have nothing more to add to these pages, which are already too long. I'm afraid I have bored you terribly, if you have had the fortitude, in any case, to reach this point. No matter. I have unburdened my soul a little, and I have written with a sort of retrospective voluptuousness about the abominable and intense scenes in which I have participated.

I do not need to assure you that <u>everything</u> in my story is <u>true</u>; I would have had no reason to lie; and you yourself will perhaps recognize the truth of all that I've written. It seems to me that I've treated myself rather harshly, that I haven't flattered myself either physically or morally.

---

34. Here, Saint-Paul inserted the following comment: "I skip certain details that are so personal that they might permit the indiscreet to discover the identity of the author of this confession. Suffice it for me to say, however, that, having verified the information that he gave me concerning his family, this family is, on the father's side, from the best and highest nobility." The passage that follows was another one copied by Saint-Paul into "Passages to be suppressed." See *Confessions*, Ms. (11), 235. We reproduce the censored part here for the first time.

Please forgive this awful scribbling but I've written to you with an open heart, as if I were confessing to a doctor or a friend, and I haven't paid attention to its form or its spelling.

Here, Sir, is what I have had to say.

> One of your most passionate admirers.

POSTSCRIPT

Do you know, Sir, what caused me to write to you from here, where I am celebrating the Jubilee of the Holy Father? It is because of the intense desire and the lust that I felt in seeing again a young man who has the most perfect and noble beauty, for whom I had the most ideal passion in the past and to whom I've never spoken nor <u>ever</u> will. I love him so much that I hate him and I wish him death, so that he would never belong to anyone else. Have you ever imagined such a martyrdom?

Third Document (1888 or 1889)

Sir:

I hope you received the package of badly written pages that I sent to you. I wrote them with pleasure, sure that, in your profound studies of mankind, its sicknesses and misfortunes, such a confession could only please you.

I wrote to you on a very boring and sad day while it rained in torrents and melancholy colors engulfed everything. The last part of this confession was written yesterday morning as a frightful rain lashed at the window of my banal and depressing furnished room.

What I wrote bizarrely reflected my mood and the sadness and boredom that surround me. I painted everything an exaggerated shade of black and revealed myself as I am perhaps, but certainly not what I am always. I am this way, and my feelings of melancholy and sadness have become the <u>basis</u> of my character—but I do come out of it often, and I don't always feel so unhappy. I am writing you this letter after a delicious dinner with a big party of friends, where I received plenty of compliments and where the generous amount of wine and the brilliance of a rich house dazzled hearts and minds. I want, therefore, to complete the study of my personality, which I consider often favored by nature, since it has made me a being who even the most audacious poets haven't been able to <u>create</u>.

[PERSONALITY]

As a man with a beautiful body, I have the mind, the charm, and all the tastes of the most delightful women. I can therefore profit sometimes from the combined gifts of both sexes even if I sometimes torment myself for being neither a man nor a woman. I like to compare myself to the ravishing heroes of mythology and to tell myself that Hyacinth, Ganymede, and so many other delightful creatures were not at all different from me and were adored by the most handsome and powerful gods.[35]

I have an aversion—the most absolute kind—to women, but I do consider women to be most like me, and I have warm, friendly feelings for many of them, who also have a tender friendship for me. Perhaps they are surprised—without suspecting why—at my reserve and my innocence in my dealings with them.

I'm in regular correspondence with several charming women, who often confide their most intimate feelings to me and whom I have always entertained with conversation that is more than a little licentious. Several of them have pretended to believe that I have courted them and have given me rather obvious signals. I immediately felt repugnance toward them and kept them at a distance. I always pretend to be in love with another woman, and I give them details about these imaginary people and tell them all sorts of things that I've learned in books or that I know about through my friends.

Once a married cousin stayed with us for several days. She slept in the room next to mine with only a wall separating our two beds, which stood in the corners of our respective bedrooms. During the night, she knocked on the wall of my room, laughing and joking, because she was very lighthearted and always played at being a spoiled child. (She has since died from meningitis.) I feared that she would get the idea to call me, and so I pretended to fall asleep immediately and to be in a very deep sleep. I believe I could have slept completely naked with her without this arousing the slightest desire in me.

I could feel the greatest affinity for ladies—I say "ladies" because other women seem to me to be gross beasts—but I could be only a friend and nothing else; nevertheless, I am aroused in a terrible and powerful way

---

35. Hyacinth was a Spartan boy loved by Apollo in Ovid's *Metamorphoses*. Ganymede was a beautiful boy, whom Zeus loved and carried off to Olympus in order to make him his cupbearer.

when there is an attractive man close by, or I simply catch sight of one, no matter what his rank in society is. However, it is true that I prefer <u>distinguished</u>, <u>well-dressed</u> men, especially <u>military</u> men.

Yesterday, when I went to the post office to send the long letter that I had addressed to you, I was struck by the good looks of one of the postal clerks. Romans are really very handsome! Today I mailed several letters just so I could go back to see him, and I enjoyed talking to him and looking at him. He is definitely a charming man!!

I have a real <u>passion</u> for men, and if I were a <u>woman</u>, I believe my loves and my jealousies would be terrifying!

Don't believe that when I use the word love, I mean only what I wrote about yesterday. I think there is a much more beautiful and much more noble way to love. Alas! I could <u>never</u> experience it because a <u>truly</u> noble and charming man, like the ones I know, would certainly not want to have anything to do with me, and I settle for depraved men. It is true that they are perhaps more amusing and better than others. That is my consolation.

Yet, I would like to be able to love somebody with a beautiful and <u>noble</u> passion. I understand all the sacrifices a person can make when he is truly in love, and I shudder at not being able to experience this, especially at not being able to be <u>loved</u> with <u>a heart-felt</u> passion and with the spirit with which I feel I could love.

I harbor some doubts now that the young military man's love for me was carefully <u>calculated</u>—a way to <u>enjoy</u> my money. Perhaps he also liked my body because I made him feel things that he hadn't before. I'm afraid that was all there was to it and he had no other feelings for me.

As for the captain, he is a <u>debauched</u> man whom I hold on to because I have nothing better right now, and to whom I belong through habit. Maybe I like him better than I realize. When he leaves, it upsets me, and these long absences are very unpleasant, even though I don't really <u>love</u> him. I've experienced true love only <u>once</u> in my life until now, and maybe I won't ever feel it again with such an intense outburst of tender and delicate feelings and such frightful jealousy.

I think the captain really loves me; he says so at least. But I've noticed more than once that he changes <u>after</u> the thing is consummated and the ardor and passion he shows me beforehand changes after he has done what he wanted. This wasn't so in the first years of our relationship, and I believe that he is only interested in his pleasure and the strangeness of my face and body, while caring less about me personally or about my feelings or affections. Besides, he exhausts me.

{Although he is so aggressive, and perhaps because of his physical strength and energy, he takes a long time to reach orgasm, even though I let myself go and ejaculate quickly. The time between his climax and mine—a few seconds only, it is true—is nevertheless enough for me to come to my senses and observe this man in the throes of passion, his face contorted in a simultaneously savage and vulgar expression that used to enchant me before, but now, when I am finished, it no longer has the same effect on me; it almost disgusts and terrifies me. I would like to get away, but it is only fair that he should be able to take his pleasure since I have had mine. This tires me out, and I lie there with a poker face, rigid and distant. At these times I hate him! When I am lucky, he ejaculates at the same time as I do and it's a real joy; on those days, I do love him, and I surrender myself entirely, body and soul, and do everything to please him. One of my regrets is that I cannot receive his ejaculation, his semen that to me is virtually the essence of his being, inside my body. This is perhaps my greatest regret, and maybe I will never stop regretting not being a woman.}[36]

After my resistance the first time and after several other attempts, he nearly gave up on trying to possess me entirely, as he wanted and as I myself desired despite the atrocious pain that I felt at these attempts that never succeeded because of the extreme fragility of my body. In order to please him, I am willing to suffer a little, but when I'm at that point—we have tried three or four times—I feel nothing but pain, and despite his efforts and his feverish urging, I have to refuse.

Perhaps you are surprised that I discuss with so much passion a man who is no longer young, even though he is worth more than several young men put together. I haven't told you as much about my other passion, which was much stronger. The reason is that the other man is no longer alive, and it took place four years ago. I always live in the present, and I still have pleasure with him. And also, I was relatively more reserved with the other one because I loved him more, and I never did nor did I ever condescend to do to him what the captain taught me and made me do, sometimes very brutally. His violence secretly charms me and makes me docile in everything he wants. I feel tiny next to him!

---

36. Copied from the original manuscript into "Passages to be suppressed" and translated into Latin. See *Confessions*, Ms. (10), 235.

THE NOVEL OF AN INVERT   83

In the confession that I've written to you, that I've chosen you to hear—because of my admiration for you and in the hope that I could be useful to you in something—I didn't want to tell you about the delicious debaucheries I have enjoyed with this man. I had decided to tell you about only the more refined one I had in the army, but, carried away by my excitement, I couldn't resist describing the delicious scenes I recall of boundless pleasure and desire, even though they often leave me sad and weary.

The <u>only</u> person who perhaps felt true love for me was the young Spaniard with whom I enjoyed myself perhaps a dozen times and who loved me <u>madly</u> even though I was only very cold toward him. I thought we were too much alike. He was a <u>virgin</u>, like me—even though he didn't want to admit it, but you could tell it from all his conversation, and men attracted him quite strongly. He was delicate, but not handsome, although he had gorgeous eyes with greenish brown irises, like precious marble.

He told me one day that when he was following me without knowing who I was—this lasted several months—and not having seen me for fifteen days (I was then in Palermo), he cried for a long time, believing me to be sick or dead. He also kept an oleander leaf I had picked, nibbled, and dropped on the ground without realizing it. He kept it as a <u>relic</u> and showed it to me, framed under glass. I always <u>laughed</u> at him, and secretly he was very repulsive to me, even though I wanted to appease him sometimes. I've since been afraid of having the same feelings myself, and this made me especially conscious of how easily I can be attracted to someone at first sight.

I've also been very <u>reserved</u> since then in my behavior in society and toward my lover. I don't tolerate any banter, and I treat him with complete <u>indifference</u>. I do the same even when we meet alone or have intimate conversations, and I let myself go <u>completely</u> only inside his apartment, in the half-darkness of his bedroom. In the past I wasn't always so reserved, but the ways of the world have taught me how to behave in these unusual and exceptional situations.

When people talk about him, I say nothing or I say something <u>bad</u> about him. People have often had to defend him from my attacks. What is worse is that I'm sincere in my criticism, and the bad things that <u>I say about him</u> are what I actually <u>think</u>. I sometimes abuse him with my words, and I'm not afraid to contradict everything that he says in front of other people. Yet as soon as we are alone and he shows himself to be the master, I let go of my impudence, which is feigned, and fall into his arms, very happy to see his excitement and lust for me. It's no doubt because of him that I don't look for other diversions, and, besides, habit has made him my master, and I only briefly desire other men who attract me.

Yesterday, in the last pages that I wrote, I described the despair and rage I felt when I saw the young man again whose beauty has always struck me. He's so <u>handsome</u> that I'm completely overcome, but I consider him more a work of art than a <u>man</u>. I really envy the woman who will have him and enjoy him, but I would rather have him as a lover than a <u>husband</u>. He is too <u>perfect</u>, and that must become <u>monotonous</u>. This doesn't mean that I can ever see him dispassionately, and I desperately want to be loved by him, to hold him in my arms, and also wish he were in love with me.

Alas! This is impossible and I have to resign myself to what I have—which isn't so very little. Maybe everyone isn't as happy as <u>I am</u>. I've loved passionately, and maybe if I had been seduced by a young man, delightful in his elegant virility, I would have experienced all the flames of jealousy and of a passion satisfied, if not <u>completely</u>, at least in a <u>fulfilling</u> way. I am loved, with a horrific and violent love, by an old warrior at the height of his virility and next to whom many other men seem weak and small. He showers me with his passionate affection, and if I weren't a <u>little</u> tired of him, I would be absolutely happy in my satisfied desires.

I do regret and will often regret the <u>denial</u> of my nature and not being able to enjoy sex in body and soul, but in the end, I'm young, pretty, charming, and rich. And if my soul is monstrous, I console myself in thinking that I'm the depraved and dainty product of a refined and delicate civilization.

In the rest of this letter, I want to tell you a little about my actual character, something that might also interest you and give you a better grasp of my strange personality. I love everything that is beautiful, and almost nothing—in any artistic genre—is beautiful <u>enough</u> in my eyes. I adore things that are exceptional, rich, and elegant. In my imagination I have built palaces more beautiful than all the existing ones, filling them with masterpieces chosen from all the masterpieces in the world. The sight of a work of art, artificial and yet real, keeps me in ecstasy for hours, and I dream about it at night.

Beauty in my eyes surpasses <u>everything</u> else, and for me <u>all</u> vices, <u>all crimes, are excused by it</u>. The one character of Balzac's that charmed me the most is the handsome <u>Lucien</u>. I still believe I resemble him, and I've always thought that the horrid Vautrin's love was more physical in nature than Balzac could have admitted to himself.[37]

Flowers please me infinitely, especially flowers from greenhouses and rare, expensive, and unusual plants. Roses and big tropical flowers especially delight me, even in paintings. I have a real aversion to lilies and all wildflowers and plants that grow in the countryside without the need for cultivation.

In the human family, I like only distinguished, well-dressed, and elegant people who, I believe, are the only ones entitled to the dignity of the name man. The others don't count for me. I make an exception for artists who, thanks to the refinement of their souls and the beauty of their work, can be allowed a little laxness in their appearance. Other people don't count at all for me, and I feel only aversion toward them. I much prefer a magnificent dog—a King Charles spaniel, for example—to all the workers and peasants of the world. The latter repel me; I make exceptions for some of the former, especially if they are handsome and muscular, something that happens from time to time. If I had been a beautiful lady, I believe I would like to try out some of them—only to send them back afterward, understandably.

For me, the word woman conjures up ideas of luxury, emblazoned coaches, satin, velvet, white and perfumed skin, perfect hands, and the laxest of morals. A woman who walks in the street seems to me to be low and fallen, and working-class women are simply horrible, even if they are beautiful in a physical sense.

It's not necessary to tell you that—however indifferent I am to everything political—I'm a royalist by instinct. To me kings and queens seem to be made differently from the rest of humanity.

I'm a Catholic without conviction, an unbeliever really. I like the pomp and circumstance of the Church, and I'm proud to belong to it. I like rich churches, those of the Jesuits especially, with their gilded decorations and polychrome marbles. And I like the solemn religious ceremonies that make something unknown and mysterious quiver inside me.

---

37. Lucien de Rubempré is the main character in Balzac's *Illusions perdues/Lost Illusions* (1837–1843) and *Splendeurs et misères des courtisanes/Splendors and Miseries of Courtesans* (1838). He had an ambiguous relationship with Vautrin, the master criminal who appears in many of Balzac's novels. Vautrin is often considered the first homosexual character in nineteenth-century French literature.

I <u>despise</u> the republic, and it always seems to me—you will perhaps laugh—to be populated by ragged, dirty creatures.

I feel comfortable only in very rich and magnificently furnished apartments, a taste that my father shares. He has spent a substantial <u>fortune</u> on artworks, especially on porcelain from the East and superb and unusual pieces from Japan. I am delighted by long passageways opening onto row after row of rooms with velvet hangings and mirrors as far as the eye can see. I adore greenhouses and overheated rooms, where I like to daydream about everything by evoking mysterious and voluptuous images. I have always been vain, and I feel a real <u>thrill</u> when I am riding in our carriage through our garden gate and people stop and stare before going on their way.

I love being admired, and I'm proud of my beauty, which I try to heighten as much as I can. I've always found in myself a resemblance to the busts of Madame du Barry—a du Barry with short hair and dressed as a boy.[38] People often exclaim that I look like a woman, and though I am occasionally annoyed by this, more often than not I'm flattered by their curious and surprised looks. One evening, a number of years ago, I was thrilled by the sensation that I caused at the skating rink in Paris. Several ladies thought I was cross-dressing and showed unmistakable signs of surprise. I was delighted by it!

In paintings, I prefer genre paintings over any other, especially if they depict rich and modern interiors. Moreover, I have a real fanaticism for the great Makart, whose sensual and troubling works enchant me. My favorite painting by this artist is <u>The Death of Cleopatra</u>, a scene that I've always admired and envied.[39]

There's a deep vein of <u>cruelty</u> in my personality. I enjoy others' pain, especially if I am the one to inflict it. When I was a child, I voluntarily tortured animals, using the most exquisite methods, and in doing so, I would feel a sharp pain that pleased and excited me.

I've always been very arrogant, and at times when business was going badly, I missed luxury terribly. It's a real necessity for me, and I can't live

---

38. Marie-Jeanne Bécu, Countess du Barry (1743–1793), was the final mistress of Louis XV.

39. Hans Makart (1840–1884) was an Austrian painter, known for his large-scale interpretations of mythological and historical themes. This work, *The Death of Cleopatra*, dates from 1875.

with less. I hate everything that is ordinary, especially everyday things, and I adore everything that is extraordinary and impossible. Often, when my parents were away from home, I would sleep all day. Then I would turn on all the lights in the apartment and stay up, drinking and eating all night long, wearing a Greek dressing gown, after having taken a hot bath scented with perfume. I paint very beautifully, especially in watercolors, and I work on ladies' albums and their fans.

I am cunning and treacherous, although at times I am naively credulous. Everyone who meets me adores me, and nobody resists my charms. I have always had my way with people by playing on their emotions, and I have always succeeded in making them do whatever I want, whereas others, imposing their will by force, don't get anywhere. I've often noticed that—for the same kind of misdeeds and failings—my friends and companions would be punished while I would escape scot-free, thanks to the innocent and melancholic air I assumed.

I've always tyrannized those who loved me; I immediately act rougher and more authoritarian. Although I am weak and effeminate, I detest weak people and like only strong ones, those who fight and win. I've always regretted not being able to console the great and the powerful after their downfall. I think if I had been Marie Louise, I would have followed Napoleon to Saint Helena. Maybe I wouldn't have done so if I had known and loved the handsome Neipperg, despite his glass eye.[40]

I admire enthusiastically, as I've already told you, all that is beautiful and delicate, but the strange thing is that ugliness, especially if is grandiose, primitive, and powerful, pleases me as much in a man as beauty does, and maybe even more so.

I have a very lively and alert mind despite my failings and weaknesses. I understand both the good and the bad in everything, and I also admire them equally, as long as there isn't anything vulgar about them.

I never could learn arithmetic beyond the four rules, and never knew how to do the third rule, even though I had a mathematics tutor for a long time.[41] I also don't understand anything about financial affairs, even though I've

---

40. Marie Louise of Austria (1791–1847) was the second wife of Napoleon I; she refused to share in his exile; instead, she lived openly with Adam Adalbert, Count of Neipperg, an Austrian officer and diplomat, in Parma, Italy.

41. The four mathematical rules are addition, subtraction, multiplication, and division.

heard them discussed in my family at length. Now, thank God, I don't hear any more about that because I no longer need to!

I can learn a poem that pleases me in five minutes, no matter how long the text is, but I can't get two lines of unpleasant prose into my brain, even if I spend hours at it. I play the piano well enough, even though I don't have the patience to practice for long. I prefer to play melancholic pieces, especially by Schubert or Mozart.[42] I also play operas and, while playing, I like to imagine the scenes and passions of the characters in the librettos. Verdi is my favorite composer, whom I adore![43] In literature, I prefer descriptions of feelings and the long and inevitable evolution of passions rather than a hodgepodge of adventures. I wanted to read the works of Ponson du Terrail, but I couldn't finish them; I found them too boring.[44]

Historical novels don't attract me in the least, except for Ivanhoe, because I want to believe that Rebecca could be one of my maternal ancestors.[45] The novels of Dumas the elder have interested me for a long time, but I find consulting historical documents and memoirs of the time much more interesting. I own countless books about Marie Antoinette, my favorite heroine, and about several other famous women. I like to collect their portraits, even the ugly ones, but I don't show them to anyone in order not to embarrass my beloved heroines. I keep those for myself. I've paid 200 francs for some books that don't interest me at all just to get a small print depicting Queen Marie Antoinette on the scaffold, based on a drawing made in 1793.

The history of France interests me the most, even though, if I could have chosen a time and a country in which to have come into the world, I would have chosen Rome at the height of its decadence, under Hadrian, for

---

42. Franz Peter Schubert (1797–1828), the famous Austrian composer, was best known for his classical symphonies and romantic songs. Wolfgang Amadeus Mozart (1756–1791) was also an Austrian composer, best known for his operas, including *The Marriage of Figaro, Don Giovanni,* and *The Magic Flute,* as well as his serenade, *A Little Night Music,* and forty-one symphonies.

43. Giuseppe Verdi (1813–1901), the foremost Italian composer of opera in the nineteenth century, was the author of *Oberto, Nabucco, La Traviata, Aida,* and many others.

44. Pierre-Alexis-Joseph-Ferdinand, Vicomte de Ponson du Terrail (1829–1871), was a popular novelist, known for his adventure series, *The Exploits of Rocambole.*

45. Rebecca was one of the main characters in Sir Walter Scott's novel, *Ivanhoe.* She was the daughter of Isaac of York, a Jew, who took care of Ivanhoe when he was injured. Later, after she was captured by his rival, Ivanhoe defeated his enemy in mortal combat in order to gain her release.

example.⁴⁶ (Henry III's court would please me too.)⁴⁷ I would have been ravishing in Roman garb, and the Roman costume I wore at a masked ball caused quite a sensation, showing off my naked arms and legs, with gorgeous sandals that revealed my bare toes with nails shining like polished agates. The captain (I call him that even though he is no longer a captain) was dressed as a gladiator, and he was superb in his maillot, the color of coffee with cream (he is actually darker than that), which showed off his magnificent body amply [endowed with firm muscles, his legs and chest clad in armor. That evening we abandoned ourselves to mutual delight.

I have a real passion for animals, for sea birds and rare dogs above all; I own some adorable Japanese pugs. In the past, I also adored children, but now I can no longer put up with them, and I never hug them, not even those who are close relatives.

Naples is my favorite city, and when I leave it,]⁴⁸ it's always with regret, even if only for a few days. It's almost oriental with its enormous palm trees and its blue harbor blazing with a strange glow that would look impossible in a painting. If Naples were inhabited by the French with their refined civilization, it would be divine; there wouldn't be a more beautiful city in the world. If it had belonged to the English at the time of the Spanish conquests, it would have been a beautiful paradise! As it is, it is, nevertheless, superb. I would like it to be better groomed and more refined; then, it would be the paradise of Mohammed.

I like nature only in its wildest remote places—a forest, for example—but once man comes into it, I prefer a perfect civilization with all its refined

---

46. Hadrian (76–138), the Roman emperor from 117 until his death, was devastated when his lover Antinous, whom we mentioned previously, was killed under mysterious circumstances. He deified him and had innumerable statues of him created throughout the empire. These statues came to represent the classic male nude of the Roman Empire.

47. King Henry III of France (1551–1589) was known for his inordinate attention to his favorites, his "mignons," who were all young and attractive men.

48. This passage was cut from the letter to Zola by Saint-Paul and kept in his archives under the title "Spécimen de l'écriture de l'auteur de la confession adressée à Émile Zola" / "Specimen of the handwriting by the author of the confessions sent to Émile Zola." It was recently found in the Saint-Paul family archives. It proves, if it were necessary, that the handwriting is the same for both "The Novel of an Invert" and its "Sequel." It allows us to transcribe the fragment accurately, and we have reproduced it in figure 2.

delicacies and distractions. I like English gardens, but the gardens at Versailles and those at Caserta have more charm for me.⁴⁹

I don't need to tell you that I am mad about your work, which I've read with admiration, even though, for me, the subjects of your latest books weren't very pleasant.⁵⁰ The book I like the most is La Curée, where I find characters with similar feelings to my own and who live in a society in which I've lived almost my entire life, the upper class in which I [was born and still live. Madeleine Férat also made the strongest impression on me.⁵¹

I am writing these pages tonight with the most intense pleasure. The room is very gay with gaslights burning, warm carpets, and the sounds of the hotel swarming with people. I'm almost happy. How long will this last? A long time, I hope. I only want to think about enjoying what I have without seeking anything else. I've written this for myself, but what I've written I'm sending to you. Will I have been useful to you in anything, or will I have wasted my time? In any case, I don't regret these hours. I've relived all my life in its frightful sorrows and guilty and frenzied joys.]⁵²

[FURTHER THOUGHTS]

I thought I could sleep, but all the memories brought up in these pages have made sleep impossible, and I have to return to the writing that makes me relive many long years in the space of a few short hours.⁵³ Besides, my abstinence for the last few weeks and my friend's trip have incredibly excited me. He hasn't yet told me when he'll return, and I feel a surfeit of desire and passion that prevents me from taking a long rest. I'll thus pick up the thread of my conversation with you, but certainly, this letter will be the last that I write to you because, if not, I'm afraid I'll never finish and I would

---

49. Caserta is a city in south central Italy, known for its royal palace and magnificent gardens constructed in the eighteenth century.

50. Writing in 1888 or 1889, he was probably referring to some of the following: *La Terre/The Earth* (1887), *L'Oeuvre/The Masterwork* (1886), or *Germinal* (1885).

51. *Madeleine Férat* (1868) was one of Zola's earliest novels.

52. This passage is the recto of the fragment that Saint-Paul cut from the Italian man's letter to Zola as an example of his handwriting (see figure 2).

53. A handwritten copy of the rest of this letter was found in the Saint-Paul family archives. It allows us to compare the original letter with the published letter. The two versions are nearly identical. Underlined words were underlined in the original; double-underlined words were double-underlined in the original; and italicized words were those that Saint-Paul selected for emphasis.

send you a real tome that would end up exhausting you greatly. I always think I've finished, but then I always find something else to tell you. In addition, I enjoy talking about my little self so much that I'll never stop describing myself as if I were looking in a mirror. I don't think anyone can ever tire of talking about oneself and examining oneself down to the most minute details, especially if the creature nature has made is as exceptional as I am. After all that I've written to you, I'm sure that you'll be able to guess the rest of my character, my ideas, and even my companions, but since this is so enjoyable, I'll go on a bit longer—more for my benefit than for yours.

You've already deduced that I'm almost as great a gourmand as Brillat-Savarin himself.[54] I don't eat a lot but I love fine wines, even those that don't seem so to me, as long as they have a famous name and a high price. I have a passion for game, especially for pheasants, and all gamy meats delight my palate. I love the rarest cheeses and the strongest smelling ones. All the accoutrements of dining enchant me, and I can't enjoy a dinner unless the table is brightly lit and the service is flawless. I adore Turkish coffee and drink a lot of it, but in small quantities and very hot. I like liqueurs, too, but in very small quantities. I've always dreamed of Roman banquets, and one of the scenes that enthralled me the most is Arbaces's bacchanal in The Last Days of Pompeii.[55] I adore that city, and I often stroll through it reflecting on its dead charm and its life snuffed out by Vesuvius.

I have the most intense passion for equestrian competitions, and athletes' beauty, their strength and perfect bodies, has a very strong effect on me. On the other hand, tumblers and acrobats in the circus inspire only pity and disgust in me. I love beautiful horses, but I prefer driving in a carriage to riding on horseback, even though I do ride rather well. I almost never miss seeing the wild circus animals, and I've always gone to watch the feeding and exercise of lions and tigers with the secret desire of seeing a little blood flow. I prefer a handsome lion tamer to all the seedy poets in the world. When I see men—and in my passion for them, I want to see

---

54. Jean-Anthelme Brillat-Savarin (1755–1826) was the most famous gastronome of the nineteenth century, known for his work *The Physiology of Taste* (1825).

55. *The Last Days of Pompeii*, a very popular painting by the Russian artist Karl Pavlovich Bruloff (1799–1852), inspired Edward Bulwer Lytton (1803–1873), the English novelist and playwright, to write his work of the same title in 1834. Arbaces "the Egyptian" is one of the main characters.

splendor, courage, strength, and beauty—delicacy in them doesn't attract me at all, since I am so delicate myself!

I love gambling passionately; the riskiest games please me the most. I'm fairly lucky at them, but money does slip through my fingers and never stays in my pockets. I've often repaid my friend's gambling debts—as small as they are. I spend little money on myself, and that is almost always limited to books, curios, and my wardrobe, which interests me a lot. I love the strict and proper <u>chic</u> of the English, whose simple and unique style we all adopt. I love the color black, which brings out my blond and pretty face. I love sparkling white linen and the finest, most stylish boots. I'm very elegant in appearance and <u>never</u> look <u>awkward</u>. I don't like jewelry on men and wear only very simple tie pins. My watch is truly a <u>marvel</u>. On my left pinky, I wear a simple iron ring with a big diamond that my mother gave me. Canes are my great luxury. I have some by Verdier, which are marvelous, especially one with a head made of superb rock crystal.

I don't believe I've told you about my <u>hands</u>, which are truly <u>superb</u>, perhaps the loveliest part of me, except for my hair and my complexion. I'm very proud of them and they're so generally admired that people often tell me that it's a pleasure to be touched by them. A great sculptor, who unfortunately has just died and whom I knew well, wanted to make a cast of them, and I have a copy of this cast in my bedroom, displayed on a blue velvet pillow. The shape is <u>perfect</u> but <u>strange</u>, long and tapering, showing no joints or muscles. My fingers are long, broad at the base but tapered at the tips. Even though my fingers are of an unheard-of delicacy and of an extreme fineness, my fingertips are <u>square</u>, and I have to cut my fingernails squarely also. My nails resemble precious stones and are so red they seem polished; from the pale half-moons at their base their color ranges through all shades of pink. Although they're square, their shape is <u>perfect</u>, and the flesh surrounding them, to the tips of my fingers, is as fine and white as an eggshell. I'm admiring them as I write this; they are truly <u>marvelous</u>. My thumb is delightful, rounded with an oval nail. My hand is like white velvet, with shades of pale, almost imperceptible, blue veins. The last phalange of each finger is curved oddly upward and is a bright pink color that contrasts with the whiteness of the rest. My palm—which was once examined by a German lady who does palm readings and conducts séances—is marked by deep, long, well-defined lines that don't break off anywhere. They are, however, crossed by one irregular broken diagonal line that bisects all the others. This lady explained these lines to me, but in a fantastical and German way, I fear. I inherited my beautiful hands and my handsome face from my paternal grandmother, who was stunning and whose arms and hands were so magnificent that even Canova complimented her one day.[56] {She was, they say, the mistress of Ferdinand II—if they only knew I dared to write this!}[57] But other than that, he did nothing for the family, and perhaps we owe him only the shape of our lips and our chins.

My grandfather was unhappy in his marriage}[58] and died very young from the distress caused by his wife, who didn't survive him for long either; she died before my birth. As I've already told you, my brothers are hearty and well built. The eldest is superb; he resembles my father; but he is perhaps a little less handsome. The other two aren't good-looking, especially the third, who takes after my mother's family, who are repulsive to me. They're all much taller and stronger than I am and were born one right after the other. I came into the world ten years after the last one, and only after my mother had suffered a terrible illness which brought her very close to death. I think it was one of those deadly fevers. All my brothers' children are attractive, strong, and well made. There is one little girl who resembled me strikingly, people say. She died when she was only eighteen months old in a matter of hours without any sign that death was near. I would like to die the same way.

Otherwise, my constitution is perfect, with a great deal of nervous energy, spirit, and dynamism. Sometimes I suffer from a great lassitude but then I recover, feeling extraordinary joy and a strong impulse to laugh.

56. Antonio Canova (1757–1822) was an Italian sculptor known for his neoclassical style.

57. In the published version, Saint-Paul deleted the name of this king, which is, however, in the original manuscript as it appears in the "Passages to be suppressed," with the following note by the author: "Ferdinand II was denounced for having the face of his maternal grandmother, Queen Maria Carolina the Great of Austria. They say he had an indomitable character." Ferdinand II (1810–1859) was the king of the Two Sicilies from 1830 to 1859; he married Marie Christine of Savoy (1812–1836) in 1832 and had a son, Francis II (1836–1894). His grandmother was Maria Carolina of Austria (1752–1814), the queen-consort of King Ferdinand IV (1751–1825) of Naples (Ferdinand III of Sicily and eventually, in 1816, Ferdinand I of the Two Sicilies).

58. Copied from the original manuscript into "Passages to be suppressed" but left in French with some minor deletions in the published versions. This passage appears on the final page of the manuscript without a number. See *Confessions*, 236.

Then I don't leave anyone alone, and I become everyone's favorite because of my talk, my flattery, and the cajoling that I shower on everyone around me. All of a sudden, I become silent and sad, and everyone is amazed by these quick and seemingly inexplicable—to them at any rate—changes. My facial expression (especially where my upper lip is separated from the nose by a little indentation) changes as the colors of the sea do on a stormy day. My eyes are almost always somber, drowned under their long lashes. You can hardly see them, and their color is indefinable, sometimes blue, gray, or green; often they turn a shade of violet.

People say I have an arrogant attitude, mocking and taunting. In reality I often use that to hide my shyness and awkwardness in public, keeping people at a distance in this way. I believe there are few people in the world as egotistical as I am. I would sacrifice everybody for one of my passing fancies, and only in the grip of one of my momentary desires do I understand sacrificing for others. In my family—who have always spoiled me—everyone complains about my coldness, and they often call me an ingrate because of it. This always upset my father because he favors me, and even in the most difficult times, he never refused to fulfill any of my demands or my extraordinary and useless whims. In truth, I have little affection for my family. I've told them that when I'm in a bad mood, the cause of which you will undoubtedly guess. I see them as the source (innocent, to be sure) of my extraordinary and perverse nature, and I can't forgive them for having made me this way. I hold it very much against them, but now I'm trying to rid myself of this awful feeling and make an effort to show them warmth and affection, which is sometimes genuine and sincerely felt.

They often hurt me deeply by discussing or teasing me about my presumed love affairs and the love that women have for me. I hate them in those moments and reply in a very brusque manner that they tolerate only from me, since they would protest vehemently if others showed them so little respect.

My father socializes very little. He's consumed with decorating and furnishing his house, and it takes all his attention. He is not interested in anything else, except his grandchildren, who adore him and whom he loves passionately. I was jealous of them and couldn't stand them.

I pay a great deal of attention to my health, even though at the age of fifteen or sixteen—before meeting the captain—when I was alone and had made those awful discoveries about myself—I wanted to die without really knowing what that meant, except that it would be a change in my intolerable situation. I quickly abandoned that feeling once I understood the horror of the void and bodily putrefaction. At that time I spent hours at night on my balcony, practically nude, in very cold weather, trying to kill myself and thereby escape my passions, which no one was satisfying then. But I didn't <u>even</u> catch a cold, and I quickly gave up such foolishness. I've since realized that as long as you're <u>alive</u>, you can have <u>pleasure</u>, and I hope to live out the <u>rest</u> of my youth. Perhaps, when I have reached the end of my youth, I'll <u>still</u> want to live all the way to the age of <u>100</u>! It's possible!

I always take <u>showers</u> and take care of myself as well as I possibly can in order to have all my strength ready to serve my passions and to satisfy my master, who is far away at this time and whose return I eagerly await. He writes to me frequently and tells me about Hungary, about his horses, and about the women in that country. {God only knows the pain he causes me! but as long as he doesn't cheat on me with other boys, then I don't care! That's the only thing I want and desire.}[59] His birthday just passed recently, and I sent him a superb whip with a beautifully carved handle. He also wrote me that despite the journey through barbaric and exhausting lands, he's in exceptionally good spirits and always looks at a lovely photograph of me that he keeps close at hand. He told me that he thinks only about returning and often dreams of <u>me</u> and of my favorite <u>cologne</u>. He rarely takes off the conservative topcoat and elegant collars that I <u>insisted</u> on.

I forgot to tell you that I would like you to give a few more details about the <u>physique</u> of your characters. Don't <u>physical</u> attributes explain the moral aspects of nations and individuals?

I've just read <u>Mademoiselle de Maupin</u> and it absolutely delighted me.[60] Oh! What a beautiful book! What lovely corruption, so sweet and delicate!

Please excuse the horrible handwriting and all the mistakes in French and in spelling, but my soul and my passions have carried me away. To write this, I haven't looked anywhere, except inside myself.[61]

---

59. Copied from the original manuscript into "Passages to be suppressed," Ms. (12), 235.

60. *Mademoiselle de Maupin* (1835) was written by Théophile Gautier (1811–1872); its main character is an adventurous cross-dressing young woman who loves both men and women.

61. The version published in the *Archives d'Anthropologie Criminelle* in 1894–1895 ends here, but Saint-Paul added the following note in his book: "There is another postscript

POSTSCRIPT

In the hotel where I am staying, I met a man who is about thirty years old.[62] *It was at the dinner table. He tried to seduce me openly, and I quickly realized what he wanted.* He's tall, has a rather nice face, very pale and elegant, with long, thin arms. He's from Milan. *If I wanted to, it would have been done right away.* But should I get involved again in a passing fling like this? My blood boils, and I'm afraid I won't be able to resist the temptation. If he came right now, it would be done quickly, I'm afraid. If the captain knew about it, that would be a fine mess! He would be capable of strangling me. In any case, we'll see tonight. I'm getting dressed now and going down to dinner. It'll be a decisive evening. It seems to me that he <u>doesn't</u> have good teeth. He has a long mustache that hides his mouth. I'll make up my mind there, at the dinner table—come what may!! Besides, this man will be leaving soon. Let's hope that he doesn't get attached to me!!

I don't have to tell you that I gave a <u>false</u> name and a <u>false</u> address at the post office where I send my letters, and besides, I won't be here in a few more days. You will learn <u>nothing</u> more about me. <u>Farewell</u>, Sir, and perhaps, <u>Good-bye</u>. The bell is ringing and I must enter into a real battle.

7 o'clock in the evening.

---

that cannot be published. Agitated by the long confession that he had just written, the author describes how in the hotel where he was staying, he met a stranger who provoked in him a very strong attraction. The tone changes abruptly: more sadness, more boredom, but passion and nervousness about the next battle against himself, a struggle that he knows that he will lose. Even fear of the captain doesn't stop him; he isn't afraid of his jealousy. Only the man's teeth make him a bit hesitant; they aren't very pretty, he says, but he's going to join him, saying: 'Never mind. Come what may!' The next day he sent Zola one last postcard in which he declared his happiness: he 'would shout it from the rooftops.' And he announced triumphantly that he had succeeded in doing what he had refused the captain, not because of modesty, but because of his fear of pain. 'There where everyone else had failed, he (the stranger whom he had met) had succeeded.' And that is the last word of the confession from this strange, revolting, and truly pitiful person." It should be pointed out that Saint-Paul is freely adapting the Italian man's words here for his own purposes.

62. Handwritten copies of this postscript and the postcard addressed to Zola have been recently found in the Saint-Paul family archives. This enables us to reproduce here for the first time the text as it is in the original. We have indicated in italics the passages that were translated into Latin in the 1896 published version.

Postcard (1888 or 1889)

To Émile Zola, Author, Paris, France

Sir,

   Not knowing your address, I've sent you by registered mail two letters that I addressed to your editors, Monsieur Charpentier and Company. I hope that both of these will get to you and that they aren't still on their way. Since your person is so well known, I am sending this one without an address. I hope that it will get to you as well. That which <u>must</u> come to pass <u>has</u> come to pass. I still have the most delicious memory of it and was perfectly happy this morning, I can assure you. I'll shout it from the rooftops. There where <u>everyone</u> else had <u>failed</u>, <u>he</u> has <u>succeeded</u>!

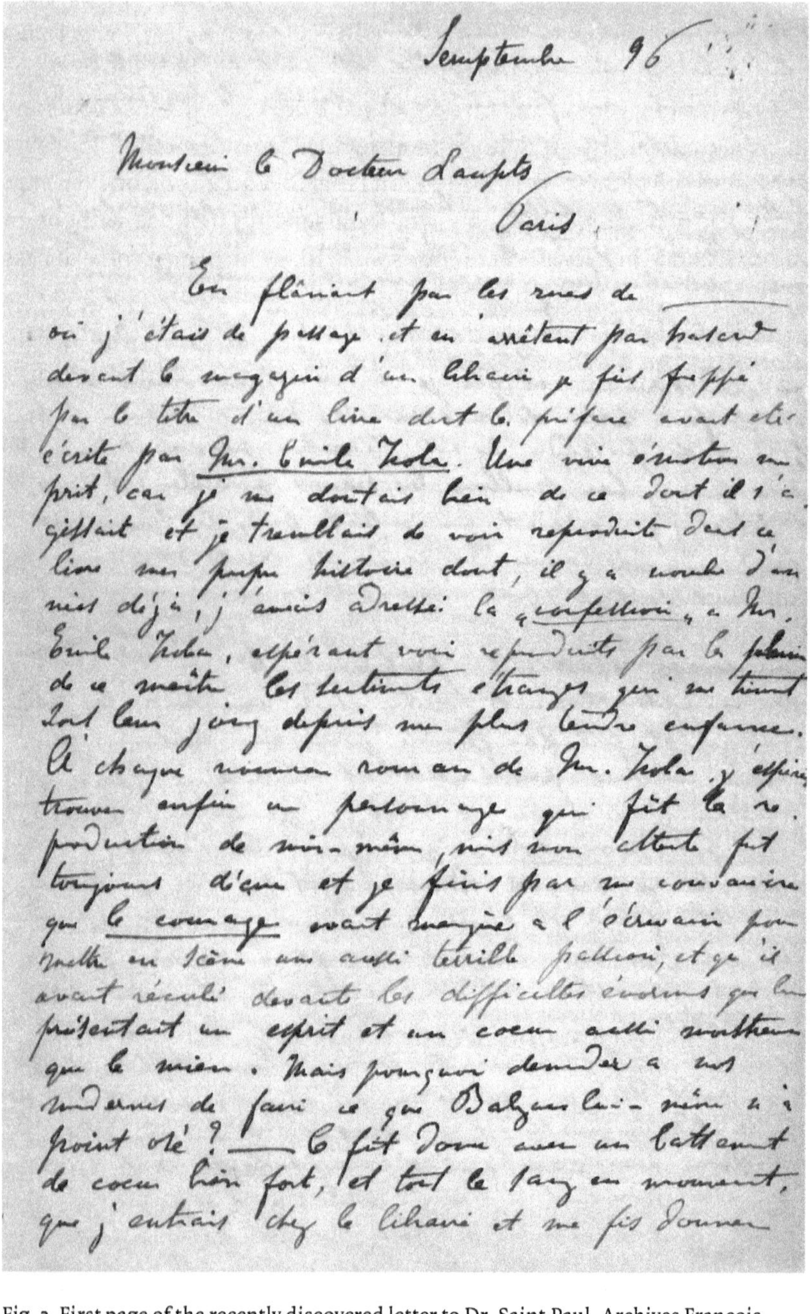
Septembre 96

Monsieur le Docteur Laupts
Paris.

En flânant par les rues de ____ où j'étais de passage et en m'arrêtant par hasard devant le magasin d'un libraire je fus frappé par le titre d'un livre dont la préface avait été écrite par Mr. Emile Zola. Une vive émotion me prit, car je me doutais bien de ce dont il s'agissait et je tremblais de voir reproduite dans ce livre ma propre histoire dont, il y a nombre d'années déjà, j'avais adressé la « confession » à Mr. Emile Zola, espérant voir reproduits par la plume de ce maître les sentiments étranges qui me tiennent sous leur joug depuis ma plus tendre enfance. À chaque nouveau roman de Mr. Zola, j'espérais trouver enfin un personnage qui fût la reproduction de moi-même, mais mon attente fut toujours déçue et je finis par me convaincre que le courage avait manqué à l'écrivain pour mettre en scène une aussi terrible passion, et qu'il avait reculé devant les difficultés énormes que lui présentait un esprit et un coeur aussi malheureux que le mien. Mais pourquoi demander à nos modernes de faire ce que Balzac lui-même n'a point osé? — Ce fut donc avec un battement de coeur bien fort, et tout le sang en mouvement, que j'entrais chez le libraire et me fis donner

Fig. 3 First page of the recently discovered letter to Dr. Saint-Paul. Archives François Émile-Zola © Nouvelles Éditions Place.

The Sequel to the Novel of an Invert

September 1896

Dr. Laupts, Paris[1]

While strolling through the streets of . . . ,[2] where I was just passing through, I stopped by chance at the display window of a bookstore and was struck by the title of a book whose preface had been written by Mr. Émile Zola. A powerful emotion overwhelmed me because I suspected what it was about, and I guessed that I would see my own story in it—the "confession" that I had sent Mr. Émile Zola a number of years ago, hoping to see the strange emotions that had enslaved me since my earliest childhood reproduced by the pen of this master.

In each new novel by Mr. Zola, I hoped to find a character based on me, but my wait was always in vain, and I ended up being convinced that this writer lacked the courage to put such a terrible passion into a novel and that he had retreated before the enormous difficulties that a heart and mind as monstrous as mine had presented him. Nevertheless, why ask our modern writers to do what Balzac himself didn't dare to? It was, therefore, with a rapidly beating heart, with my blood surging through my body, that I entered the bookstore and bought the book you wrote, Dr. Laupts. The title of one of its chapters, and especially the name of Mr. Zola, had already made me guess its contents.

---

1. The title on the envelope containing this document in the Zola family archives was "Lettre au Dr Laupts: Suite des confessions d'un homosexuel / Letter to Dr. Laupts: Sequel to the Confession of a Homosexual." It was probably written by Zola's son Jacques because it is stamped "Collection du Docteur Jacques Émile-Zola / Collection of Dr. Jacques Émile-Zola." Since the entire manuscript has been found, we can now translate the entire text according to the original formatting.

2. The name of the city is left out of the original document.

I didn't dare look at these pages; I was so afraid of seeing my own story reproduced in its totality. This fear was quickly assuaged, and I had a real sense of relief. I thank you, Sir, for your discretion because I would have truly regretted seeing the confession published entirely. It's a confession that in a moment of excitement and delirium I had sent to a great writer, a confession I hadn't been afraid to write and release. But hadn't I the right to ask for even greater discretion? You can certainly publish the terrible scenes (and yet so beautiful!) that have an interest for science; you can also relate the cruel and tender feelings that were and still are my despair and my joy; but you could have left out everything that was too personal, the names of cities, for example, and many other things that have no value in the study of psychology and are extremely risky for me personally, details that a determined and resourceful person could manage to uncover. That is something I would regret bitterly, whether for myself or others.[3]

You are a scientist, Sir, and (from what I can gather from the way you express yourself) a decent and tolerant fellow. I want you to understand, therefore, that I read your excellent book and I thank you for the discretion you exercised, which, I'm not afraid to repeat, could have been greater still. Like all sick persons who see in their doctor a friend (even if he knows that the illness is incurable), I feel friendship and gratitude for those who study the treacherous affliction that torments me. And like a good friend, I try to help by showing them what they are making such great efforts to find and what I, on the other hand, know so well through an innate science. Years ago I sent a confession to a very talented writer; today I am writing to a scientist. What I sent to Mr. Zola, you decided to call a novel, and it certainly is a story. I will now send to you, Sir, a few observations about myself and my paternal and maternal ancestors. This might interest you and help you understand many things.

I repeat that I am counting on your absolute discretion that in all cases, you will name neither the place nor any other thing that could reveal, or even give clues to, my identity. You're a man of science, and because of that, I want to reveal myself in all my physical beauty and moral ugliness, but this doesn't prevent me from wanting to conceal my identity from the world that I despise

---

3. Saint-Paul deleted this passage from the published versions of 1910 and 1930. As mentioned in the introductory comments to part 1, this and other passages set in sans serif font were not published until 2017 and have not been previously translated.

too much to give it a chance to despise me in turn—besides, I scarcely deserve it.

What shall I say about how I felt, seeing my <u>confession</u> published? At first I was terribly afraid of having written too much and of giving too much precise information about myself, my family, and my home, and I cursed my recklessness, my mania for writing, and, especially, Zola's indiscretion. Thank God, I was soon <u>almost</u> reassured because unless your book fell into the hands of someone in my family—which I doubt will happen—the details are so vague that it is almost impossible to find out anything about me and my family.

The feeling I experienced next—<u>my insufferable vanity</u>, as you like to call it—was pleasure at seeing myself published <u>just as I am</u>—though I would have much preferred being brought to life in the pages of a novel and not in a treatise of medical science. In the end, that was what was decided and I can't dispute it. Still, having been by the side of Hyacinth, the sweet friend of Apollo, or of Alexis, the handsome lover of Virgil,[4] and then to find myself after that in the pages of an anthropology text in the company of a Parker or a Taylor,[5] that was a bit hard, believe me, Sir! I am not complaining; I am simply stating a fact; *that's all!*[6]

[When I wrote to Mr. Zola, I was about twenty-three years old; I am now thirty,][7] and with more experience and peace of mind. I might be able to add to what I wrote to him then a few interesting things that will open up new horizons. You imply that studies on the mixing of the races are very interesting. I can tell you something about it, and I want to bring to light for you the ancestors that I previously described in a very summary fashion. <u>We are what our parents made us</u>. Science understands and excuses many things from this perspective; there is nothing more fascinating for the expert and

---

4. As noted earlier, Hyacinth was a Spartan boy loved by Apollo in Ovid's *Metamorphoses*. Alexis was the shepherd boy in Virgil's second *Eclogue*, with whom Corydon, another shepherd, fell in love.

5. Charles Parker was one of the young men whom Oscar Wilde was accused of soliciting; his testimony at the trials led to Wilde's conviction. Alfred Taylor was Wilde's codefendant accused of introducing male prostitutes to him; he was also convicted. They were mentioned in Marc-André Raffalovich's account of Wilde's trials published as the third chapter in Saint-Paul's 1896 book.

6. "That's all" was in English in the original manuscript.

7. The passage enclosed in square brackets here was deleted from the 1910 edition but was reinserted into the text in the 1930 edition.

the scientist than to see a corner of the mysterious veil that covers all these issues. You owe me many thanks. I'm very vain, you say; this is certainly true; but vanity isn't my sole emotion: there are many others that motivate me to write to you. It's very enjoyable to create characters and attribute imaginary virtues and vices to them, as novelists do. Isn't it much more interesting to delve into oneself and describe the passions that consume us and make so many men worthy subjects of investigation? And this mania: What becomes of it when nature has made us abnormal, that is to say, people whom science studies relentlessly, the people from whom science wants to tear off the mysterious veil covering their heart and soul, the veil that conceals them from common people's eyes? Ah, Sir! To feel different from everyone else is sometimes satisfying, but how many hours of anguish are often the penalty for a few moments of pride and infernal pleasure! Enough! Let's end our talk of philosophy and accept life as it is and not as we would want it to be! Each of us has his tastes inscribed in his brain and heart; whether he fulfills his urges with regret or with joy, he must fulfill them. He should let others act according to their own nature. It's fate that creates us and guides us throughout our lives: to fight against it would be little more than fruitless, foolish, and reckless!!

[Many things have happened since I wrote my last postcard to Zola during one of the most critical times in my life. Many changes happened around me; I myself have not changed at all. I remain the same. Semper eadem.]⁸ Morally I have, however, matured, that is to say, I have become calmer, less impulsive, and my personality has taken on a seriousness that I didn't have before. My heart seems to have dried up; perhaps debauchery or too many strong, unnatural, and stormy passions have led to physical damage that will cause my death someday, like most of those of my family whose hearts (the ones in their bodies) have been stilled.

What I can tell you, however, is that I'm more egotistical than ever, that my heart is truly at ease, and that I have come to think of it as a shriveled organ that feels something only in response to an intense emotion. Then I feel pains that are like heart spasms. However, except for those times, I am very calm and could even say very happy. My mind is the same way. I know now what I am and what I want. I have made up my mind, and I look for as much happiness in life as I can, without worrying about the rest.

---

8. Latin for "Always the same." This passage was deleted from the 1910 edition but reinserted into the 1930 edition.

Memories of my past <u>hardly</u> disturb me, and the men, whether living or dead, who came into my life by joining me in pleasure now concern me very little. I live in the <u>present,</u> not reflecting at all on the past and not thinking very much about the future. If in my soul the memory of my past sometimes reappears as if in a mirror and I see even the past joys as evil and the pleasures cruel, this painful feeling lasts only a short while and is quickly forgotten. Perhaps my brain itself is atrophied and no longer conjures up images with vivid crude clarity! What should I tell you about my <u>passion</u>? About this passion that occupies all my waking hours, every minute of my life, never giving me any respite? <u>It is still there</u>, but although it is very intense at certain times, it no longer has the terrible power it had before and can no longer be compared with my earlier frenzy, when even the sight or the thought of an undressed man made me burn with all the flames of Hell.

Events in my life, the losses, one after another, of members of my family and a certain amount of physical and mental exhaustion, have contributed to calming or rather weakening my nerves, resulting in a partial state of tranquility. In the past, my nerves seemed to be made of a mixture of sulfur and fire; today I'm rather tired, and even though earlier I could hardly keep still for two minutes, today I spend hours on end stretched out on a sofa, daydreaming and smoking cigarettes.

[Literature still interests me a great deal. I have journals in many languages everywhere. I devour a large number of books. Paintings (by other artists) please me immensely. But the art that thrills me the most is music. I spend long hours listening to my favorite scores on the piano and conjuring up the episodes of different dramas that play out in my imagination as the music evokes them with an intensity resembling a hallucination. This lasts a long time, until fatigue overwhelms me and makes me fall into a half sleep, from which I emerge aching all over but with the most delectable feelings of laziness and calm.][9] I like Wagner, but our great composers, especially Verdi and Bellini,[10] move me more.

My health is excellent except for a few spells of sluggishness and fatigue that affect me from time to time and that I dispel by taking a warm perfumed bath and drinking many, many cups of Turkish coffee. I have a good

---

9. Deleted from the 1910 edition but reinserted into the 1930 edition.

10. Like Wagner and Verdi, Vincenzo Bellini (1801–1835) was a composer of opera, known for his "extremely long melodies," according to Verdi.

appetite but do not eat much, and I love exquisite and delicate food. I don't go out very much when I'm at <u>home</u>,[11] but I travel frequently and my boredom comes along with me to Europe's most important cities. I'm alone at present.

My parents are dead; one died shortly after the other. My father died from a heart disease that no one suspected or even recognized the symptoms of; he felt fine in the evening but died that night from an aneurism. My mother followed him just a short while later; an untreated cold that turned into a chest ailment quickly sent her to her grave. I really regretted her death; she was very kind and very sweet, and I'm sorry to have so often misunderstood her. I was her favorite son, and she certainly showed it. As for my father, he became extremely irritable during the last years of his life. You could hardly speak to him, and he was so bitter that I approached him only with trepidation whenever I decided to do it, which wasn't often. Our relations had been a bit frosty for some time, and no doubt the lack of sensitivity I demonstrated toward him was responsible for this. Later, I will talk a little more about him and my mother, especially their families. Let me first finish speaking about <u>myself</u>, and then I will come back to them. After the death of my parents, I remained <u>alone</u>, but being rich and independent, I've been able to arrange my life as I wish—in a manner that is a little strange, like everything I do.

All the tastes I confessed to Mr. Zola earlier are with me still. They have become even more pronounced. I still love luxury, and the apartment where I live is a real <u>museum</u> that would charm the most demanding artist. Statues, paintings, family mementos, rare books, magnificent furniture, Persian rugs, etc. . . .—all these things are part of the decor. I have a small circle of close friends, and of course, I have a <u>favorite</u> among them—one who has a lovely beard.

Some charming women friends come to play music with me, to look at my engravings and art objects, to sing and to chat with me. I've inspired some foolish passions in these women, who are distressed by my coldness and who would throw themselves into a fire—to no avail, besides—in order to bring that to an end. I am still a virgin—oh! what a strange word for my pen!—and I will remain one always. <u>Mr. Raffalovich should fear nothing on that score!</u>[12] To me, women are what they've always been: delightful

---

11. The word "home" is in English in the original.
12. Marc-André Raffalovich (1864–1934), a poet of both French and English verses, an essayist, and an early sexologist, was best known for his work on homosexuality,

companions and good friends, from whom I flee only when they show any sort of amorous inclination toward me and let me know they would prefer a less platonic friendship. I entertain only married women. This allows me to explain my extreme coldness as being due to my friendship with their husbands and the honor I don't want to betray. What a comedy! Several of these women are quite enamored of me, and for a long time one of them was thought to be my mistress.[13] I laughed a great deal at the rumors that were spread about us because our entire relationship was based on the music we made together and our frequent, quite innocent conversations. But because this gossip disturbed me, I had her keep her distance and saw her only very rarely. Simply the idea that people could suspect she meant something to me was enough to make her almost repulsive.

My nature is perverse, as it has always been, but it has gained in moderation, tranquility, and sophistication. I spend months in the most complete abstinence, in the most absolute chastity. It seems I have water in my veins instead of the molten lava of the past, but when the opportunity arises—a simple glance, an ambiguous handshake, a whisper—that is enough to awake the demon of unbridled lust in me—and I burn as if I had sulfur ignited in my body.

I knew Venus and her formidable fires
Of the blood that she inflicts with such inevitable torments![14]

Uranisme et unisexualité: Une Étude sur différentes manifestations de l'instinct sexuel (1896), translated by Nancy Erber and William A. Peniston as Marc-André Raffalovich's *Uranism and Unisexuality: A Study of Different Manifestations of the Sexual Instinct* (2016). He was also the author of the chapter on the Oscar Wilde trials in Saint-Paul's book *Tares et poisons* (1896). In his personal life, he was the lifelong companion of John Gray, the young working-class poet who was befriended by Oscar Wilde in the early 1890s (he was later a Catholic priest in Edinburgh). Gray was reputed to have been the original model for Dorian Gray in Wilde's novel *The Picture of Dorian Gray*.

13. The author placed the following text in a footnote in the original manuscript after "one of them": "a very petite, cute woman, very witty and mad about literature and music."

14. The lines "Je reconnus Vénus et ses feux redoutables / D'un sang qu'elle poursuit tourments inévitables" are a reference to the play *Phèdre* (1677) by Jean Racine (1639–1699). In his notes on the novel *La Curée*, Zola indicated that he intended it to have echoes of this play in his novel. The two main characters of Zola's book have an incestuous relationship like the one in *Phèdre*. The characters in the novel also watch the play in the novel.

Do you want a horrendous example? I was at the deathbed of a person related to me by blood and affection when I received a letter that gave me a pleasant surprise and filled me with emotion. It was from a young friend of mine whom I had previously treated badly and who, after many years, was passing through the town where I lived. He remembered me and asked me if I would enjoy, as he would, meeting again. All of a sudden, my head was on fire and my blood began to boil more than that of Saint Januarius![15] I forgot about everything, even the sickbed, which turned into a deathbed on the following day. I even forgot my affection and my duty and everything else. I lived only for the next day—the day of our meeting.

My young friend arrived, greatly changed in appearance, with a handsome mustache and a small beard like that of Henry III, dressed in the most perfect elegance, with a self-assurance and a brash attitude that I had never noticed before.[16] [He's in the diplomatic corps, and, as it seems, has not wasted his time. We talked about unimportant things, but he looked at me with a dreamy gaze that I recognized, and as I complimented him on his handsome appearance, he told me: "It's you who are still handsome, more handsome than ever!" I got up to show him an album because I felt a certain discomfort being near him, as I had on other occasions, but when I came close to him, he grabbed both my hands, kissed them ardently, and murmured sweet nothings into my ear. I was very moved (not, however, as I was with the others), and I caressed him as well. I found him very fine and very delicate, and this displeased me about him, even though our senses were already aroused. And for lack of anything better, I was content with this adventure. Since there were people nearby, I had to take my leave of him, and we separated, promising to see each other again two days later.][17]

It was the day of the funeral when I saw him. On the previous evening in the room where the young creature was laid out—a brightly lit chamber filled with beautiful flowers—I felt as if I was at a festival, and I trembled

---

15. Saint Januarius (ca. 270–305) was an early Christian martyr executed during the reign of Diocletian (ca. 305). His relics are preserved in a church in Naples. The reference is to the miraculous liquefaction of the dried blood, which is supposed to bubble up during the annual celebration of his feast day, as well as on two other holy days during the church calendar.

16. The "young friend" in question was the "Spaniard" about whom the author wrote in his letter to Zola.

17. Deleted from the 1910 edition but reinserted into the 1930 edition.

with pleasure to think that <u>I was alive</u> and that sensuous pleasures were waiting for me the next day. And yet I had cared very much for the being who had passed into eternal slumber after such horrible suffering. I had almost watched him being born and I had always cuddled and spoiled him—but isn't lust stronger than <u>anything else</u>? The more illicit it is, the more it eats away at your heart and kills all other emotions.

I surprised everyone with a carefree attitude that contrasted with the other mourners' sadness. I had to leave in order to hide the excitement, almost joy, that I felt at having seen again such a charming man who had once loved me to distraction and whom I had almost driven away with my contempt. [At that moment I desired him passionately, and I don't know what I would have done if he had not come. He finally arrived, but I felt cold in his presence as I had in the past and even colder, even though he showered ardent caresses and passionate kisses on some parts of my body and received my caresses with delight, he still gave in to me on other points only with extreme resistance, betraying his very strange and <u>truly</u> incomplete nature. He was a deficient being—but maybe there was something too similar in our natures that prevented us from making each other truly happy.

He told me about a romantic encounter he had had in the capital of his country with an engineer, whom he had met at the Opera and whom, he told me, he had loved passionately. He showed me his portrait. He was very handsome with brown hair and looked very manly. He had, as my friend told me, taught him <u>a great many things</u>. They still wrote to each other, and my young friend burned with desire to see him again. This anecdote extinguished my lust completely, and we said good-bye after exchanging a few friendly kisses and nothing more. We felt as if we belonged to the same sex, and this idea (which had led to our first separation) estranged us <u>forever</u>. So the young diplomat left . . . abruptly,[18] without even writing me a brief farewell. I've since learned that he was sent to a country far away—across the ocean! May he enjoy himself! That's what I wish for him with all my heart!

As for me, I've known true passion only <u>once</u>, with its delights and its torments, with its jealousies and its transports, when we are <u>two</u>, and yet become <u>one</u> with the person we love. With my artful ploys and powers of seduction, I once awakened an emotion in a young and simple man (but so

---

18. The author left the name of the city out of this passage.

chivalrous and so handsome) that he himself perhaps didn't understand, a mixture of admiration and gratitude, sensual love and true friendship.[19] I passionately shared this feeling and by exciting my friend's mind and senses into a frenzy, I aroused in him the most feverish, unrelenting lust. This seemed completely natural to him, I can assure you, and he wasn't at all surprised, since it happened with no forethought and virtually against his will—and perhaps even against my own. I truly <u>loved</u> him then with my head, my heart, my senses, with everything. It was like a nightmare, a dream, and when I woke up far from <u>him</u>, my passion had burned itself out, and there remained only ashes in my heart—but not in my blood, which burned and burns still. What would I not give in order to feel once again one minute of this happiness, which is the equivalent of centuries of beatitude! For an instant of these joys, I would renounce an eternity of happiness in the company of all the saints in Heaven! Alas! I feel old in my heart and in my soul; and vice, not <u>passion</u>, still attracts me.][20]

"The captain," as I will always call him, died not long ago from a horrible illness that required a cruel operation. He was given chloroform but never woke up and died of an unstoppable hemorrhage. He had to live far from me because of his debts and other financial difficulties, but I went to visit him sometimes because I missed him and always enjoyed seeing him again. He was a real <u>demon</u>, but I liked him because of the enormity of his vices and the energy and strength that never left him. He would be old now—it is better that he is dead! He'll be a worthy comrade for Satan, and he'll even teach him a thing or two!

The adventure at the hotel was only fleeting, alas!—but it left more traces than the others before it.[21] By opening up new horizons, it made me what I

---

19. Here the author is referring to the "sergeant" about whom he wrote in the letters to Zola.

20. This long passage was deleted from the 1910 edition but reinserted into the 1930 edition.

21. This long passage about "the adventure at the hotel" was deleted almost entirely from the 1910 edition, but parts of it were reconstructed for the 1930 edition. Instead of trying to indicate all those editorial changes, we have placed most of this section in sans serif font. Saint-Paul added the following note: "The original document relates at great length details that I will not reproduce. It is with acute precision that the author describes the preliminary acts, the first attempt that almost succeeded, the second attempt that succeeded completely, and the following nights, etc." Where relevant, however, we added footnotes containing additional information.

am and what I will never stop being. The liaison was <u>short</u> but <u>decisive</u>. The man was still young, enterprising, and bold. He didn't stop staring at me all through dinner. He noticed my discomfort and the glances that I gave him from time to time. At the end of the meal, he approached me under some pretext and began to engage me in small talk. I could barely say a word because I was so nervous, and I replied to his conversation in almost unintelligible monosyllables. But without saying anything explicit, we understood each other. I felt it. I spent the rest of the evening strolling through the streets, and even though it was quite cold, I was burning like a lit fuse. Toward 11 o'clock, I found myself back at the hotel, and I can assure you that I was at the end of my rope. My heart was thumping in my chest; my head was on fire; my whole body was in a state of overstimulation that is impossible to describe. I entered the lobby without glancing at anyone, and I pretended to look at the illustrated newspapers that were on the table. From the corner of my eye, I had already noticed him sitting on a sofa, and he was looking at me over his newspaper. I felt a shock to my stomach. Without even thinking about it, I gave him a long glance and left slowly. He left the lobby almost as soon as I did, and he followed me at a distance, nonchalantly watching me climb the stairs. I did this very slowly, turning around only once to see him as I climbed the stairs and went down the long hallway where by chance—by a happy chance, I should say—our two rooms were located. I went into my room and did not lock the door, naturally.

The minutes crawled by like centuries, it seemed, and I worried that I was wrong to sense in this man a passion that was, after all, only the desire that occasionally motivates the stupidest and most ignorant people to chat with a person with a pretty face. But my instinct wasn't wrong—it had not deceived me! I had hardly begun to undress when I heard a scratching at my door. I felt myself freeze up; I can't express what I felt at that moment. I was quiet, mute as a fish, when the door opened and the man appeared. Now as I write this, it seems to me that I'm still in that moment, so powerful was the sensation that I felt in my body and soul. I was half-sitting in an armchair next to the bed, looking at the man who had closed the door and then stood silently with a forced smile on his parted lips. I saw it all in a flash and stayed where I was without saying a word; I just kept watching him. He had a gray coat and a hat on his head and stood by the door, not moving, looking at me without batting an eye and still smiling in a strained manner.

"What do you want?" I asked him at last, making an effort to speak. I spoke in a low, trembling voice—I knew very well what he wanted, and he understood what he could dare to do. He came toward me very slowly without saying a word. I sank into the armchair and bowed my head, not daring to look at him. He came right up to me, sat on the left arm of the chair, and, taking hold of my head, tilted it upward and kissed me on the mouth without saying a word. I can't describe to you what I felt, but it was a little like the delicious and delirious sensation that I have felt other times when the man I desired came close. We stayed like that for a long time, seeking each other's lips hungrily and exchanging kisses on the mouth with mad, almost ferocious, lust.

I had the strength to say to him, "Lock the door!" He stood up and did what I asked. He returned to the bed and sat on the edge, speaking in a low, halting voice. I answered the same way. We talked, but certainly neither of us grasped what we were saying; besides, it didn't matter! We embraced each other; we kissed again, thrusting tongues into mouths; and then, after covering the candle with a green lampshade that plunged the room into semi-darkness, he began to undress while I dived under the covers, panting with desire, hoping for something new and unknown. I watched him put away his clothes and his shoes, and thought him very handsome indeed; a real man with attractive, bulging muscles and large and powerful limbs silhouetted by the flickering light. He came toward the bed discreetly and climbed on it, caressing me a thousand times, kissing my head and my neck, laughing under his breath, and murmuring sweet nothings in a low, husky voice. He stretched out next to me and hugged me as he nestled deeper, little by little, under the covers. When he felt the warmth of the bed, he sighed with satisfaction, and while still holding me in an embrace and kissing my head and face with pleasure, he wrapped his long and hairy legs around my body, which was as cold and smooth as marble. He didn't need any more stimulation! He was very passionate but behaved like a lover with his mistress, very tender and considerate. He tickled me delightfully, rubbing his beautiful mustache against my cheeks and my head with a passion and a happiness that pleased me infinitely. I could no longer control myself, and soon I reached my climax. He noticed it, and with a great deal of discretion let me take a rest while whispering a thousand silly things in my ear and trying to reawaken my desires with caresses, compliments, and delicate touches that made me laugh and squirm. Desire returned to me quickly, and I was once again in a state of intense overexcitement in just a few minutes.

I did everything that I know for him, and that was not a little (given the teacher I had had and the amount of steady practice). But he wasn't satisfied with that. Thanks to his pleas, his wiles, and his skill, he succeeded in his attempt, which was, after all, made a little easier by the previous efforts made on other occasions that had never succeeded. Besides, I was completely willing, and I reacted to his desire with an intense desire of my own because if he wanted to possess me completely, I wanted it as much as he did. Perhaps his physique fit better with mine; perhaps he was more patient; or perhaps I was more willing. The fact is that little by little the path was opened up and the conqueror entered the castle so long under siege but now captured, if not entirely, at least a good part of the way. This maneuver was repeated several times, always more successfully, owing to this man's skill and the positions he knew and could show me. Our lovemaking lasted a good part of the night, and only at dawn did he dress and return to his own room, not without my checking the hallway to make sure it was empty. We parted without saying a word to each other, and I fell into a deep sleep, not awakening until 11 o'clock the next morning.

My body was sore and my head was heavy, and in order to revive myself, I had to take a hot bath. That did marvels for me, and every trace of fatigue and pain disappeared immediately. After rubbing my entire body with a bottle of *eau de cologne*, I felt full of life and joy. I had never been happier and regretted only having taken so long to learn this new pleasure, which, more than the others, was intended to fulfill completely and without reservation the men who attracted me and responded to my passion.

At lunch the man didn't show up—a fact that didn't bother me too much, especially since I would have been a little ashamed to see him in broad daylight. He did return for dinner that evening, and we hardly glanced at each other. But as soon as I went to bed, I heard him coming into my room, and since I wanted him, he undressed quickly and lay down next to me. He was even more daring than he had been the night before and wanted to take his pleasure in the same way that the labors of the previous night had made easier and more enjoyable. I endured patiently, <u>almost with joy</u>, the pain that I was still feeling, but my entire being was so aroused and so frenzied that the pain hardly registered and the pleasure was <u>immense</u>. He must really be an expert at this! Because he didn't rush anything and with subtle twisting motions and barely perceptible caresses, he achieved orgasm after having felt and given the most intense pleasure. He used a little tube of *cold cream* that he had brought with him the night before and that served us well.[22] He

---

22. *Cold cream* is in English in the original document.

was perfumed with rosewater, and I can still imagine that scent in my nostrils. It was a new sensation for me to feel his life <u>flow</u> into mine, and I was happy to feel myself possessed entirely and in such a complete way.

What delighted me most of all was the joy that he seemed to feel, the ardor and the passion with which he led up to and performed the act. He was supposed to leave the following day, but he couldn't make himself do it, and he stayed with me another three weeks, despite the pleas from his family and others who needed him. Except for two or three nights, we always slept together during that time. He changed rooms and took one next to mine, <u>separated</u>, or perhaps better put, <u>united</u> by a door that connected the two rooms. What we did together always seemed very natural to us, and we would talk and laugh before and after as if nothing had happened. It was only when we were making love that we whispered, and our faces and our behavior changed completely and became strange. We seemed to be <u>changed</u> then, our frenzy was so great and our entire bodies in states of such intense arousal. I was almost always the first to go to bed, but often, when I came back to the hotel, I would find him in my bed already, smoking a cigarette. I love the smell of cigars, and the perfume of mild fine tobacco pleases me infinitely. I would then seek his tongue with mine, and he seemed to be perfectly happy and satisfied. We would always begin with kisses—on our hands and mouths, <u>everything</u> was done in the most expert way, and when there was nothing left to do, and when we felt close to swooning from so much excitement, our remaining strength was used to consummate the supreme act, which was now habitual, with actions of such precision that it gave us only the greatest pleasure instead of the original pain. After that, we would stay entwined together and often fell asleep from exhaustion and excitement. Ah! the delicious nights we spent there!

A whole new life began for me there when the act to which nature and fate drove me was consummated. [When I pass by this hotel, I always look up at the windows of the two adjoining rooms where I accomplished my life's goal for the first time: to take and to give a <u>sterile</u> pleasure—<u>one superior to all the others</u>. And furthermore, may I make a confession to you? I really didn't like this man at all. He was <u>very</u> good looking, still young,[23] with muscles of iron and skill and incredible technique. He introduced me to pleasures that I thought I would have to renounce. Still, I had no

---

23. The author gives his age as "36 years old" in a footnote in the original manuscript.

feelings for him, and if, during the night, another man, equally as strong and equally as handsome as he was, had come to take <u>his</u> place, I would have accepted him with no regrets.]²⁴ But as soon as I was <u>alone</u> in my bed and I felt this man getting ready to come to me, then my lust overwhelmed me and I would have renounced mother and father and nailed Christ to the cross again for his sake. Such is the power nature gives to lust, especially when that lust exceeds the usual limits and exists only for itself and by itself, with no other purpose. Finally, he had to go, and he left with a feeling of regret that I only partly shared. He returned to his family and wrote to me from time to time.

I have seen him since; he's married, but that didn't prevent him from chasing after me one day when our paths crossed by chance in the same city. He wanted me to come with him to the hotel where he was staying, supposedly to show me the purchases he had just made. As soon as I entered his room, he took me in his arms without saying a word and smothered me with kisses. Even though it was the middle of the day, we went to bed as we had done before, and, after extraordinary caresses, we united in a complete and supreme act of passion that we repeated twice that afternoon.

He talked to me about himself and his brilliant position, and since I had asked him about his wife and child, he said: "<u>For you, I would throw them both into the water.</u>" I couldn't help laughing—but I shuddered as well. He left that very evening, and I have not seen him since.

There it is! The story of my greatest fall, the final act in a drama that began before my birth!!

Perhaps I am trying your patience by repeating the same thing, but I must tell you that I love still and I love often, but only with my <u>senses</u>. My <u>heart</u> and <u>soul</u> are no longer susceptible. Is it true that one <u>loves</u> only once in one's life? I have become more and more <u>passive</u> and let myself be taken rather than hunt for prey, as I used to. As soon as a man in whom I immediately detect this vice and this passion looks at me, and as soon as our glances meet in a certain way, I feel a blow to my stomach; my blood rises to my face and head; my ears begin to tingle; my extremities freeze; and then I would be able to follow this stranger through countless dangers, over mountains and valleys, across deserts and forests of the wildest kind; I would follow him into the flames of Hell! But when I have satisfied my passion, I become extremely

---

24. This passage was placed at the end of the version that Saint-Paul published in 1910 and 1930.

cold toward him and toward other men. Men repel me until lust lures me again and I throw myself into their arms, almost without my realizing it. Often a great sadness overwhelms me (when I think about my solitude, and my lack of <u>true</u> affections), but that doesn't last long, and soon a desire for life and pleasure reawakens in me, and I spend hours, delightful hours, imagining new pleasures and savoring their fulfillment.

There is no point telling you about the adventure that occupies me now. I bring to it a wild passion and an extraordinary taste, but my <u>entire</u> self is not engaged as it was before, and I don't feel the same cruel and bitter intensity in this affair as I had with the only man I truly <u>loved</u>.[25] Still, I am happy that he is <u>dead</u>! He will live forever handsome and young in my memory, and after all, what could life have offered him in the future? His family situation was not very promising; there was nothing in his future to offer him happiness, and after he met me and lived a very strange, fantastic, and exceptional life for several months, wasn't dying the best that he could do? Destiny took over, but don't you think that if it hadn't been for the <u>other man's</u> hand, his <u>own</u> hand would have fired the pistol that ended his life? As for me, I am sure of it, and I don't believe that he could have <u>ever</u> reentered normal life. I had bewitched him <u>too</u> completely, and his soul had been too altered and molded by <u>me</u> for him to be content with a life of ordinary pleasures. May he rest in peace! If only the images I engraved there aren't still coming back to haunt the vestiges of his brain![26]

As for me, as long as I have youth, vigor, and beauty, I will be happy to be <u>alive</u>, even with a corrupt and sick heart and mind! Morally, this is what I am now. Physically, I have changed even less. People think that I am, at most, twenty-four years old, and as I have already told you, I have a very youthful and charming look. My face has kept all its fine features and perfect symmetry; my eyes are lively and expressive; my complexion is still rosy and delicate; my hands are lovelier than ever. I feel more and more like <u>a sexless idol,</u> but nevertheless <u>an idol</u>, who asks only for pleasure and adoration. That is what people are doing at this moment, because all of those who annoy me, even the servants whom I tyrannize, worship me. But as

---

25. He is referring to the "sergeant" described in the letters to Zola.

26. In the original manuscript, the author added the following text in a footnote: "He was a decent fellow! I had written to him a number of passionate and ardent letters that could have greatly compromised me. He returned them to me at my request. I was terribly ungrateful to him." Saint-Paul inserted this note into the text.

for me, I no longer adore anyone. Let me love—that is all that I can do from now on!

Before finishing the description of my psychology, I must tell you, Sir, that you are wrong when you insinuate that I must like to dress in women's clothing and disguise myself in that way for those whom you like to call my accomplices. I can assure you that you are very grossly mistaken, because I am horrified by men disguised as women, and I naturally apply this feeling to myself. I like the most serious, the most correct, the most masculine kind of elegance—English chic, in fact. Everything that seems out of place in a man disgusts me, and I reject all feminine outfits and useless ornaments with contempt. I dress as a gentleman,[27] not as a man-girl. I have never worn bracelets, and only one diamond and one superb emerald that I inherited not long ago shine on my fingers. (I like this last gem as much as *Dorian Gray* liked his, and in reading that beautiful book, I was struck by his taste for emeralds—a taste that I share.)

What I say about my clothing I can also say about my face. No one, in seeing me, could guess the feelings that I harbor in my breast, and my face, as charming as it is, is still that of a young and handsome man.[28] If those of my sex turn around to look at me and smile at me, it's because of the bold and persistent looks that I give them when a fire burns deep inside me. My appearance is not at all effeminate. Rather, I have the look of a handsome horseman or an elegant page more than anything else. I am of medium height with long thighs, and my slim, smooth body has nothing ambiguous about it, even though I do have radiant satin skin, which, besides, most people don't see and only a few privileged souls have been able to touch and admire. As I've already said, I inspire love—a very intense affection—in women, and from this alone, you can understand that I don't look like a girl.

And now, Sir, after the masterpiece, let us examine briefly those who made it.[29] This will certainly help you understand many things and explain how nature makes us. In recognizing the oddity of those who preceded them

27. In English in the original manuscript.

28. The author added the following text in a footnote in the original manuscript: "especially for the last few years."

29. The following paragraphs about the author's family were almost entirely deleted from the 1910 edition, although some of the text was included in the 1930 edition. We have placed most of it in sans serif font. Where relevant, we have added footnotes indicating additional information. See also the family tree in this volume.

in the stream of generations, one begins to understand the <u>strangeness of those</u> who came after and were created by them. <u>I beg you to use the utmost discretion</u> with everything that follows. I put my trust in your honor.

As I have already described elsewhere, my family is originally from Spain but came to Italy in the fourteenth century. One branch remained in Spain, where it continues to flourish. Ours—the one in Italy—split into several branches, of which only two still exist: the senior branch and the <u>junior</u> branch, to which my family belongs. All these branches had <u>illustrious</u> members among them—but it's pointless to discuss them. That was long ago and could have no interest for you. For a long time now, the brilliance of the family—like that of three-quarters of noble families—has dimmed, and political revolutions have plunged it into an even greater obscurity. My great-grandfather lived quietly in the provinces when important events obliged him to take refuge in a part of Italy ruled by the English. A queen famous for her beauty and her debauchery had called them there—only to regret it afterward.

It was there during the first years of this century that my great-grandfather married a noble Englishwoman who brought him little in terms of a dowry, but much in terms of a ravishing beauty! I own a miniature portrait of this charming woman, and with her hair dressed in the Greek style, her very pronounced upturned nose, her divine eyes, and her perfectly oval face, she truly had an enticing allure: one would have said a <u>keepsake</u>[30] designed by <u>Kate Greenaway</u>.[31]

Her only son, who was born a short time after his parents' marriage, resembled her in an extraordinary way: he was entirely an <u>English gentleman</u> in his looks and tastes. He truly had an aristocratic attitude, and his portraits strikingly resemble those of <u>Lord Wellington</u>.[32] He was passionate about horses, dogs, and ladies, and all physical exercise. He piled up a number of debts, and his generosity toward everyone was proverbial. He was—I am assured—an enchanting and brilliant man, a great seducer of women,

---

30. In English in the original manuscript.

31. Kate Greenway (1846–1901) was an English writer and illustrator of children's books.

32. Arthur Wellesley (1769–1852), third child of the Earl of Mornington, advanced quickly in the British army during the Napoleonic wars and was commander of the allied forces during the Peninsular War. He was made Duke of Wellington in 1814 and conquered Napoleon at Waterloo in 1815. He served as prime minister from 1828 to 1830.

but also very kind, charming, and handsome. He, even more than his father (who was dominated by his wife), brought <u>Anglomania</u> into the family—because anything that wasn't <u>English</u> was banished from the house and treated with the greatest contempt.

He was married at a very young age to a very young widow from a <u>very prominent family</u>.[33] She was a remarkable beauty but a few years older than he. My grandmother wasn't wicked, but she had an angry and violent temper, easily aroused, and when she became angry, the whole house trembled. She could, however, be generous, and when she hurt someone (which, I am told, happened often), she felt sorry afterward and made every effort to be forgiven—only to begin again the very next moment. She was very proud of her birth and bragged about having Norman blood in her veins, something that in certain countries is considered <u>the last word</u> in nobility. It's the blood of the conquerors! She was terribly jealous of my grandfather, even though she herself was not above suspicion—but is it true? She was both enthusiastic and fantastic, domineering and violent, tyrannizing everyone and imposing her will <u>through</u> her haughtiness and temper tantrums. A large portrait of her by a famous painter depicts her in a blue velvet dress, her hair dressed in the English style with roses in it. Her face is a beautiful oval shape; her chin is very strong and exquisitely shaped; her mouth is rather large and as red as blood (the entire lower part of her face resembles mine); her eyes are deep blue and remarkably cold; her hair is superb and bright blond. Her nose contrasts with her face just a little, because it is a little short, straight with wide nostrils. Her shoulders, arms, and hands were <u>famous</u>, and the

---

33. In the original manuscript, the author inserted the following note: "From her first marriage, she had a daughter whom she couldn't stand and so she married her off very early in order to get rid of her. This daughter died young, leaving a son who caused his mother's death in childbirth. This son, who had forty lovers, was a real *Sardanapale*, loving women with a fury and young men with equal passion. He is very handsome and courted me for a long time. I ended up by yielding to him, and I can assure you that he has the strength, the tastes, and the passions of Roman emperors. We see each other little, because he lives far from me, but we have traveled together. He doesn't have a family." Sardanapale (Sardanapalus or Assurbanipal) was the Assyrian king from 669 to 631 BCE. He was always represented by the Greeks as a debauched and effeminate king. Allegedly, he organized a collective suicide of his court, including his concubines and his eunuchs, when the Babylonians threatened to capture him. His story is the subject of a painting by Eugène Delacroix entitled *Death of Sardanapalus* (1827).

painter reproduced them well. She was truly a beautiful woman, even though she looked neither good nor kind.

In going through family mementos and skimming <u>thousands</u> of letters in order to keep some and burn others, I was glad to come across a letter written by the young King Ferdinand to her in which he talks about his young and charming fiancée, Christina of Savoy.[34] "<u>The princess is certainly beautiful</u>," the royal fiancé wrote, "<u>but she is not my type</u>." Could this mean something? I don't think so. Besides, she was several years older than the king—but this would not be reason enough to reject the claims of malicious gossip. What is <u>very</u> certain is that my father, who was born soon after his parents' marriage, resembled them both in a striking manner—physically and morally. He had the brilliant and lighthearted nature of his father, compounded by the sudden tantrums and flightiness of his mother. He was <u>very</u> handsome, a true English gentleman, brilliantly endowed with intelligence, who hadn't perhaps all the gravity one would have wanted. His character had a strange sensitivity; he was high-strung and emotional in a way that was truly effeminate.[35] He used to have genuine <u>crazes</u> for one thing or another and would enthuse just as easily over the most different and contradictory things. Full of hope, life, and gaiety in one moment, he would descend into a bad mood and state of despair the next. Very talented but not level-headed, in one hour he would go through a thousand different sensations, wracking his nerves. He had all the talents that a well-developed intelligence combined with a sophisticated upbringing could give a well-born man whose education was varied and vast. He read a great deal: history, literature, philosophy, science; everything interested him. He loved all beautiful things, and he was an avid collector (this taste was shared by almost all members of our family, even distant relatives), and his home was always filled with magnificent objects for which he had spent a considerable amount of money. He spent money prodigiously and was so recklessly generous that

---

34. As mentioned, Ferdinand II (1810–1859) was the king of the Two Sicilies from 1830 to 1859; he married Marie Christine of Savoy (1812–1836) in 1832 and had a son, Francis II (1836–1894).

35. Note in the original manuscript: "I speak of his character, you understand, because he also loved women. Once, being with me in London, he showed me a house near Trafalgar Square where he went once with a girl and where, having heard a suspicious noise in the room next door, he immediately left without having used this girl and only partially paying for her. This story shocked me in a way that I can't tell you, and I don't understand how he could have told me this thing."

he was almost always mired in financial difficulties that forced him to speculate and risk his good name in enterprises that could have compromised him. He had to move frequently, and even though fortune smiled on him more than once, he would rake in the money with one hand and spend it with the other. And even if he had had the wealth of the Vanderbilts,[36] he would have found a way to get in an awful lot of trouble for himself. He was also a thorough <u>Anglomaniac</u> and admired nothing that didn't come from England. <u>He had a younger brother who turned out badly</u>, did a number of stupid things, and, as a last resort, disappeared somewhere where he died of apoplexy after having converted to the most excessive and unusual form of piety.

My father married, or rather, was married off, around the age of twenty. My mother's family certainly had a significant influence on us, and I will write more in detail about it than I have about my father's family. My maternal grandfather was born in a European country that was still quite <u>Oriental</u>. He came from a Jewish family that had accumulated tremendous wealth trading in precious gems. He was a widower with three children when at the age of <u>seventy</u> he remarried a very young girl of the same race and religion; an unscrupulous mother allowed it. A daughter—my mother—was born from this marriage. Naturally, the rest of the family disapproved of this marriage, especially his children, something that enraged the old man so much that he broke with them and left to his last daughter everything he could keep from the rightful inheritance of his other children. After his young wife's death (prematurely, she was barely eighteen), he channeled all his affection onto this girl, who was born charming and became even more so as she grew up. If I can believe a <u>daguerreotype</u> of my maternal grandfather (I have burned it since), he must have been an unusually ugly man—a real monkey. Truly he had a "Turk's head" with a big nose, fat lips, a sparse beard, and long ears.[37] Nevertheless, he had a sly and intelligent look, with a mocking smile on his thick-lipped mouth. He died at eighty-two, leaving my mother

---

36. Cornelius Vanderbilt (1794–1877), the first of the line, made a great fortune by building a maritime and railroad empire. During the nineteenth century he was one of the wealthiest men in the world.

37. A "Turk's head" was a fairground attraction; the phrase was used to denote something that was cartoonishly ugly. In this case, the expression might also be an allusion to the country of origin of the family.

to the care of her maternal grandmother, who was indeed the strangest creature in this world.

I must spend a little time describing this bizarre woman whom I saw occasionally during my childhood, but never without feeling a sort of fright. It always seemed to me as if I was seeing Queen Jezebel as depicted in the Bible with her made-up cheeks and her almond eyes.[38] She was married at twelve and gave birth to her only daughter at thirteen. She remained a widow for a long time and never wanted to remarry, no doubt in order to be able to indulge in her disorderly instincts. Without any formal education, she had a diabolical wit and spirit. The strangest things were said about her in the family, and when we visited her (which wasn't often because she lived several days' journey away), I always peppered her entourage with questions, and little by little they told me all the stories circulating about this strange creature. They said that she had been a real Messalina and had a character dominated by impudence, haughtiness, audacity, and an incredible lack of scruples.[39] Her father committed suicide,[40] and one of his brothers did the same after the discovery of his incestuous affair with one of his own sisters, an affair that resulted in a child who, happily for herself and others, died soon after her birth. All these stories really interested me, and I almost admired this made-up old woman who reminded me of the days of Jezebel and Athaliah,[41] whose blood she might have had in her veins.

She used to sit (she was already very old) in a big armchair, swathed in big fur-lined robes even in summer, her head wrapped in a red silk scarf that

---

38. Jezebel, a Phoenician princess, was married to Ahab, king of Israel from 874 to 853 BCE. In Kings, it is reported that she introduced the cults of Baal and Astarte into the kingdom of Samaria, persecuted the adherents of the Jewish religion, led Ahab astray, caused him to turn away from the true God, and tried to put to death the Prophet Elijah.

39. Valeria Messalina (ca. 20–48 CE), the third wife of the Roman Emperor Claudius and the mother of Britannicus, was known for her scandalous behavior, which provoked her downfall. Suspected of plotting against the emperor, she was executed in 48 CE. She was infamous for her unusual sexual appetite, that is, her nymphomania, and tradition classifies her as an "Augusta meretrix" or imperial whore.

40. Note in the original manuscript: "There are suicides in my father's family as well, but they are distant relatives. A young and handsome man killed himself. We don't know why."

41. Athaliah, the daughter of Jezebel and Ahab, was the wife of Jehoram, king of Judah (843–837 BCE). According to 2 Kings and 2 Chronicles, she was an idolatress and a usurper.

accented her still magnificent, shiny, black hair. The apartment in which she lived was completely modern, but, strangely enough, on a gilded chest there were five or six Egyptian statuettes, like the ones in museums, small bronzes with a greenish tinge because of their antiquity. They were horrible figures, sitting or standing, with animals' muzzles and the moon between their horns! They almost frightened me, and I have since thought of the time when <u>God's people</u> feverishly worshipped in the debauched sects of strange and monstrous gods, whose images I encountered centuries later in this modern and luxurious apartment. What strange people these Jews are! I saw this great-grandmother just a short time before her death, in her ninety-sixth year, and I will never forget the impression she made on me. She was really like an Egyptian mummy then, <u>she was so dried up and wrinkled</u>.

Her skin, which had an ivory color, was plastered on her bones; her eyes, green and luminous like those of cats, still shined and sparkled with intelligence, and at that age she still used makeup and lined her eyes extravagantly with henna. Nothing except her jewel-like eyes and pointy nose, as sharp as a knife, recalled the beauty she once had that, everyone says, had been <u>marvelous</u>. She had a devilish wit, and even though she believed in neither God nor the Devil, she was superstitious in the way savages are. Isn't it strange how the lack of religion is often tied to monstrous and ridiculous rites? It's that way with all religions, and I know several examples even in my father's family.

When she died, this woman still had a full head of hair, which she dyed and perfumed. And she spent her days polishing and shining her nails, which were extraordinarily long and thin. Until the very last days of her life, she groomed herself and behaved with excessive coquettishness. She washed with milk and bathed in strawberry water, allowing herself to be adored and perfumed like an idol. She kept all her wits until her death and discussed everything with an innate wisdom; she had seen a lot, traveled a lot, and I believe that the Devil himself had taught her everything she knew! My mother, quite young at the time, was entrusted to this strange creature. Luckily, she was enrolled in boarding school, and my great-grandmother continued her adventurous life in distant lands.

I could not tell you what this woman (whose temperament kept her young and slim until old age) did during those years, but I think that, given her character and her tastes, she didn't play the Vestal virgin and gave in to her tendencies with no inhibitions. Since she didn't have any religion, she was wary about speaking about her Jewish heritage, and her intelligence and incredible daring enabled her to gain entry everywhere or to make herself admired everyplace where she insinuated herself.

During one of these countless journeys, she met my paternal grandmother; they become friends; and soon <u>Jezebel</u> reigned supreme over the entire family and their circle. She dazzled everyone with her wealth (she was rich and also spent her young ward's income without a second thought), her strange beauty, and her even stranger arrogance. Even though she was no longer young, she was <u>enormously</u> attractive. And—judging from what she was like in her old age—at fifty, she must still have been beautiful. A photograph I have of her at about the age of thirty shows a long and very narrow face, a fine and elongated oval, long and deep-set eyes—two emeralds—a chiseled nose, and a charming mouth. She had more of an Assyrian or an Egyptian appearance than a Jewish one, with shiny, black hair and green eyes, the likes of which I have never seen elsewhere.

She was the one who arranged my parents' marriage. At first the difference in religion caused some problems, but they were quickly overcome when it was decided—without consulting her—that my mother would become Catholic. Questions of money were also soon settled according to this woman's wishes. She disclosed only what she was willing to and hid the rest. My mother brought a substantial dowry to the marriage, and it has since grown through inheritances. The family's crest was thus gilded anew. My mother's baptism and marriage took place abroad so that when she arrived at my father's house, no one (except the family) knew what she was or where she had come from.[42] She was at that time—they say—ravishing, and she kept her youthful air of innocence until her death. Her fine, narrow face, shaped like a goat's, her <u>beautiful</u> blue-green eyes, her delicately chiseled features, her rosy complexion, and her golden brown hair never hinted at her race, which acquaintances would have suspected only because of her slightly hooked nose and something odd about her light-colored eyes whose pupils often contracted into a blue pinpoint. Then her eyes looked black and were lovely. Her head resembled an antique cameo that always had a virginal expression. Her personality was very sweet and very good, simple and friendly, very different from that of her grandmother. She always loved my father with the utmost tenderness, even when he was in a bad mood and

---

42. Note in the original manuscript: "There was a mystery around this woman for our entire society. My mother had a foreign name which, by a strange coincidence, was that of a noble family."

treated her harshly in a way that revolted me more than once. However, she knew his faults and excused and gladly pardoned them. She doted on her children—especially on me—a fault that my father shared and that made him forgive all our transgressions, my brothers' often egoistic and disrespectful actions and my strange behavior, especially the aloofness that I often showed him.

[My mother had reservations about being baptized and decided to do it only after she saw my father, who at twenty was the handsomest young man one could hope to find. Perhaps the fear her grandmother inspired in her couldn't have succeeded in forcing her to do something she found repugnant. Besides, she remained what she had been since birth—a <u>deist</u> par excellence who always had a limitless admiration for the <u>people of God</u>, as she called them. The triumphs of "Israel" filled her with joy, and she didn't hide it, but she was more impassioned by <u>her people</u> than her religion. When the book by Mr. Drumont was published,[43] she said: "Here is the most beautiful praise you could give to the Jews; even their enemies are forced to acknowledge their superiority over other races! To claim, as this man does, that they have conquered and reduced to servitude the people among whom they live? And besides!" she added, "if <u>you</u> wanted a <u>God</u>, you had to come looking for Him among <u>us</u>!"—all of which made my father and the others laugh uproariously.][44]

In the first years of their marriage, three children were born, which I have already mentioned. [[My brothers are all married and all made excellent matches. The eldest has a serious and charming son, very intelligent with a calm and thoughtful mind; the second one has two lovely daughters; the third is a widower without children. Five of my nephews died at a young age from various illnesses: croup, peritonitis, meningitis, etc. . . . My brothers are healthy, well built, and robust. The eldest takes after my father's family; he has hard, dark blue eyes like my grandmother; he has a terribly egoistic personality—caustic, haughty, and disagreeable. He carries himself <u>very</u> well, but his morals have nothing attractive about them—<u>un pallone pieni</u>

---

43. Édouard Drumont (1844–1917) was a French journalist, writer, polemist, and politician, founder of the anti-Dreyfusard, anti-Semitic, and nationalist newspaper *La Libre Parole* / *The Free Word*, and of the association Ligue Nationale Antisémitique / The National Anti-Semitic League. In 1886 he published the book *La France juive* / *Jewish France*, which was a tremendous success.

44. This paragraph was placed in a footnote in the 1930 edition.

di vento,⁴⁵ as my father used to say about him. He bullies his wife, who is charming, and is in turn bullied by his son.

My second brother is entirely Italian and southern with an outgoing and gay personality that makes him loved by everyone who knows him and meets him. His wife is less beautiful, but he <u>tolerates</u> her, all the while cheating on her frequently but without causing a scandal.

My third brother, luckily for him, lost his wife, who was annoying and sad, and he will <u>never</u> remarry—at least that's what he says. This last one is a direct descendant of the <u>Orient</u>; he is short and stocky like an Assyrian bas-relief and rather unattractive since his very handsome head clashes with his very vulgar body. He is often melancholic and eccentric; he travels a lot and has spent a lot of time in Africa.

<u>All</u> my brothers love <u>women</u> and are normal in that respect. They have all had many mistresses, and though married, they are still womanizers.]]⁴⁶

As for me, I have in my veins both Italian and English blood mixed together; I'm completely <u>Aryan</u>, and my body resembles the most charming Greek statues: but I'm more like the statuette of <u>Hyacinth</u> in the Naples Museum⁴⁷—do you know this delightful bronze?—than the statue of the <u>Hermaphrodite</u>.⁴⁸ As I grew, my hips narrowed and my torso is certainly that of an ephebe and not of a woman. It's smooth and firm like marble, and my nipples are

---

45. In Italian in the original manuscript. Literally, it means "a balloon filled with wind"; colloquially, it means "windbag."

46. In the original manuscript, this entire section is enclosed in double brackets with a line going through them, followed by this note: "I beg you not to show this paragraph to anyone."

47. The statue mentioned here has recently been identified as a bronze statue of "Dionysus" (cat. no. 5003), found in Pompeii and exhibited at the National Archaeological Museum of Naples. We are very grateful to Dr. Andrea Milanese, curator at the National Archaeological Museum of Naples (MANN) and head of the Museology and Historical Documentation Office, who identified it for us. At the end of the nineteenth century, the statue was thought to depict "Narcissus"; however, according to art historian Benoît Delcourte, heritage curator at the French Ministry of Culture, it is difficult to differentiate between statues of Apollo, Narcisses, Hyacinthus, and Dionysus, all of which depict nude young men.

48. Hermaphroditus, the son of Hermes and Aphrodite, inherited at his birth on top of Mount Ida of Troade the beauty of both of his parents. While bathing in Lake Caria, the naiad Salmacis fell in love with the adolescent, but he rejected her advances. She took him by force and beseeched Hermes to be united with him forever. The wish was granted, and from then on they formed a single bisexual being.

imperceptible. On <u>certain parts</u> of my body, I have a real forest of blond, wiry hair, but my arms, my chest, and my legs are white and smooth as well as firm and taut. My bone structure is delicate, but my brilliant white skin covers hard, firm flesh: there is no <u>fat</u>. To the touch, my body is as hard as marble and—a strange thing—even in bed it keeps its freshness; when I am with a man, my face becomes flushed and hot and my ears and <u>other</u> parts of my body red and congested; my chest and my legs remain cold, and my hands and feet are often <u>freezing</u>. My lips are often burning, and then they seem to swell up, so much blood is rushing into them. They are as red as blood, and my ears—which are small and charming, do not protrude from my head, and have delightful lobes—often become red as well.

I almost never sweat, and I detest cold and humid weather. Summer is my favorite season, and I thoroughly enjoy breathing the hot and dry air of warm countries. I cool the air in my apartment with blocks of ice, and I often sleep in a hammock under a long row of laurel trees, forming an arbor in my garden.

I have still kept a passion for flowers. I always have them <u>everywhere</u>, and my apartment is filled with the strong scents of magnolias and roses. Several people have felt faint when they enter my home; but I, on the other hand, can sleep soundly in this perfumed atmosphere without feeling the least bit uncomfortable.

Then I dream of impossible things, and all the lovely objects that surround me seem to come to life on their own. Handsome young men step out of their paintings and start to kiss me, statues come down from their pedestals, and even the flowers speak to me in a mysterious language. I spend divine hours in this way, and all the arts are put to use to enable me to enjoy life. I live an imaginary and monstrous life, but isn't it a privileged one? I'm at times <u>perfectly</u> happy and calm, but at other times I hardly feel that way, and I'd like something <u>new</u> but don't know <u>where</u> to find it. Ah! Why didn't nature give man at least ten senses? Five are too few. And what good are they? God! How bored am I!

It's fortunate that you wrote your book, which I found by accident, and now I can spend some time discussing things with you! I wish I could go to another planet and see what is there! Our world is too well known, <u>too</u> visible; all the great cities resemble each other; the countryside is horrible; there is so little real beauty on earth! I spent hours on end in galleries and museums looking at famous masterpieces. They often seem mediocre—I'm dreaming of something much more perfect! But when I find one that pleases me, I return to it several times and never get tired of looking at it! I wish I could give life to *Hercules Farnese* and see him flex his enormous muscles—but perhaps I would like him to be even more colossal.⁴⁹

One of my servants is a very young man of <u>perfect beauty</u>—you can well believe it! He is the son of a peasant, but he is so handsome that Antinous pales next to him. I never tire of looking at him, and I am very fond of him. He is blond with orange eyes, well proportioned, a truly ideal beauty. I have a lot of affection for him. I hired him because of his beauty, but I <u>admire</u> him only as a masterpiece come to life. He doesn't arouse <u>any</u> feelings in me, and I think of him as the most <u>beautiful piece of furniture</u> in my house. He has a very vulgar mind, but he is so handsome that I would be crushed if he left me, so I shower him with money and presents to keep him with me—so I can continue to look at him. He is a delight for the eyes, and one of these days I'm going to have a painting of one kind or another done of him.

A foreign painter has recently done my portrait. He wanted to exhibit it, but I didn't. I don't like being on display for everyone, and I quickly brought this beautiful work home, where—since it is in my bedroom—few people have seen it. The painting has a dark background—a very dark green. I'm seated in an oak chair with green velvet upholstery with my back almost turned to the viewer. I'm in black, wearing a fur-lined coat; my head is in three-quarter view and stands out marvelously against the somber and subtle background, as do my hands. The light effects are superb. My hair seems to shine like dark gold, and my fawn-colored mustache outlines my rosy, seductive mouth. People have compared this portrait to the work of Van Dyck⁵⁰—and maybe he would have welcomed a model with such well-proportioned features and beautiful complexion! But there I go again! My <u>vanity</u> and my <u>intolerable egoism</u> make me talk about nothing but <u>myself, myself again, always myself</u>.

---

49. *Hercules Farnese* or *Hercules at Rest* is a type of statue, the original of which is an ancient Greek sculpture attributed to Lysippos (fourth century BCE). Hercules is represented leaning on his club, which is covered in the Nemean lion's skin, and holding in his hand, behind his back, apples from Hesperides's garden, which he had just picked. One copy from the third century BCE created by Glycon of Athens was discovered in 1546 in the ruins of the Caracalla baths. It entered the Farnese collection and is today on view at the National Archaeological Museum in Naples.

50. Anthony Van Dyck (1599–1641) was a Flemish painter known for his portraits of King Charles I of England and his family.

Still I must tell you about other members of my family and finish their story before coming back again to <u>myself</u>, a subject that delights and grieves me. My grandfather died several years after his eldest son's marriage, and his wife followed him to the grave just a short while later. Both of them died rather suddenly: my grandfather from heart disease that had afflicted him for two years but worsened and turned fatal when we least expected it; my grandmother died from a terrible apoplexy. She had made life very hard for my mother; she nagged her endlessly about the most minor things, which made the young couple establish their own household. My grandmother lived with her second son, who was her favorite and whom she adored maybe because of all his faults, which were so numerous. I have already described the edifying end of my uncle, who combined religious piety with worshiping Venus and Bacchus. He married abroad and left no children. And that was fortunate!

[[When I was born, my grandparents had already died and my brothers were already grown because I came into the world ten years after my last brother's birth—but I have already explained that. I will add only that my relations with my family are rather cold. I hardly ever see my brothers and really don't care for them. Months go by without any of us knowing whether the others are alive or dead. Still, I have to admit they behave <u>better</u> toward me than I do toward them. I have always shown an exaggerated coldness toward them—a sort of aversion—especially toward the eldest, whom I can't stand. I don't care about my nephews—I am more than indifferent—because the ones I loved the best are dead—or rather it seems to me now that I loved them because they are no more! Our family name depends on <u>one sole offspring</u>, and maybe my nephew is destined to become the head of the <u>entire</u> family since the senior branch is dying out. As to what I have, <u>never</u> will I leave a <u>cent</u> to anyone in my family. I would like to be able to annihilate everything with me and destroy all I own before I die. That being impossible, I will leave what I have to someone who doesn't expect it. How this thought amuses me! I hope at least to live to be as old as Methuselah.]][51]

---

51. There was a note here in the original manuscript, which read: "At her death, my paternal grandmother decreed that none of her personal effects were to be given away and that they were to be left in her cupboards as if she were still alive. This was done. After several years, we wanted to see what became of them all: they were all ruined, eaten by mites, or rotted away. We had to throw them all away. It was my mother who told me this."

This paragraph was placed in double brackets in the original manuscript and underlined, probably indicating that the contents were to remain secret. Parts of the

Jezebel, the old crone, was almost one hundred when she died and kept all her wits and the verve of her devilish nature until the very end. She died surrounded by Oriental luxury, with many of the things she had collected heaped around her. [She had developed a passion for silver and had collected an enormous quantity of exquisitely engraved silver and gilt silverware. At her death, she left behind magnificent gems, furs, and gorgeous lacework. In one of the jewelry boxes that belonged to her, I found so many pretty things, including a superb, stunningly crafted coral phallus. It was in a gold setting with a ring attached on the top, indicating it was meant to be hung on a chain around the neck. Perhaps it was an amulet.][52]

I inherited many of my great-grandmother's treasures after her death, including her Egyptian idols and a large scarab with hieroglyphs that she claimed—I don't know why—had belonged to King Amenhotep.[53] In the last years of her life, she lavished all her affection on an enormous Angora cat that never left her and that really resembled a lion. She loved it passionately and fed it roasted chicken and small live birds. She fired a cook who had been with her a long time because he had forgotten to cook chicken for this feline archduke. His Highness, not finding his dinner ready at the accustomed hour, flew into a diabolical rage and howled so loudly that it ignited his mistress's temper. I inherited this cat and brought him to Italy, but since my Persian cat was jealous and couldn't stand him, I had him put down and then stuffed—he doesn't bother me anymore.

So I have reached, dear doctor, the end of this long conversation that, I hope, hasn't bored you too much. In writing to you, I have relived in my imagination the most remarkable moments in my life—something that I do with pleasure, especially if the imagined scenes are related to my passion and evoke in my mind the memory of exciting incidents in my strange existence.

---

text were included in Saint-Paul's 1930 edition with the following note: "I could not, even in summarizing it, reproduce the text. It is the history of a family, and despite the attractive, picturesque, and seemingly sincere description of the revealed psychologies, it is not suitable to publish these recognizable particularities without the family's knowledge just because it gave birth to an invert."

52. This paragraph was placed in a footnote at the bottom of Saint-Paul's edition with the following introductory comment: "I am extracting from the manuscript written by the author the following few lines."

53. Amenhotep was the name of three pharaohs from the eighteenth dynasty (ca. 1570–1370 BCE). The reign of Amenhotep III was known as one of the greatest eras of peace and prosperity for ancient Egypt.

I have brought to life for you the people to whom I owe my life, and this should interest you somewhat because there are some very curious types among them.

The West and the East with their very different bloods and civilizations are combined in me—could it be that their clash is the cause of my strange personality? The other members of my family are <u>ordinary</u> beings: why was I thus born with my blood on fire and my soul haunted by the strangest memories, obsessed by dreams of debauchery that is tamped down by fatigue from time to time but <u>never</u> extinguished? <u>Who</u> could probe this mystery? And will it remain impenetrable forever?

I often have noble and lofty feelings, and my thoughts reach heights that few men have glimpsed. I like to imagine what I could have been and could have become if nature had undertaken one last effort with me. I feel <u>almost</u> like a man, and my heart pounds inside my chest. But my soul loses strength very quickly, and the most I could wish for is to have the <u>body</u> that suits my <u>soul</u> so that I would stop being an anomaly. Sometimes I also want to <u>masculinize</u> my soul so that it would match my apparent sex: it is an effort that drains me, and I abandon it immediately because the realization of my wish seems <u>impossible</u>. I am crushed then and feel real anguish and discomfort that doesn't last long. Nature made me this way, and we cannot rebel against what she has done! From now on, I will accept what I am: a strange being, neither man nor woman, or, rather, both man and woman at the same time, with strange inclinations, loving men with a woman's passion but also with an impetuousness, an enthusiasm, and an ardor that women don't feel, emotions that only a man's strength and energy could muster.

If I had been ugly, my painful existence would have been awful. But I am handsome, very handsome, and I inspire passions that perhaps women haven't ignited to such a degree. Isn't it already a lot to have these joys in life and to count myself among the <u>fortunate</u> ones on earth? Almost everyone complains about something and regrets being, or not being, this or that—have I not had moments (and do I not have them still) when I have regretted <u>nothing</u> and have enjoyed life in the most intense fashion? Maybe I am one of those who have lived the <u>most</u> and the <u>best</u>! Let's set morality aside—it is only a word—and tell me if many men have taken from life as much pleasure as I have! [Isn't pleasure <u>everything</u> here on earth? And doesn't it justify <u>everything</u>? What do we ask of life if not pleasure? And when we have it, what do we want more of? Ah! How foolish I was to have despaired in the past, but how I have made up for lost time!

My thoughts often turn to the East and the strange people who are so influential in the history of the world and whose blood I often feel burning in my body, which is too fine and delicate for it. I envision all the debaucheries of Tyre and of Sidon in which the Jews have so often participated, <u>fornicating</u> with the gods against whom the prophets railed.[54] How many times have I not recalled the rites of Astarte and Moloch while contemplating the small bronze idols, burnished green by the passage of time, that now stand on the mantle in my living room?[55] I travel in my imagination to the time when people celebrated the gods' bloody rituals; and the priests of Baal smile in my imagination more often than those of Christ![56] I am a staunch <u>materialist</u>; in other words, I am absolutely convinced by <u>atavism</u>.

The memory of these two different civilizations haunts my brain, and these two strains of enemy blood do battle in my veins. Why should the heroic and religious history of relatively recent times matter to me when I feel this ancient ferocity, the strangest and most passionate perversion stirring in my blood? Nature has created a being where disparate elements have corrupted each other. But isn't it rather the clash of two civilizations, <u>equally</u> corrupt, from which I was born? There are plenty of poisons <u>everywhere</u>, and if the ardor, brashness, and passion that consumed me and continue to consume me come from far away, originating in the earliest history of the world, do they only come from there? The graceful and classical vices of Greece, the hypocritical libertinage of England, the impetuousness and crimes of Italy—have they not also contributed to making me what I am? What is very certain is that I live a sterile life, and except for <u>pleasure</u>, nothing good comes from me. When I <u>love</u>, I <u>corrupt</u>, and my entire being is like a beautiful flower with a fatal scent.

---

54. Tyre and Sidon were ancient Phoenician cities, whose destruction by other city-states throughout the centuries was usually attributed to their decadence.

55. Astarte, also called Ishtar or Ashtart, was the goddess of fertility and war in the ancient religions of Mesopotamia. Her cult was strongly condemned by the prophets of the Old Testament. Moloch was a local deity, the god of the Ammonites, denounced by Jeremiah and other prophets.

56. Baal was a name given to many local deities in Canaanite, Phoenician, and Aramaic religions. Generally, he was an agrarian god of fertility or storms or a protector of a city or a state. His worship was carried out on mountain tops and in woodlands, and the prophets of the Old Testament continued to denounce him throughout the history of ancient Israel.

THE SEQUEL TO THE NOVEL OF AN INVERT 131

I have <u>nothing</u> more to tell you, dear doctor, and my task is finished. I'll have nothing new to confess in my life. I'll still have loves, adventures, maybe even passions, but have I not already examined my entire <u>being</u> and revealed it? And what else could I reveal that you don't already know? I've told you the <u>causes</u> and the <u>effects</u>; now you must study them for the benefit of science and humanity. It's a beautiful thing to make the world better or at least to want to do so. As for me, such as I was born, I will live, and as such, I will die.][57]
Good-bye now and good-bye forever.[58]

[ADDENDUM]
Here are my physical attributes, invariable or slightly variable, as they were recorded in my <u>personnel record book</u> in the regiment in which I served:[59]

Hair:
  –color: dark blond
  –form: curly
Eyes: blue-gray
Complexion: rosy
Teeth: healthy
Eyebrows: light brown
Forehead: regular
Nose: ditto
Mouth: ditto
Chin: round
Face: regular
Unusual features: two beauty marks on the left cheek
Cranial measurements:[60]
  –front-to-back: 19 cm. maximum [7½ in.]
  –side-to-side: 15 cm. maximum [6 in.]

---

57. In the 1910 and 1930 editions, Saint-Paul ended the narrative here.
58. This line was deleted from the published versions.
59. Most of this addendum was deleted from the published versions and has been enclosed in angle brackets, but a few passages were placed in earlier parts of those published versions, and these passages have been placed in sans serif font.
60. We have placed in square brackets the equivalent measurements in the U.S. customary system.

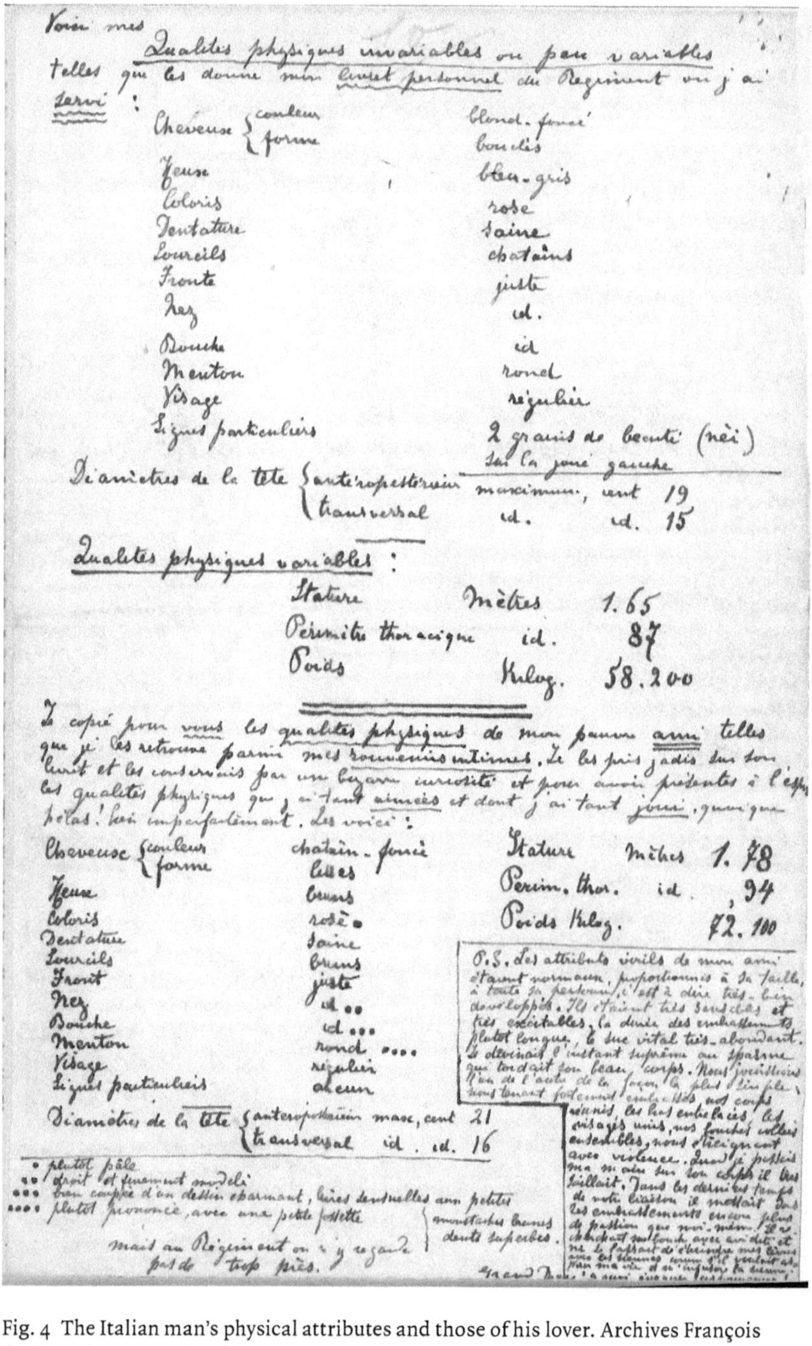

Fig. 4 The Italian man's physical attributes and those of his lover. Archives François Émile-Zola © Nouvelles Éditions Place.

Variable physical attributes:
    Height: 1 m. 65 cm. [5 ft., 5 in.]
    Circumference of chest: 87 cm. [34¼ in.]
    Weight: 58.2 kg. [128 lbs., 5 oz.]

I am writing down for you the physical attributes of my poor friend,[61] as I found them among my private mementos. I copied them from his record book and kept them because of a bizarre curiosity and a desire to keep alive in my memory the physical qualities that I loved so much and that I took so much pleasure in, albeit, alas, an imperfect pleasure. Here they are:

Hair:
    –color: dark brown
    –form: straight
Eyes: brown
Complexion: rosy (rather pale)
Teeth: healthy
Eyebrows: brown
Forehead: regular
Nose: ditto (straight and finely shaped)
Mouth: ditto (chiseled, a charming shape, with a little brown mustache, teeth superb)
Chin: round (rather pronounced with a little dimple, but in the regiment they didn't look too closely)
Face: regular
Unusual features: none
Cranial measurements:
    –front-to-back: 21 cm. maximum [8¼ in.]
    –side-to-side: 16 cm. maximum [6⅓ in.]
Variable physical attributes:
    Height: 1 m. 78 cm. [5 ft., 10 in.]
    Circumference of chest: 94 cm. [37 in.]
    Weight: 72.1 kg. [158 lbs., 15 oz.]

P.S. My friend's genitals were normal, in proportion to his height and to his whole body, that is to say, very well developed. They were very sensitive

---

61. He means the sergeant with whom he had an affair during his military service.

and easily excitable; the duration of erection was rather long, his vital juices abundant. I could sense the exact moment of his orgasm that contorted his beautiful body. We took our pleasure together in the simplest way, gripping each other tightly, our bodies united, our arms wrapped around each other, our faces touching, our mouths pressed together, holding each other with all our strength. When I stroked his body with my hand, he trembled. Toward the end of our affair, he put even more passion into his embraces than I did. He sought my mouth hungrily—and wouldn't stop pressing my lips with his, as if he wanted to breathe in my life and infuse his into mine. Good God! What has inspired these memories!

So here we are after a number of years! Since then, I have grown around two centimeters taller, and my chest now measures 88 cm. [34⅔ in.] My actual weight is about 65 kg. [143 lbs., 5 oz.] The circumference of my waist, which I just measured, is 83 cm, [32⅔ in.] taking the measurements from <u>just above</u> my navel, and my hips don't seem to be the same as they were then. My chest is <u>deeper</u> than it is <u>wide</u> and because of that I look <u>thinner</u> than I am. My breasts are <u>not at all</u> feminine, unnoticeable, flat, although smooth and well-formed. My torso is charming; the ribs are hardly visible; and my whole body is supple, elegant, and well-made. I say it again: I have <u>no</u> signs of physical degeneration; [I resemble an <u>ephebe</u> and I am not misshapen.][62] My legs are somewhat long but not too thin, and my feet are like my hands—that is to say, <u>very</u> attractive. My stomach is round, and when I amuse myself, looking in the mirror, trying to make my <u>male attributes</u> disappear between my thighs, then, only then, is there something, not quite feminine, but ambiguous about me. My posterior is beautiful with a lovely shape and not at all over-developed. When I want to, I can arch my back in a most unusual way and perform extraordinary contortions.

My genital organs are completely normal, of average size, with great sensitivity, and they are aroused by the most minor stimuli: reading an erotic passage, imagining a scene of debauchery, etc. . . . When a man who attracts me and whom I attract comes near, my genitals become as rigid as an iron bar, with a vigor and pressure that one wouldn't expect in me. My sexual fortitude is

---

62. Saint-Paul included this sentence in an earlier part of the published versions, and he added a footnote at the bottom of the page: "The author of the document gives details about his anatomy and sexual physiology that indicate that they are completely normal."

very great—my whole family brags about having this characteristic—I'm ready at any moment, and only need a few minutes of rest to regain my strength, as long as the relations I'm engaged in aren't <u>too</u> violent and <u>too</u> prolonged. My <u>sperm</u> flows from my body copiously, and its release gives me extreme pleasure. When someone loves me and possesses me <u>completely</u>, I experience extraordinary pleasure, but that is more in my <u>mind</u> than in <u>the rest of my body</u>.

What delights me the most is the <u>anticipation</u>, the <u>emotion</u> that precedes the <u>act</u> and all that comes before. I start thinking about it hours, often days beforehand, and as the time of the rendezvous approaches, my emotions reach a peak, my desires are completely overwhelming with an unheard-of intensity. Yet for me to reach that height of passion, there must be some mystery, an intimate setting, a solitude without fear, a semidarkness, a completely special <u>milieu</u>. I prefer going to <u>their home</u> rather than receiving my friends in <u>mine</u>; I prefer their bedroom or a hotel room to my own. Every man lives in a setting that <u>suits</u> him, and when I take my pleasure with a man, I want to enjoy the environment in which he lives, breathe the air he breathes every day, live <u>his</u> life, actually.

There are some nice men for whom I have only a simple friendship, feeling completely unmoved near them; the presence of a debauched man who attracts me lights a fire in my veins. I have taken and <u>given</u> pleasure in a <u>thousand</u> ways, but what delights me the most is to observe the various passions I arouse, to see how they reveal themselves and how they are satisfied. In those moments when I feel at ease, I enjoy watching the <u>man</u> closely, and with virtually no exceptions, the men all look the same. I always see him panting for breath, his eyes unfocused, his mouth half-open, his face in a rictus of lust, unaware of his words and actions. I have noticed that those who approach me for the first time in an amorous encounter mumble unintelligible words and appear terribly uncomfortable and uneasy; this disappears after a few minutes, replaced by the most unbridled lust and the most obscene gestures. That discomfort and unease are no longer apparent in our second encounter because we have become used to it <u>all</u> and what we are doing seems completely <u>natural</u>. When <u>we</u> are ensconced in a cozy, safe bedroom, [we forget <u>everything</u> else and only one idea, or rather, <u>one feeling</u> remains: a desire that <u>nothing</u> can stop and that must be satisfied, no matter the cost. <u>Pain</u> no longer exists at that moment, and for a long time now, my body is accustomed to what used to terrify it before. It is now a temple dedicated to lust and it inspires in me the respect that is due all sanctuaries.]⁶³ I keep from it all filth—except that of men—and the most painstaking and devoted care I give has made it almost <u>an idol</u>.

[Despite the passion that burns inside me, the lucky ones have been few in number and carefully chosen. I made some exceptions in my travels abroad. One day I met a young and handsome ticket controller on the train in Belgium⁶⁴—and I pestered him and spurred him on so much that finally he went to bed with me. I spent three nights with him in a very small lodging house, almost a hovel, where he lived and where I went to join him. This was really entertaining for me.

My friends have all been or are men of the world, <u>of the best society</u>, people with perverted and sophisticated tastes, but <u>virile</u>, completely <u>manly</u>, such that I feel delicate, weak, and soft next to them. They yielded to all my whims, and I bullied them in an absolutely unbelievable way. My <u>friends</u> have been few in number, and there have been rarely more than one at a time. Those were genuine love affairs with all the preliminaries and twists and turns of ordinary relationships. Jealousy, remorse, quarrels, breakups, letters, messages, <u>nothing</u> was missing. And it all took place without <u>anyone</u> around me suspecting a thing. I've even pretended to be <u>devout</u> in order to mislead others more thoroughly and succeeded in this completely. Now I no longer need to account for my behavior to <u>anyone</u>, and I'm free to do whatever I want with no restrictions. May the gods be praised!

In my relationships, I want a young man, but <u>always</u> a few years older than myself. I want him to be independent and rich enough so that I need not suspect his motives. I want a <u>passionate lover</u> whose lust I enjoy stimulating, watching his desire increase, teasing him—and then satisfying him. All this thrills me, but the man must attract me. If not, he is quickly dismissed in a most cavalier manner. I am very arrogant with those who are <u>too</u> enamored of me. If someone seems to be neglecting me, I suffer from the most awful jealousies and hatreds; I imagine committing a crime. If we were living in the olden days, I surely would not hesitate to have it done or do it myself. I only fantasize, then, about daggers and poison, especially the latter. But these emotions are rapidly dispelled, and <u>I</u> am the first to go from <u>feelings</u> to <u>carnal pleasures</u>.]⁶⁵

---

63. Saint-Paul moved this passage to an earlier part of the narrative.
64. In Saint-Paul's version, he changed "train" to "tramway."
65. Saint Paul moved this passage to an earlier part of the narrative.

A completely naked man doesn't attract me <u>much</u>. I prefer him in a shirt or underpants under which I enjoy imagining a thousand things, to put my hand inside to touch and stroke him—something that delights me the most. [I have had the captain, my handsome hero, the man at the hotel—Sardanapale, as I call him—and two more—one who <u>was</u> and the other who <u>is</u>—these are the relationships that thrill me the most. I don't count the young Spaniard, who was an unbearable fellow, and two or three—let's make it four—transitory affairs of no importance. Except for the little diplomat and the young sergeant, all the other men have possessed me completely, including the ex-captain after the adventure in the hotel.][66] I have had pleasure with these men in the most complete way and have given myself to them body and soul. There isn't an inch of my body that has not taken part in the most refined lust, but if the body is satisfied (and at present it is perfectly so), the soul is not, and <u>it</u> is <u>never</u> at peace. Something is missing—and I myself don't know how to define it. Maybe it is the feeling of abnormality that plagues me; what is certain is there is something <u>unfulfilled</u> in me, and I still yearn for <u>something else</u>, some impossible pleasure yet to experience, because all my senses are, alas!, limited. I have been embraced <u>too much</u>, kissed <u>too much</u>, adored <u>too much</u>; my lips burn with the lust that men have tasted there; my chest is bruised by kisses that are almost bites; so much human sap has flowed into my body that it would engender a great many people in very little time! I have consumed entire generations in this way—maybe this is what torments me and ruins all my joy! But is it truly bad to make the flood of generations sterile? Wouldn't it be better to snuff out all humans at conception, to destroy <u>everyone</u> while <u>we</u> savor the utmost pleasure? To enjoy and destroy at the same time: Isn't that magnificent? And the idea that when we eat the <u>forbidden fruit</u>, we are hurling ourselves into the void, and the death of humans who would one day overrun the earth, isn't that enough to multiply tenfold the joys of lusts that were the glory of Sodom? Instead of a cradle, the human body will be our coffin. I myself have contributed to this and do not feel any remorse for it.

Of <u>everything</u> that I have written to you, I beg that you use it with the utmost <u>discretion</u>, especially the passages that I have <u>indicated</u> and <u>all</u> the postscripts at the bottom of the pages. I have trusted you. Do not betray this confidence.

---

66. Deleted from the 1910 edition but reinserted into the 1930 edition.

Other Particularities

Sometimes brushing against someone, his movements next to me, especially if he is gorgeous, affects me like a narcotic.[1] When I feel him moving near me, I experience a languor, a voluptuous powerlessness to which I yield with delight. It has a hypnotic effect on my whole being.

The sight of the most beautiful woman in the world would not trouble me at all; I would not even desire her. Nevertheless, I have a very fiery temperament.[2] Only the beauty of a young man—his vigor and his physique—delights me from an aesthetic point of view, naturally. I believe I could never love a woman. However, from the perspective of emotional satisfaction, men are repulsive. Abnormality, an error of the heart,[3] a strange esthetic, compared to human beauty. All in all, a pure love, absolutely chaste, ethereal, or other-worldly attracts me to the male sex. Of

---

1. This fragment was found in the Saint-Paul family archives in a bound volume entitled "Docteur Laupts. Notes et documents de psychologie normale et pathologique. 1895–1897. Tome 2" / "Dr. Laupts: Notes and Documents on Normal and Pathological Psychology, 1895–1897, volume 2" (volume 1 contains the bound copy of his 1896 book). It is placed between Zola's preface and documents relating to the negotiations with the publishers. It was first published in *Archives d'Anthropologie Criminelle* in 1896 in an article entitled "Enquêtes sur les fonctions cérébrales normales ou déviées" / "Investigation of Normal and Abnormal Brain Functions," 97–100, with minor editorial changes that are indicated in the following footnotes. It was signed by "X." It is clear from the handwriting that it was written by the young Italian man, but it is unclear where this text belonged in the original letters to Zola.

2. In the published version, Saint-Paul changed this phrase to "Nevertheless, my temperament is very passionate."

3. Instead of "an error of the heart," Saint-Paul wrote "an inherent vice" in the published version.

course, if the young man is ugly, I would prefer a woman to him; if he is handsome, I am in ecstasy.[4]

4. In the published version, Saint-Paul changed this sentence to the following: "Of course, I'd rather meet a beautiful woman than an ugly man. But instinctively, to be fundamentally honest in acts and intentions, I am ecstatic at the sight of a young and handsome man."

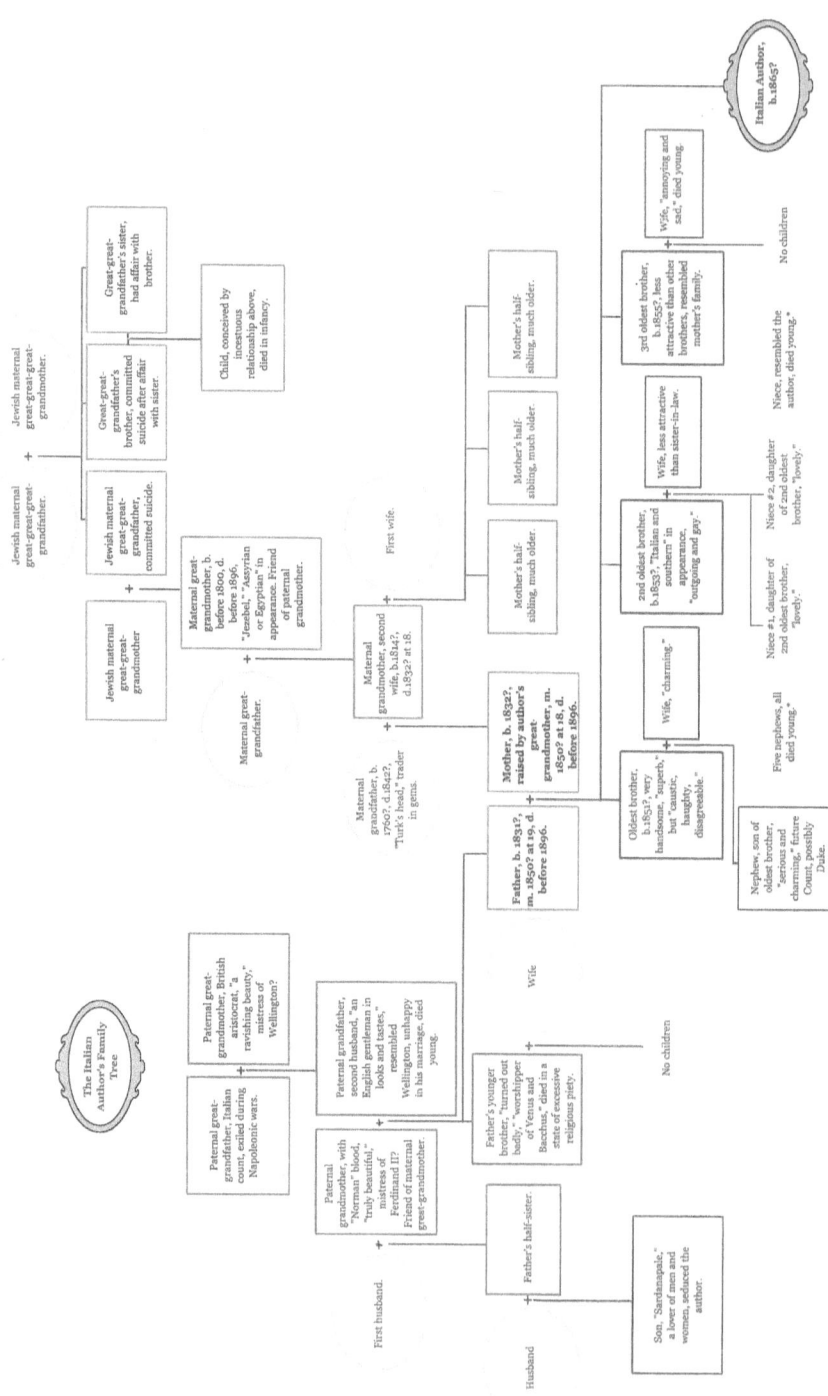

Fig. 5 The Italian man's family tree. Designed by David H. Peniston.

The Italian Man's Family Tree
Michael Rosenfeld

When he wrote to Saint-Paul in September 1896, the author included a much more detailed description of his family history than the one he had given Zola in 1888 or 1889, the details of which might enable us to uncover his identity sometime in the future.[1] Those details are as follows. The anonymous writer belonged to a preeminent aristocratic Neapolitan family, whose senior branch had the rank of duke, while his own, the junior branch, had the rank of count. The family was originally from Spain, where some members still lived; the family arrived in the Kingdom of Naples in the fourteenth century, when the Angevins ascended to the Neapolitan throne.

During the Napoleonic wars, from 1806 to 1814, when Ferdinand IV, the king of Sicily,[2] had to flee Naples and take refuge in Palermo, where he established his court, the narrator's great-grandfather had followed the court to Palermo and had married "a noble Englishwoman who brought him little in terms of a dowry, but much in terms of a ravishing beauty!" (Sequel). According to the narrator, this Englishwoman was pregnant when she married: "Her only son, who was born a short time after his parents' marriage, resembled her in an extraordinary way: he was entirely an English gentleman in his looks and tastes." The narrator gave an additional, intriguing detail about his great-grandmother's son: "His portraits strikingly resemble those of Lord Wellington." Should we deduce from this that she bore the illegitimate child of Arthur Wellesley, the duke of

---

1. We have done research, together with Italian researchers, to try to identify the author of the text and his family on the basis of some of the specific details he provided. No Italian aristocratic family listed in the Registry of Italian Nobility, the *Annuario della nobiltà italiana, anno XII* (Bari: Direzione del Giornale Araldico, 1897), corresponds to the details he has provided. We are unsure how representative this registry is, as there are indications that families had to pay a fee to be listed.

2. After 1816, he became King Ferdinand I of the Kingdom of the Two Sicilies.

Wellington? The writer certainly wished to believe so, but his evidence was self-serving and weak. He had obvious delusions of grandeur, and this specific family story is particularly questionable.

The child in question was the narrator's grandfather, and he, in turn, married a young English widow of Norman ancestry.[3] She had two sons; the older one was the Italian man's father, who, he implied, had royal ancestry. "She was, they say, the mistress of Ferdinand II – if they only knew I dared to write this! But other than that, he did nothing for the family, and perhaps we owe him only the shape of our lips and our chins" (Novel). The narrator added, probably to dispel any suspicion of illegitimacy, that physically his father took after both his parents.

His family was on the verge of bankruptcy when the narrator's father married a wealthy Jewish woman, originally from "a European country that was still quite Oriental" (Sequel). We believe that this may be a reference to Turkey since he also used the epithet Turk's head to describe his maternal grandfather. The dowry of this young woman saved the family from financial ruin.

The narrator had three older brothers; the first, born in about 1852, was fourteen years older than the author and had at least one son, who was the sole heir to the title of duke from the senior branch of the family. The second brother had two "lovely" daughters; and the third brother, who was ten years older than the narrator, was widowed without children. The author stated that he was thirty years old in the September 1896 and that he had been twenty-three when he wrote to Zola in 1888 or 1889. Both his parents had died by 1896, and his elder brother had inherited the title of count.

His social position and the illustrious history of his family are important concerns to the writer of these confessions, who believed that they had a great influence on his personality and attitudes. He also believed that they might explain, to a certain extent, his sexual nature. It is possible that the Italian man used "Inquiry Into Sexual Inversion: Questionnaire," published in *Tares et poisons: perversion et perversité sexuelles*, as a model for the information he provided about his family in his 1896 letter to Dr. Saint-Paul (first edition). This impression is further reinforced by his statement: "I will now

---

3. She had a daughter from her first marriage whom she married off and who had a son. The narrator called this young man Sardanapale and provided additional details about him. He had an affair with him (Sequel).

send to <u>you</u>, Sir, a few observations about myself and my paternal and maternal ancestors. This might interest you and help you understand many things" (Sequel).

The Italian explained that his queerness was inherited, tracing it back to his ancestry, his mother's plebeian and Jewish roots, and his parents' decision to marry: "<u>We are what our parents made us</u>. Science understands and excuses many things from this perspective; there is nothing more fascinating for the expert and the scientist to see a corner of the mysterious veil that covers all these issues" (Sequel). The narrator used explicit anti-Semitic tropes in the descriptions of his maternal Jewish ancestry and relied on theories of "racial purity" to explain his perceived aberrant nature. He did, however, admire his mother's defense of her Jewishness, even ironically quoting the virulent anti-Semite Édouard Drumont. Writing before the virulent anti-Semitism that erupted at the height of the Dreyfus Affair in France, the Italian reflected the stigmatization of Jewish people at the time, a prejudice that was similar to how gay people were then perceived.[4]

Dr. Saint-Paul also pointed to theories of hereditary degeneration in his writing on this case, citing the Italian's eccentric great-grandmother, under the provocative nickname "Jezebel," as a source of the man's affliction. Instead of sharing his mother's admiration for her Jewish ancestors (she converted to Catholicism to marry his father), the narrator revealed his contempt: "My mother's family, who are <u>repulsive</u>" (Novel). Referring to his mother's manias, he blamed them on her Jewish heritage: "I always think this is one of the qualities or defects inherent to the race from which she is descended and for which I feel no sympathy, and even a secret aversion" (Novel). He claimed that the intermingling of the races was the one of the causes of his unique persona: "The West and the East with their very different bloods and civilizations are combined in me—could it be that their clash is the cause of my strange personality?" (Sequel).

To emphasize the eccentricity of his mother's Jewish family, he included several details about his maternal great-grandmother, whom he nicknamed "Jezebel" and who died at the age of ninety-six, a short while before he wrote his 1896 letter. This legendary lady was the second most important

---

4. The amalgamation of homophobia and anti-Semitism has been studied recently by Chantal Meyer-Plantureux, *Antisémitisme et homophobie: clichés en scène et à l'écran* (Paris: CNRS Éditions, 2019), and Alain Pagès, "L'Affaire Dreyfus. Une histoire médiatique," *Les Études du CRIF*, no. 61 (October–November 2020).

character in the letter; 10 percent of it focused on her life story. "Jezebel" was married at the age of twelve and bore only one daughter, the Italian's grandmother, when she was only thirteen. This daughter died when she was eighteen, leaving her own child, the narrator's mother, to be raised by her father. When the Italian's maternal grandfather died, "Jezebel" assumed an important role in family affairs: "He died at the age of eighty-two, leaving my mother to the care of her maternal grandmother, who was indeed the strangest creature in this world. I must spend a little time describing this bizarre woman whom I occasionally saw during my childhood, but never without feeling a sort of fright" (*Sequel*). This "Jezebel" was a quasi-mythical character who arranged her granddaughter's marriage to an Italian aristocrat, the narrator's father. Saint-Paul also stressed Jezebel's influence and her eccentricity in his analyses published in 1910 and 1930, seeing her as emblematic of the hereditary causes that resulted in the Italian man's degeneration.

PART II
Selected Works by Dr. Georges Saint-Paul

*Translated by Nancy Erber and William Peniston with
introductions by Michael Rosenfeld and Clive Thomson
and an analytical and biographical essay by Clive Thomson*

We have chosen a variety of texts by Dr. Georges Saint-Paul that provide a historical context to the theories on homosexuality he developed in his 1896 book, in the subsequent editions of 1910 and 1930, and in articles published in scientific journals. These selected works allow a deeper understanding of the doctor's theories on same-sex love, as well as their evolution from 1894, when he was a junior military doctor, to 1930, when he was a retired general and widely respected humanitarian.

Fig. 6 Photographic portrait of Dr. Georges Saint-Paul as a medical student at the School of Military Medicine in Lyon in 1891–1892, around the time that he first met Émile Zola. Georges Saint-Paul family archives © Michael Rosenfeld.

Dr. Georges Saint-Paul, Man of Science
Clive Thomson

BIOGRAPHY

> Your eminently friendly nature
> —Alexandre Lacassagne, writing to Georges Saint-Paul, 1893

Georges Saint-Paul arrived in Lyon to begin his studies at the School of Military Medicine in 1889. He probably met Professor Alexandre Lacassagne that same year. As we shall see, their meeting was crucial for Saint-Paul, who, in the next two years, attended a heavy schedule of courses on topics such as comparative anatomy, internal and external physiology, surgery, natural history, hygiene, ophthalmology, toxicology, and legal medicine.[1] Saint-Paul came from a well-to-do bourgeois family. His father was a high-ranking civil servant in the city of Tours. As a student in Lyon, Saint-Paul quickly gained a reputation for being intelligent, hard-working, assiduous, and very well-organized.[2] He already possessed a number of other personal qualities that would serve him well in the years ahead—he was ambitious, quick-witted, confident, and very adept in establishing cordial relations with his professors and fellow students.

In the spring of 1891, after Saint-Paul had completed all his compulsory course work, he chose the subject for his doctoral thesis. Most of Professor

---

1. Micheline Chanteloube, *L'École du service de santé des armées de Lyon: Album du centenaire* (Lyon: Charles-Lavauzelle, 1988), 28. The curriculum at the School of Military Medicine included the usual medical courses, as well as courses on military training (both theoretical and practical). Saint-Paul also studied French history, French literature, and the German language.

2. Saint-Paul's correspondence, diaries, reading notes, and other manuscripts are located in the Saint-Paul family archives (hereafter SPFA). I am most grateful to the family for giving me access to these archives.

Lacassagne's other students tended to work on conventional topics, such as "Cranial Trauma," "The Criminal's Brain," "Identity and the Study of the Skeleton." More adventurous students chose to do research on issues relating to sexuality: "Modes of Evolution of the Sexual Instinct," "The Legal and Medical Study of Castration," "The Sexual Abuse of Young Girls," "Criminality and Abortion."[3] Saint-Paul, however, made a very different choice. His subject—"interior language"—harked back to an ancient philosophical problem that had been studied for centuries. Originally it had been explored by Plato and more recently by Étienne Bonnot de Condillac, Louis de Bonald, and Jean-Martin Charcot. Saint-Paul decided to approach the topic through the lenses of several disciplines: philosophy, literature, physiology, sociology, anthropology, and linguistics. The philosophical dimension of his project is evident in the title of his thesis: "Essays on Interior Language." The term "Essays" had both philosophical and literary connotations. Paul Bourget, for example, had published his *Essais de psychologie contemporaine / Essays on Contemporary Psychology* in 1883.[4] From a methodological point of view, Saint-Paul located his project in the relatively new field of psychology, which was in the process of being constituted as an autonomous academic discipline. Théodule Ribot was appointed to the very first professorship of "experimental and comparative psychology" at the Collège de France in 1889. At this time, there were no courses on psychology at the School of Military Medicine in Lyon.

Saint-Paul asked Lacassagne to be his thesis adviser. It was a judicious decision because Lacassagne already had a prominent international reputation as a professor of legal and forensic medicine and was engaged in pioneering work in the hospitals and prisons of Lyon. Reports on the results of his research and on that of his colleagues were appearing regularly in the *Archives d'Anthropologie Criminelle*, the journal that he created in 1886.[5] His discoveries

---

3. See "Table des thèses soutenues pendant l'année scolaire 1892–1893," *Thèses de médecine de Lyon*: 1892–1893 71, no. 775 (1892–1893).

4. Paul Bourget, *Essais de psychologie contemporaine* (Paris: A. Lemaire, 1883). Some other examples are Gabriel Séailles, *Essai sur le génie dans l'art* (Paris: Baillère, 1883); Étienne Vacherot, *Essais sur la philosophie critique* (Paris: F. Chamerot, 1864); John Stuart Mill, *Three Essays on Religion* (London: Longmans, Green, Reader, and Duyer, 1874). Most of the titles cited in this chapter, including those of Saint-Paul and Lacassagne, are available on the *Gallica* platform at the Bibliothèque Nationale de France.

5. *Archives d'Anthropologie Criminelle et des Sciences Pénales / Archives of Criminal Anthropology and Penal Sciences* is the title that Lacassagne gave to his journal in 1886, when it

received positive attention from the medical community in France and other countries. Thus Saint-Paul gained entry into one the most prestigious scientific communities in Europe. Lacassagne's career was an example that showed Saint-Paul the importance of cultivating and maintaining a network of colleagues in the medical and scientific community.

Thanks to Lacassagne's contacts, Saint-Paul's name appeared for the first time in a Paris newspaper. Léon Riotor published reports on Saint-Paul's doctoral research in *Le Journal* on October 20 and in *Le Figaro* on December 10, 1892. The article in *Le Figaro*, entitled "The Brains of Writers: Physiological Confessions," reproduced the answers to the questionnaire on interior language that Saint-Paul submitted to Émile Zola, Alphonse Daudet, and François Coppée. Riotor wrote: "Lacassagne's usual approach to making his research projects public is to have a student work under his supervision. The student explains the objectives of the project and puts his signature on it. The disciple whom Lacassagne has chosen for this project is Dr. Georges Saint-Paul, an outstanding student from the School of Military Medicine in Lyon."

Lacassagne ensured that his students got a solid foundation during their medical training with him, especially in regard to the interdisciplinary methodologies that were emerging in a new kind of research to which Saint-Paul was very attracted. This new area went under a variety of names: psychological physiology, the physiology of the brain, the science of the brain. Lacassagne's attitude toward thesis supervision also involved giving his students considerable freedom to work on their own. The independent-minded Saint-Paul greatly benefited from such a pedagogical approach. He described Lacassagne's supervisory style in the dedicatory note on the first page of his thesis:

> It is with respect that I place Professor Lacassagne's name at the head of my thesis which I wrote in the School of Military Medicine at the University of Lyon. I sincerely hope that my work has the same qualities as those of our director, who has supervised with great enthusiasm, year after year, so many

---

was first created. In 1893 the title was changed—a sign of the times—to *Archives d'Anthropologie Criminelle, de Médecine Légale et de Psychologie Normale et Pathologique / Archives of Criminal Anthropology, Forensic Medicine and Normal and Pathological Psychology*. It is commonly known as *Archives d'Anthropologie Criminelle / Archives of Criminal Anthropology*, which is the title that we have used throughout this study.

> research projects. I refer to his judicious advice, the enormous breadth of his wisdom, and his practical and artistic intelligence. Without him, my research would not exist. I wish to express to him my profound gratitude for the precious materials that he helped me acquire and for the total freedom with which I was able to synthesize my findings. I cannot find the words to describe adequately the memories that I now have of the many hours I spent with dear friends in the friendly and supportive atmosphere that Dr. Lacassagne created for us. I am grateful for the friendship that he extended to me. He was, and he will always remain, the Master.[6]

Saint-Paul's style here is highly original if we compare it to that of his classmates, who expressed their gratitude to their supervisors in simpler terms. Saint-Paul's style is more literary, as can be seen in the figures of speech (hyperbole, repetition, etc.) that he deployed while describing his professor's attributes. The tone of the dedication is elegant and respectful, and it concludes on a very personal note when Saint-Paul highlighted the friendship that he and Lacassagne enjoyed. A few pages later, in the introduction to his thesis, Saint-Paul again thanked his supervisor profusely and included a long quotation from one of Lacassagne's lectures in which he stressed that medical doctors have important ethical responsibilities to their patients. In short, Saint-Paul's objective is to make it known to all that he enjoyed a very special relationship with his professor.

In the years immediately following the thesis defense, which took place on December 28, 1892, the personal and professional relationship between the two men became even closer.[7] Lacassagne invited his student to

---

6. Georges Saint-Paul, *Essais sur le langage intérieur: Thèse présentée à la faculté de médecine et de pharmacie de Lyon et soutenue publiquement le mercredi 28 décembre 1892, pour obtenir le grade de docteur en médecine* (Lyon: Stock, 1892). The thesis has two dedicatory notices. The first one is for Lacassagne; the second, for Saint-Paul's parents: "To my mother, to my father, I dedicate these *Essays*. G.S.P."

7. The tone of the letter of January 7, 1896, that Lacassagne sent to Saint-Paul is typical of their exchanges at this time and shows how close the two men and their families were: "Thank you, my dear Saint-Paul, for the expression of your affectionate words and for your warm wishes to me and my family. Even though you are far away, you have occupied an important place in our lives. Know that you will always occupy it. . . . Know that you can always count on my support." Lacassagne's letters are in the Saint-Paul family archives.

contribute to his journal. Between 1893 and 1909, Saint-Paul published at least six articles in the *Archives*.[8] It is also clear that Lacassagne was largely responsible when the professors at the medical school awarded Saint-Paul's thesis the silver medal early in 1893.[9] The following excerpt from the speech made by Lacassagne at the medal ceremony contains high praise for Saint-Paul:

> This thesis belongs to you. My role was quite small. I put you in touch with a few of my colleagues and I gave you some advice during those many hours we spent in the classroom. This is how I got to know you and to value you. In our daily work together that lasted a whole year, I observed you to be very intelligent, decisive, and sensitive. Your eminently friendly nature is quite contagious and facilitates the creation of affectionate bonds. We professors do not believe that the classroom is the only place in which we develop relationships with students. . . . I treated you like a friend because I saw you up close for a significant amount of time. On this very special day, let me assure you that my friendship with you will never falter.[10]

When Lacassagne claimed only to have put Saint-Paul "in touch with a few . . . colleagues" and to have given him some advice, he was obviously

---

8. Saint-Paul's first article in *Archives d'Anthropologie Criminelle* is "Quelques mots sur M. Jacques Inaudi," vol. 8, no. 2 (1893): 192–96.

9. Between November 1892 and July 1893, a total of 105 doctoral theses were defended at the School of Military Medicine in Lyon. Lacassagne is identified as supervisor for 14 of them. Between 1881 and 1913, he was the supervisor for over 200 theses. See Philippe Artières and Gérard Corneloup, "Liste des thèses produites sous la direction d'Alexandre Lacassagne au sein du Laboratoire de médecine-légale de Lyon," in their exhibition catalog, *Le Médecin et le criminel: Alexandre Lacassagne, 1843–1924: Catalogue of an exhibition at the Bibliothèque Municipale de Lyon, January 27–May 15, 2004* (Lyon: Bibliothèque Municipale de Lyon, 2004), 222–30.

10. This text is in Lacassagne's handwriting and shows signs of having been composed in haste. It is attached to the first page of Lacassagne's personal copy of Saint-Paul's thesis (located in the Lacassagne Archives in the Bibliothèque Municipale de Lyon). The text is probably part of notes that Lacassagne used to make his speech during the ceremony when the silver medal was presented to Saint-Paul. Attached to this copy of the thesis are two letters from November 1894, addressed to Lacassagne by Saint-Paul, in which Saint-Paul thanked his supervisor for the medal ("which, thanks to you, I was awarded") and offered his best wishes. I thank Michael Rosenfeld for providing me with copies of the documents.

minimizing how much he helped his young doctoral student. Because of his position as director of the *Archives d'Anthropologie Criminelle* and his frequent appearances at national and international congresses, Lacassagne was extremely well known and respected in European medical communities. It was thus due to his professor's contacts that Saint-Paul, while doing the fieldwork for his thesis, was able to interview an impressive number of prominent medical specialists, including Arnold Aletrino, Alfred Binet, Jean-Paul-Henri Coutagne, Raphaël Lépine, Alfred Mignon, and Charles Viry.

At the beginning of 1892, when Saint-Paul was in the early stages of his thesis research, he worked efficiently and quickly. First, he familiarized himself with the most recent scientific publications on the nervous system and on the physiology of the brain. He then conducted over two hundred interviews, using the questionnaire that he designed in collaboration with Lacassagne. He interviewed the older generation of medical doctors who lived in Lyon and Paris and a large number of journalists and writers (Émile Zola, Maurice Barrès, Paul Brulat, François Coppée, Alphonse Daudet, Léon Daudet, Jean-Louis Dubut de Laforest). He obtained the participation of several close friends (Jean Arrufat, Francis Biraud, Henri Massenet, Francis Miramond de la Roche). He even had his parents complete the questionnaire.[11] Saint-Paul managed to involve so many well-known contemporaries in his research for two reasons. As already indicated, he exploited fully his professor's contacts and, perhaps even more important, made good use of the personal quality that Lacassagne pointed to while presenting the silver medal to his student in 1893—his "contagious" and "eminently friendly nature."

In January 1893, right after his thesis examination, Saint-Paul took up a position as intern at the Val-de-Grâce School of Applied Medicine and Pharmacology in Paris. Later the same year he moved to Mézières in the Ardennes region of France, where he occupied for the next two years a full-time appointment as medical doctor with the 91st infantry regiment. In October 1895 he received a promotion and was sent to Algeria, where he spent two years before being transferred to Tunisia. In April 1901 Saint-Paul returned to France, and for the following twenty-five years he

---

11. In the Saint-Paul family archives, there are 239 questionnaires, most of which contain the handwritten responses of the individuals whom Saint-Paul contacted during his research. A few questionnaires are in Saint-Paul's handwriting. In these cases, he recorded the responses that his interviewees dictated to him.

served in a series of important positions with the military in Tours, Villefranche-sur-Mer, and Paris. His last posting was in Nancy in 1926 as the chief medical officer with the rank of general in the 20th army corps. He was awarded the prestigious War Cross medal for his service during World War I, and in 1929 he was promoted to the rank of commander in the Légion d'honneur.

During his six years in North Africa, Saint-Paul stayed in close contact with Lacassagne and the research communities in Lyon and Paris. After Professor Ribot invited him to write book reviews, Saint-Paul, under the pseudonym Dr. Laupts, produced a series of sixteen reviews for the *Revue Philosophique de la France et de l'Étranger*.[12] His reviews are carefully crafted and reveal a significant ability for both synthetic and analytic thinking. They also cover an impressive range of topics: the anatomy of the brain, the nervous system, hysteria and epilepsy, astigmatism, theories of degeneracy, and so on. The tone of the reviews is unfailingly respectful and diplomatic. He did not engage in the kind of polemics that can be seen in the debates among some of his colleagues. Saint-Paul also maintained his own program of research during these years. He produced some thirty articles between 1894 and 1910, all of which appeared in the best medical journals of the day: *La Tribune Médicale, Le Progrès Médical, Les Annales Médicales Chirurgicales du Centre, Les Annales Médico-Psychologiques, La Revue de l'Hypnotisme, La Revue Scientifique, Le Bulletin Médical*. In these articles, Saint-Paul continued his research on interior language,[13] while at the same time writing about

---

12. Saint-Paul was in contact with Ribot in 1894, as he indicated in a letter dated November 26 addressed to Lacassagne: "I have been writing reviews for M. Ribot. . . . I saw Ribot in Paris" (Fonds Lacassagne, Bibliothèque Municipale de Lyon). Saint-Paul and Ribot continued to communicate with each other for several years. In 1896 Saint-Paul dedicated *Tares et poisons* to Ribot: "To Ribot, Professor at the Collège de France, Director of the *Revue Philosophique*, with gratitude and affection from Dr. Laupts." In 1904 Ribot wrote the preface for Saint-Paul's book *Souvenirs de Tunisie et d'Algérie* (Paris: Éditions Charles-Lavauzelle, 1904): "I could not refuse to express my friendship and respect for a collaborator who is well known for his important research on *interior language*, and for his other psychological studies, which have created collegial bonds between us. . . . The significance of this book is that it was prepared with care and great honesty" (9).

13. In 1904 Saint-Paul published *Le Langage intérieur et les paraphasies: La fonction endophasique* (Paris: Alcan, 1904), a greatly expanded version of his thesis. The thesis contains 149 pages, and this new edition has 316 pages.

other topics, such as the ethical responsibilities of medical doctors, personality disorders, hypnotism, and suicide.

Saint-Paul undoubtedly realized that the publication of his doctoral thesis and a few book reviews was not going to give him the career profile for which he hoped. Lacassagne and Ribot, his two most important mentors, became prominent by regularly producing substantial monographs. Saint-Paul knew very well that he needed to follow their example. The idea for his first book perhaps occurred during his meetings with Zola in 1892, when he was doing research for his thesis. During one of these encounters, Zola gave Saint-Paul the manuscript containing the detailed autobiography of a young Italian gay man, which he had received a few years earlier from its author. Saint-Paul probably sensed that this extremely well-written and somewhat sensational narrative could be of significant interest to his colleagues in the medical community. He wasted no time in moving forward with the project, even though it dealt with an area—sexual inversion—that he had not previously studied in any detail.[14] In 1896, with the publication of the autobiography in *Tares et poisons: Perversion et perversité sexuelles: une enquête médicale sur l'inversion*, Saint-Paul's reputation reached an entirely new level.

The Doctoral Thesis

> A positive revolution is taking place.
> —Gilbert Ballet, *Le Langage intérieur et les diverses formes de l'aphasie*, 1886

It is worth taking a close look at Saint-Paul's doctoral thesis because it represents an important moment in his career. The fact that Charcot, Binet, and Ribot, among others, had recently made major contributions to the study of interior language did not deter Saint-Paul from tackling the same topic. In the preface to his thesis, he emphasized the idea that medical researchers must link their work to that of philosophers and creative artists. He illustrated this point by expressing his appreciation for Lacassagne's work, which was infused, he wrote, with a "spirit that is both artistic

---

14. In *À la mémoire de Zola*, Saint-Paul wrote that, when he was studying with Lacassagne in Lyon, he examined a few cases of sexual inversion. See "In Memoriam: Émile Zola" in part 2 of this book.

and practical." The following quotation by Diderot appeared at the beginning of the first chapter: "The medical doctor has a duty to write about metaphysics. It is he alone who sees phenomena and that (human) machine that can be serene or angry, weak or robust, healthy or ill, delirious or stable, imbecilic, enlightened, stupid, noisy, mute, lethargic, alive or dead."[15] A few pages later, Saint-Paul drove his point home: "In our modern societies, the role of the doctor needs to be expanded: he must be a philosopher."

Saint-Paul then focused on his methodology and stated that his scientific approach imitated that of the researchers in the pure sciences: "I believe that, as with the fields of chemistry or of any other science that are worthy of the name, physio-psychology must adopt a clear and precise terminology and give to each word a particular definition, so that all confusion is avoided." [16] He then summarized briefly what he saw as the most significant recent publications on his topic. His next step was to present the rather rudimentary taxonomy of psychological types that he deduced from his field research: he claimed that the individuals whom he interviewed fell into three categories: they were "verbal," "visual," or some combination of both.[17]

---

15. The quotation by Diderot is from his article "Philosophie de Locke," which appeared in his book *Opinions des anciens philosophes*. See *Oeuvres complètes de Diderot* (Paris: Le Club Français du Livre, 1972), 14:501. Saint-Paul did not indicate the edition of Diderot's works from which he took the quotation.

16. Saint-Paul, *Essais sur le langage intérieur*, 14. Saint-Paul was fond of creating neologisms, such as *physio-psychologie*. Some other examples are *endophasie, formule endophasique*, and *visuelisme*.

17. Here is a brief summary of the main argument of Saint-Paul's thesis on interior language. There are, he claimed, three "psychomotor" centers in the brain that "store sensations," each of which has a specific function relating to language: (1) "the interior parietal lobe" processes "the visual representation of words;" (2) "the first temporal circumvolution on the left" processes and conserves the auditory traces of words; (3) "the third frontal circumvolution on the left" stores "articulatory movements that allow for the pronunciation of words." When any one of these centers has a lesion, the result is a specific pathology: (1) "verbal blindness"; (2) "verbal deafness"; (3) "motor aphasia." A series of metaphors is used to describe these "centers" (or "regions") of the brain, the main one being a comparison of the brain to "an office" or "a depot" where each sensation arrives and then takes "a ticket" that assigns "a word" to the sensation. The brain is conceived essentially as a locale that guarantees the conservation or the storage of words. Saint-Paul went on to state that, "in normal humans," there are "sensations," "memories," or "impressions" (which are linked to objects) that are

Saint-Paul's style of writing conveys his sense of excitement, enthusiasm, and optimism for the field of research within which he was working. He was convinced that the most interesting and innovative research of the day was being carried out by psychologists. On the one hand, he displayed a certain modesty when he admitted that he was deeply indebted to the work of his predecessors and that his thesis was a rather small contribution when viewed within the larger field.[18] On the other hand, he did claim that his discoveries were original and that his methodology was more rigorous than that of his predecessors. He was proud of the questionnaire that

---

"nonverbal," adding that it was logical to suppose that these images functioned exactly like words. He concluded that "normal humans think by means of words and images and that humans are both *verbal* and *visual*." At this point, Saint-Paul laid the theoretical cornerstone that allowed him to organize the overall direction of his project and to formulate his basic research question: In what proportions do humans fit into each of the categories of the verbal and the visual? What is the relative frequency of each type? As a precaution, toward the end of his discussion of theoretical and methodological questions in his first chapter, Saint-Paul advanced the hypothesis of a third, "mixed" type—what he called the "indifferent." This last type included those people who do not fit neatly into either of the other two categories.

18. Saint-Paul acknowledged that he read the works of several doctors and specialists on this subject (Charcot, Galton, Ballet, Ribot, Binet, Egger, Stricker). He did not, however, indicate the titles of the studies he consulted. It is therefore impossible to identify which studies in particular influenced his thinking about how the brain functions. The studies that he probably read include Victor Egger, *La Parole intérieure: Essai de psychologie descriptive* (Paris: Baillère, 1881); Salomon Stricker, *Du langage et de la musique* (Paris: Alcan, 1885); Gilbert Ballet, *Le Langage intérieur et les diverses formes de l'aphasie* (Paris: Baillère, 1886); and Alfred Binet, *La Psychologie du raisonnement: Recherches expérimentales par l'hypnotisme* (Paris: Alcan, 1886). In 1925 Saint-Paul wrote the following comment about Charcot's contribution to the topic: "[Charcot] perceived that the language function, a function that is characteristic of the human species, was crucial for the study of the brain or, to be more precise, the starting point for discoveries" (Georges Saint-Paul, "Charcot, fondateur de la cérébrologie," *Le Progrès Medical*, no. 28, July 11, 1925). A recent and very interesting study sheds light on the affinities between the ideas of Egger and those of James Joyce in *Ulysses*: Laura Santone, *Egger, Dujardin, Joyce: Microscopia della voce nel monologo interiore* (Rome: Bulzoni Editore, 2009). Additionally, Jacqueline Carroy, "Le Langage intérieur comme miroir du cerveau: une enquête, ses enjeux et ses limites," *Langue française* 132 (2001): 48–56, provides a valuable account of the historical context of research on interior language in the 1890s, as well as a detailed analysis of Saint-Paul's contribution to the topic.

he created with Lacassagne, even though he admitted that it was not perfect.[19]

In his conclusion, Saint-Paul articulated what he considered to be the real value of his research. Earlier publications on interior language, he wrote, tended to be too abstract and speculative, whereas his study was more concrete because it was based on the careful analysis of data collected during extensive fieldwork. In addition to his discovery of the three personality types, Saint-Paul wrote that his study was important because it revealed interesting aspects of some famous personalities and their habits. In this sense, his point was well taken. For example, Zola gave detailed explanations about how he wrote his novels, as well as information about childhood memories. Lacassagne recounted some of his dreams, identified his favorite books, and explained the feelings he experienced while lecturing to his students.

While producing his thesis under Professor Lacassagne's supervision, Saint-Paul mastered a particular scientific method that he subsequently refined and applied in his study of sexual inversion. He also acquired an impressive body of knowledge about physiology and psychology, and, more specifically, about the most recent investigations into brain functioning. He also improved his ability to express his ideas clearly and to construct a coherent argument. While his thesis shows signs of being written in haste—this can be seen in a number of stylistic infelicities and in some gaps in the logic of his argument—he adopted a much more coherent and balanced style in his book on inversion. These are just some important differences between the thesis and the book on inversion. There are also significant similarities. In both studies, the overall objective is to advance research on the psychology of the human mind through the empirical study of individual cases.

What is perhaps most interesting about these projects, however, is that Saint-Paul abandoned—without seeming to realize it—a strictly

19. On page 21 of his thesis, Saint-Paul indicated: "In collaboration with Dr. Lacassagne, I wrote the questionnaire," and he gave the date of March 15, 1892, as the exact date when the questionnaire was created. Saint-Paul's questionnaire on interior language is made up of six sections, each containing a series of specific questions: (1) The organs of the senses (sight, sound, the other senses); (2) Sensory memory (visual memory, auditory memory, other types of memory, various questions); (3) Interior language (verbal audition, visual verbal imagination, verbal articulation); (4) Dreams; (5) General aptitudes; and (6) General information.

psychological perspective. In his study of interior language, he ended up providing valuable documentation about the personal and social activities of his interviewees.[20] The same tendency can be seen in his examination of inversion, where his interest is primarily in the personal habits and social activities of the two homosexuals who are the focus of his study – the young Italian man and Oscar Wilde. This ethnographic preoccupation would characterize Saint-Paul's investigations after he published *Tares et poisons* in 1896. Following his sojourns in Algeria and Tunisia, he published two studies, both of which have little to do with the discipline of psychology: *Souvenirs de Tunisie et d'Algérie / Recollections of Tunisia and Algeria* (1909) and *Par les colons: l'Algérie aux Algériens et par les Algériens / Through the Eyes of the Colonists: Algeria for the Algerians and by the Algerians* (1914).

Perversion and Perversity

> The question of sexual inversion is on the agenda.
> —Augustin Hamon, review of *Tares et poisons* in *La Société Nouvelle*, September 1896

Saint-Paul's objective at the time he undertook his book on inversion was to finish it as quickly as possible. He was well aware that his posting to Mézières in late 1893 was temporary and that he could end up being transferred to a military base much farther away from Paris. Proximity to the capital meant easy access to the network of contacts that he needed in order to work efficiently on his project. By the end of 1894, he had a clear idea of the structure and content of his book. As he had anticipated, he received news of his promotion in the fall of 1895. He left for Algeria in late October. On October 15, 1895, shortly before departure, he signed a contract with the Carré publishing house for his book on inversion.[21]

Using the network of professional colleagues that he had carefully built up through his relationship with Lacassagne, Saint-Paul made a number of clever decisions that he hoped would guarantee his book a certain degree

---

20. It is important to point out that the large majority of Saint-Paul's interviewees belonged to a specific socioeconomic class—the well-educated bourgeoisie—and most of them were men. Only eight women were interviewed.

21. See Michael Rosenfeld and Nancy Erber's introduction in this volume.

of success. The first step in his strategy was to ask Zola to write a preface. Zola was, of course, the most celebrated author of the time. In consultation with Zola, Saint-Paul invented a title for his first case study—the one devoted to the young Italian man's autobiography—a title with literary connotations, The Novel of an Invert, designed to attract the interest of a broad reading public.[22] To generate advance publicity for the book, Saint-Paul arranged to have this autobiography published in serial form in Lacassagne's journal, Archives d'Anthropologie Criminelle. Between March 1894 and May 1895, the contents appeared in six segments. To illustrate his theory of sexual inversion, Saint-Paul decided to devote his study to this case and that of Oscar Wilde. The scandalous events surrounding Wilde's trials appeared in the Paris newspapers over several weeks beginning in March 1895. In another step that was designed to attract attention to his book, Saint-Paul invited Marc-André Raffalovich to assist him by providing information about Wilde. Raffalovich, one of the more high-profile specialists on sexual inversion at that time, had begun publishing his innovative and somewhat controversial writings on the topic in Archives d'Anthropologie Criminelle in 1894.[23]

The first chapter of Tares et poisons contains references to the work on inversion that had been published previously by Karl Heinrich Ulrichs, Albert Moll, Alfred Binet, Benjamin Ball, Théodule-Armand Ribot, Alexandre Lacassagne, Richard von Krafft-Ebing, Valentin Magnan, Marc-André Raffalovich, and Julien Chevalier. Saint-Paul's summary of these publications merits a closer examination for at least two reasons. First, his overview captures succinctly the most significant new ideas that were circulating around him in this quickly evolving field of investigation. Second, his

---

22. The form of the title invented by Zola and Saint-Paul was very common in late nineteenth-century France. Examples include C.-E. Guichard, Le Roman d'un homme d'état (Paris: Garnier, 1861); Edmond About, Le Roman d'un brave homme (Paris: Hachette, 1881); Octave Feuillet, Roman d'un jeune homme pauvre (Paris: Lévy, 1887).

23. Raffalovich's articles on homosexuality in the journal were "L'Éducation des invertis," Archives d'Anthropologie Criminelle 9 (1894): 738–40; and "Quelques observations sur l'inversion," Archives d'Anthropologie Criminelle 9 (1894): 216–18. In 1896 he published Uranisme et unisexualité: Étude sur différentes manifestations de l'instinct sexuel (Lyon: Storck, 1896); translated by Nancy Erber and William A. Peniston as Marc-André Raffalovich's Uranism and Unisexuality: A Study of Different Manifestations of the Sexual Instinct (London: Palgrave Macmillan, 2016). See also Patrick Cardon, Discours littéraires et scientifiques fin-de-siècle: Autour de Marc-André Raffalovich (Paris: Orizon, 2008).

summary shows the extent to which he took pains to familiarize himself with the most recent research of his sexologist contemporaries in France and across Europe.[24] In general, he contented himself with brief mentions of the ideas he apparently considered outdated (those of Ulrichs, Mantegazza, Lombroso, Binet, etc.), and unlike some of his colleagues, he did not engage in polemics against those ideas with which he disagreed. However, he meticulously summarized and foregrounded the aspects of the theories that influenced his own thinking about inversion, specifically those of Chevalier, Lacassagne, and Raffalovich.

Saint-Paul was clearly impressed in particular by Julien Chevalier's doctoral thesis, which had been published ten years earlier,[25] quoting a long extract from the thesis in which Chevalier referred to the bisexual nature of the human fetus in its early stages of development. Saint-Paul speculated that one of the many possible causes of inversion could be linked to this biological fact. He then extended Chevalier's point and suggested that all human beings have the potential to develop homosexual tendencies—a totally new idea at the time that would have offended the majority of Saint-Paul's medical colleagues. Saint-Paul aligned himself with both Chevalier and Lacassagne, who emphasized environmental causes over hereditary ones in their accounts of inversion. He highlighted Lacassagne's way of classifying the types of sexual inverts: "It is one of the most simple, clear, and practical classification systems, and probably the most scientific."[26] He expressed a particular admiration for the work of Raffalovich, whom he described in the following way: "He is a psychologist; he adopts a broader

---

24. Saint-Paul provides quotations from a variety of French and non-French sources but does not give detailed bibliographical references. He studied German during the time he was a medical student in Lyon and would therefore have been able to read German publications in the original. He also had at his disposal the French translations of some German titles, such as Albert Moll, Les Perversions de l'instinct génital, étude sur l'inversion sexuelle (Paris: G. Carré, 1893); and Richard von Krafft-Ebing, Étude médico-légale, "Psychopathia sexualis": avec recherches spéciales sur l'inversion sexuelle (Paris: G. Carré, 1895).

25. Julien Chevalier, De l'inversion de l'instinct sexuel au point de vue médico-légal (Paris: Octave Doin, 1885). Chevalier issued an adaptation in 1893 under the title Une Maladie de la personnalité: l'inversion sexuelle (Paris: G. Masson; Lyon: Storck, 1893), a copy of which Saint-Paul owned in his library.

26. Dr. Laupts, Tares et poisons. Perversion et perversité sexuelles (Paris: Georges Carré, 1896), 23.

and livelier perspective that is respectful of facts and reality; he dissects the minutiae of phenomena; his knowledge of the sexual instinct and of man in general is thus more precise."[27]

Saint-Paul's ideas on sexual inversion do not represent a radical departure from what his colleagues were proposing. He did, however, express reservations about some aspects of their positions. He suggested that Krafft-Ebing's taxonomy could be improved, and that Moll was simply wrong when he claimed that the only valid category was that of the born invert. Saint-Paul's thinking was also much less categorical and dogmatic than that of most of his contemporaries. He frequently reminded his colleagues that there were many aspects of inversion that remained unexplained, such as why some inverts experienced sexual pleasure exclusively in the passive position. He also pointed out that much more research on the role played by heredity in inversion needed to be done. Saint-Paul was convinced, finally, that current sexologists simplified the complexities of the phenomenon, which, he claimed, had multiple causes and which must be studied from a cross-disciplinary perspective. On these particular points, he was consistent with the approach that he adopted in his doctoral thesis.

Saint-Paul went on in his first chapter to present his two cases—that of the born invert and that of the occasional invert. The way in which he crafted his argument created the illusion that he deduced his categories from his observation of a variety of cases, but it is clear that his classification system was basically the same one that several other doctors had adopted before him. He claimed that the born invert typically played the passive role in sexual relations between the partners, whereas the occasional invert was most often the active partner. He conceived of the occasional invert as a "pure accident," and he was clearly much more interested in such cases. He suggested that they were more complex and—more important—were capable of being cured, providing that the behavior was of short duration. In the final paragraphs of this first chapter, Saint-Paul reminded his readers of how Greek love functioned in antiquity, and he then advanced his claim that there were, in fact, three types of inversion—the born "passive" invert, the occasional "active" invert, and the occasional "passive" invert.

---

27. Laupts, *Tares et poisons*, 277.

He affirmed that the last type was exceptional and therefore very difficult to explain.

Saint-Paul described in detail the questionnaire he used for his survey.[28] He pointed out that the questionnaire was to be used primarily by medical doctors, but he also invited anyone interested in the topic of inversion to apply it. This questionnaire was more sophisticated than the one he created for the study of interior language because it solicited information on the ancestry of inverts, their physique, their mental states, and so on. The preamble to the questionnaire asked medical practitioners to identify the theory of inversion to which they adhered. Saint-Paul's innovative approach here makes it clear that there were several theories of inversion, and that the doctor needed to be aware of the perspective that he espoused. The final questions on the survey were designed to have the interviewee think about how he judged himself and to reflect on what he saw as the causes of inversion. Such questions imply that, for Saint-Paul, the relationship between the doctor and the invert was to be seen as a dialogue. Such a view of the patient-doctor relationship was rare at that time.[29]

Chapter 2 of the book contains a transcription of the narrative of the young Italian man, followed by Saint-Paul's commentary. Chapter 3 presents the personal history of Oscar Wilde and an account of his trials. The Italian man's case is an example of the born invert, whereas Oscar Wilde's case corresponds to the occasional invert type. Saint-Paul admitted to finding both individuals somewhat sympathetic, and in his explanation of the causes of inversion, he attributed greater weight to social environment than to hereditary factors.

In chapter 4, "Inversion Explained by Philosophers," Saint-Paul summarized the theories of his contemporaries but did not criticize them. He emphasized the affinities between his own theories and those of others: the theories "do have significant differences but it is satisfying to see that all other theories recognize more or less explicitly the distinction between

---

28. See "First Edition (1896)," in part 2 of this volume.

29. Whereas the complete collection of responses to Saint-Paul's questionnaires on interior language has been preserved in the Saint-Paul family archives, the responses to his questionnaires on inversion appear to have been lost. See the introductory essay in this volume.

the born invert and the occasional invert and that the answers to my questionnaire on sexual inversion confirm absolutely the theories that I espouse." It is clear that Saint-Paul was taking care to show respect for the publications of his colleagues. In the conclusion to this chapter, he affirmed: "We must not forget that '*normality*' or '*the normal*' does not exist in reality. There is no such thing as a perfectly or fully normal type in the human species."[30]

The final chapter of Saint-Paul's book contains a summary of the arguments presented in the preceding chapters. He repeated his belief that it was futile to attempt to cure born inverts because such efforts would only worsen the already "corrupt" condition of the invert. Saint-Paul's attitude toward occasional inverts, however, is different and innovative—he recommended that they be given psychotherapy: "The anger, the sexual excitement, and the fears will diminish and even disappear if the occasional invert is allowed to talk, if he is given material to read, or if he is given advice. It is undeniable that one intelligent human being can influence another one."[31]

Saint-Paul believed that he had produced a very important book on inversion, and he expected that it would create a sensation among members of the medical community. His disappointment when it was greeted with almost total silence was understandable. In January 1897 he expressed his disappointment in a letter to Zola: "I believe it was virtually impossible for me to be more circumspect in my language, and, please excuse the choice of word—'conservative'—in my theory."[32] While it is true that Saint-Paul's basic theoretical positions on inversion did not differ dramatically from what had appeared in previous studies, some details of his argument triggered disagreement. For example, Augustin Hamon, who wrote the only review to appear in 1896, claimed that Saint-Paul's distinction between "perversion" and "perversity" was meaningless. He also criticized the study for its lack of concrete proposals to prevent or cure inversion. In addition, Saint-Paul's positive references to Raffalovich's work attracted nothing but

---

30. Laupts, *Tares et poisons*, 196, 277.
31. Laupts, *Tares et poisons*, 308.
32. Saint-Paul to Zola, January 28, 1897, Collection "Dr. François Émile-Zola." See the introductory essay in this volume.

scorn from Hamon: "*Uranisme et unisexualité* by André Raffalovich is a document of very little scientific value, except perhaps for the fact that it was probably written by a uranist."[33]

The best way to assess Saint-Paul's contribution to the study of inversion at the fin de siècle is perhaps to focus more on his methodology and less on his theoretical positions. Inversion, he believed, was a serious illness, and the doctor's ethical obligation was to study it in order to find a cure. He was convinced, like many of his medical colleagues, that the scientific investigations into inversion taking place in France were superior to what was happening elsewhere. There were, however, some aspects of his thinking that did set him apart from his contemporaries. He did not refer to the old idea of "degeneracy" in his explanation of the cause of inversion, nor did he think it useful to see inversion as a phenomenon caused largely by hereditary factors. He was not interested in making correlations between the behavior of inverts and physiological traits. Saint-Paul criticized some of his contemporaries for their obsession with creating elaborate taxonomies and for treating those taxonomies as ends in themselves. Although he did subscribe to the view that there existed two categories of inverts (born and occasional), the primary thrust of his research was to seek a deeper understanding of the occasional invert and to propose a cure. What can be seen as innovative and progressive is the meticulous attention that Saint-Paul exercised in preparing the questionnaires used in his field research. There is considerable merit, as well, in the way that Saint-Paul presented his two main case studies in *Tares et poisons*. He spared no detail in describing all aspects of the lives of the young Italian and Oscar Wilde. Some of his turns of phrase are striking: "To love oneself is to be an invert."[34]

One of the particularly revealing moments in Saint-Paul's discussion of inversion occurred when he wrote about "desire," as in the following sentence: "The intensity of our desire is perhaps the most specific aspect of our subjectivity."[35] What he was implying here was that the sexual desire

---

33. Augustin Hamon, review of *Tares et poisons* in *La Société Nouvelle* (September 1896): 428–29. In a private letter to Saint-Paul dated July 1, 1896, Hamon wrote: "Raffalovich is a sodomite" (SPFA). Raffalovich referred to himself and other homosexuals as "uranists."

34. Laupts, *Tares et poisons*, 337.

35. Laupts, *Tares et poisons*, 98.

of the invert had its own unique characteristics, and that it should be studied as such. Saint-Paul's position was therefore forward-looking. It foreshadowed those developments in twentieth-century psychoanalysis that gave priority to the concept of desire (for example, in the theory of Jacques Lacan). In this sense, Saint-Paul's thinking was ahead of its time.

First Edition (1896)

EDITORIAL COMMENT BY CLIVE THOMSON
AND MICHAEL ROSENFELD

Saint-Paul first published his "Inquiry Into Sexual Inversion: Questionnaire" in the *Archives d'Anthropologie Criminelle* in 1894 and then an updated version in his book *Tares et poisons* in 1896.[1] Intended as a guide for medical practitioners while interviewing their patients with an "abnormal inclination" toward people of their own sex, the aim of the questionnaire was to gather detailed information on the causes of these feelings. The questionnaire reflected the scientific thought of the time that focused on heredity as the main origin for what was perceived as a neurological or cerebral abnormality. What is especially revealing in these theories are the queries about feminine traits in gay men or masculine ones in lesbians. Such questions were based on a belief that certain physical characteristics could be interpreted as signs of homosexual tendencies. Saint-Paul's more modern approach is revealed toward the end of the survey (section H), where the doctor recommended that patients be asked how they perceive their same-sex attraction, how they explain it, and what they see as its cause. This interest in the psychology of these women and men showed a certain measure of empathy for them, as well as a willingness to give them a voice by publishing their responses in his book.

We have not yet discovered the replies to the questionnaire in the Saint-Paul family archives, nor in the Lacassagne archives at the Bibliothèque

---

1. Dr. Laupts [Georges Saint-Paul], "Enquête sur inversion sexuelle: questionnaire-plan," *Archives d'Anthropologie Criminelle* 9 (1894): 105–8; Dr. Laupts [Georges Saint-Paul], *Tares et poisons. Perversion et perversité sexuelles* (Paris: Georges Carré, 1896), 39–45.

Municipale de Lyon.[2] There are some indications that the Italian was guided by the questionnaire while writing his 1896 letter to Saint-Paul. Some of the other men who wrote to the doctor refer to the questionnaire in their letters.

We have also translated Saint-Paul's acknowledgments to his colleagues that were published at the end of the first chapter of his book. Saint-Paul's openness to a variety of theories can be seen in the way he consulted colleagues not only in France but also in Russia, the United States, Austria-Hungary, the United Kingdom, and Germany.

The introduction to the Italian's text contains Saint-Paul's opinion of the Italian as someone with "tainted instincts." This view was nuanced as he also defined the Italian as someone who was "able to determine his psychology" and who had a voice, which he repeatedly stated was "*true, entirely authentic.*" Even though he censored parts of the text and delegitimatized some of the Italian's feelings, he did not suppress those passages in which the Italian expressed his right to love freely. Saint-Paul categorized different kinds of "inverts," conceding that those he considered "born inverts," such as the Italian, were not to blame for being a woman in a man's body (a definition the Italian categorically refuted). The doctor criticized "born inverts" when they seduced men who were attracted to their feminine characteristics, a behavior that he defined as "perversion" or "perversity." Once seduced, these men developed a "predisposition" toward homosexuality that could be transmitted to their children. Another scientific hypothesis to which the doctor adhered was that homosexuality was contagious, a theory he developed further in the introduction and in the conclusion to the second edition of his book in 1910.

Inquiry Into Sexual Inversion: Questionnaire

Dear Reader:[3]

The research that I have undertaken in the laboratory of forensic medicine at the University of Lyon includes several psychological surveys, the

---

2. Saint-Paul had requested that the replies be sent to Dr. Lacassagne in Lyon in 1894 and to his editor, Georges Carré, in Paris in 1896. Thus, if they still existed, they would be in either his archives or Lacassagne's archives.

3. This questionnaire was originally published in "Enquête sur inversion sexuelle: questionnaire-plan" (1894) and was republished with major changes in *Tares et poisons*

first of which has already yielded significant results. It owes some of its interest to the considerable number of famous writers who agreed to participate in it by providing insight into their inner speech. Our work, however, is aimed at everyone, no matter his profession. One simply needs a keen sense of observation.

The question that concerns us today is that of "*sexual inversion,*" that is to say, the abnormal inclination, platonic or not, of one person for another person of the same sex. However, in a general sense, we are studying all sexual deviations.

Let us also hope, Sir, that you will be willing to help us as promptly as you can with observations, notes, documents, and confessions that you have collected in social circles that your profession, as a writer, professor, lawyer, or doctor, has enabled you to examine and study.

In any case, Sir, we hope that you would agree to answer the questions in the first paragraph, at the very least. After that, we have included an outline intended to facilitate the organization of the information that you would consent to send us, but you are free to ignore this schema in part or in its entirety.

With our sincere thanks, we end our request by asking you to write your answers only on one side of each page, if possible, and to indicate very clearly the sections that you would like to keep anonymous, or, if you wish, you could keep your entire response anonymous. And finally, please direct all replies to Dr. Lacassagne, Professor at the University of Lyon, Faculty of Forensic Medicine, Quai Claude Bernard, Lyon.[4]

[I. A GUIDE INTENDED TO FACILITATE ANSWERS

This paragraph should be answered by all respondents.

With reference to Lacassagne in *Vade mecum du médicin légiste / My Guide to Forensic Medicine* and the section on forensic investigations in Chevalier's work, page 448 onward, we find the following:

A. Heredity.—Family Tree.—Ancestry going back two to three generations. Collateral branches. Notions of heredity; do not limit it to direct or similar heredity; try to bring out the development of neuroses and

---

(1896). We are translating the second version here.

4. In the 1896 edition, the parts that follow and are enclosed in brackets are found in a note. We have reproduced them as part of the text. Most of this does not appear in the 1894 article.

psychoses. Search for the existence of nervous or psychopathological traits, convulsive sicknesses (chorea, general paralysis, apoplexy), signs of degeneration (unusual sensations, mental deficiencies, moral defects, eccentric behavior, vagrancy, mental debility, outbursts of delirium), alcoholism, inbreeding, exaggerated age differences, etc. . . .—Indicate the manner of death for relations: apoplexy, suicide, dementia, etc. . . .

B. Personal Antecedents (biography).—Intra-uterine development (mother's frights, traumas, acute illnesses). Birth at term or not. Infancy: walking, talking, teething.—Convulsions, episodes, symptoms of meningeal chorea.—Intellectual aptitude at school.—Upbringing. Education.—Tendencies, bad instincts, vices, insubordination, wickedness, lying, vagrancy, thievery.—Impulsive acts.—Puberty: development.—Repeated psychic disorders: emotionalism, exaltation, religiosity, fears.—Nervous disorders: headaches, migraines, convulsive fits, hysterical attacks, delusional episodes. Concussions.—Hysterical traumas.

INITIAL SIGNS OF SEXUALITY. REGARDING
CURRENT CONDITION

A. Physical condition.—Focus primarily on secondary sexual characteristics and note the signs of degeneration and physical defects. Morphology. General Appearance. Height and bone structure. Head: cranial, facial, or palatal asymmetries.—Ears.—Jaw: prognathism, dentition, harelip. Facial features: appearance, look. Voice: timbre, volume. Breasts: their development. Pelvis: width, height. Genital organs: various defects. Hernias. Fingers and toes: anomalies of the extremities. Skin: body hair, beard

B. Physical functions.—Health.—Investigate signs of functional degeneration. Temperament. Physiognomy, attitudes, gestures, manner of speaking, gait, deportment. General sensitivity.—Lack of feeling, hyperesthesia. Senses: impressionability, perversions. Anomalies in the interior of the eye. Repeated headaches.—Migraines, dizziness, vertigo, insomnia. Muscle contractions: convulsive movements, tics, spasmodic contractions, cramps, tremors. Circulation: pulse rate, palpitations. Digestive functions: appetite, overindulgence, alcoholism, constipation. Functions of the skin: sweating. Genital functions: potency, excitability.—Nocturnal emissions.—Venereal excesses. Neurasthenic ailments: tension headaches, painful sensations in the fingers and toes, constant fatigue, gastric phenomena, palpitations, etc. . . .

C. Mental faculties.—Tally and evaluate the psychic defects and episodic syndromes. Moral sensitivity.—Perversion of feelings.—Emotionalism, imaginary fears, obsessions, fixed ideas.—Irritability.—Fits of rage. Feelings of affection or family feelings.—Sympathies and antipathies. Survival instinct or destructive instinct.—Prodigality or greed.—Meanness, meekness, or mockery.—Hypochondria, melancholy, defiance.—Persecution complex.—Hallucinations: Intelligence.—Intellectual level.—Lapses: lack of balance.—Investigate memory, attention, imagination, cognitive ability (to accept or reject ideas), to analyze or to synthesize, to generalize, to speculate.—Syllogistic ability: judgment, paradoxes.—Particular talents: mathematical, musical, etc. . . .—Delusional beliefs.

Activity and Character.—Volition, instability, perseverance.—Timidity and courage.—Laziness.—Periodic episodes of enthusiasm or discouragement, of agitation or pressure, of expansion or contraction.—Inequalities: lack of a sense of decorum, eccentricities, vagrancy.—Irresistible impulses.—Moral sense, ethical failings.—Excesses of subjectivity; egoism, vanity, ambition; hyperbolic personality. Moral perversions.—Base passions.—Immorality and cynicism. Moral insanity. (Chevalier)[5]

What are your ideas, theories, and hypotheses on these questions? What do you think are the causes of this illness, of its extent, and of its cures?

Do you have documents relating to inversion, such as confessions of inverts? Can you send them to us?

II. OBSERVATIONS ABOUT A SPECIFIC SUBJECT

A. Personal and hereditary antecedents, from the physical and moral perspective.—Current age.—Sex.—Race.—Profession (if possible).

B. Physical attributes (born inverts with defects).—Physical and anatomical anomalies: effeminacy, slightness of form, enlarged hips, rounded breasts, atrophy of the muscles, sparse body hair, etc. . . . , in men; . . . the opposite traits, masculine aspects in women.[6]

---

5. Another student of Dr. Lacassagne, Julien Chevalier, wrote his dissertation on "the inversion of the sexual instinct" in 1885 and revised it for publication as Une Maladie de la personalité: L'inversion sexuelle / An Illness of the Personality: Sexual Inversion in 1893.

6. Note in the edition of 1896: "Please mention carefully, if possible, all the deviations, all the deformities, of all the organs, particularly those of reproduction."

C. The subject's history. Childhood.—Anomalies.—At what age did they appear? Vices that occur frequently in schools and dormitories.—Perversion of the sexual instinct. *Love for a person of the same sex who seems to be a paragon of this sex* (that is, the masculine-loving male invert who loves very strong and very masculine men, and the female invert who loves very feminine women).—*Love for a person of the same sex who resembles the opposite sex* because of his physique, his emotions, or his personality (that is, the male invert, either feminine-loving or pedophile, who loves effeminate men, or the female born invert who loves women with masculine characteristics).—Love that the subject tolerates.—Love that is forced on the subject.—*Indifferent love* that, depending on the circumstance, takes as its object someone of the same sex, or someone of the opposite sex.—Love for an old man, an animal (bestiality), a cadaver (necrophilia), or an inanimate object (azoophilia). Hatred or indifference toward the sex that should normally be loved. Love that requires the sight of blood or the smell of offensive odors.—Fetishistic love (love of an appendage: of a foot or a hand).

At what age did the first outward signs of sexuality appear? At what age did the first deviant tendencies appear?

Repressed tendencies. Satisfied ones.

Sexual acts, the subject's role (active or passive): regrets, jealousies, etc. . . .

Adolescence, Youth, Maturity.—Same outline as the preceding. In addition: For women: menstruation: regular or not? At what age did it begin? Pregnancies or abortions; menopause, puerperal insanity, etc. . . . Occasional inversion due to particular circumstances, in particular, seclusion in an abnormally single-sex environment.

For both sexes: adolescent crises; marriage or celibacy; impotence; sterility. The appearance of abnormalities; diminution, aggravation, or disappearance of these abnormalities.

Old age: same outline as the preceding. In addition: inappropriate sexual interest in children.

D. The category in which the observed subject places himself:

Born inverts with physical defects: feminine-form if he is a man; masculine-form if she is a woman.

Born inverts without physical defects: if he is a man: one who is searching for a man who is more masculine than he is, or one who is searching for a man who is less masculine than he is. If she is a woman: one who is searching for a woman who is very feminine, or one who is searching for a woman who is less feminine than she is.

E. Coexisting functional abnormalities: hallucinations, tics, manias, signs of degeneration, according to Magnan.[7]—Deviations, associated perversions, whether in-born or acquired.

F. Illegal acts committed and subsequent criminal penalties: condemnations: fines, imprisonments.

G. Instincts. Maternal instinct (absent, enhanced, or reduced?)

Instinct for self-preservation (deviation: fear, egoism, avarice, alcoholism?)

Constructive instinct.—Destructive instinct.—Altruistic instinct (philanthropy).—Character: courage, caution, perseverance.—Intelligence: intellectual, literary, scientific, or artistic aptitude.

H. *How does the subject see himself? How does he explain himself? To what does he attribute his anomaly or anomalies?*

We will gratefully accept and acknowledge all the information that is received, even if it is only indirectly related to the topic or if it deals only with a specific part of the program that we have just outlined.[8]]

[ACKNOWLEDGMENTS]

[A certain number of people were willing to answer us, with either observations or confessions that they had received. Some sent us studies that were very original. We are going to examine the most interesting ones, but before doing that, I must thank:[9]

Émile Zola for the interest that he showed in my study. I owe him a great deal for everything that he has so kindly sent me: for the letter that has become a very remarkable preface to my work, and for the confession that a sick man with congenital inversion sent him and that I am publishing under the title *The Novel of an Invert*. His well-deserved popularity, his sincerity that is not compromised by any false modesty, his boldness, and his

---

7. Valentin Magnan (1835–1916) was the chief doctor at the Hôpital Sainte-Anne in Paris, a mental asylum, where he formulated a theory on the effect of hereditary degeneration on the mental health of his patients. He also wrote a treatise on "sexual abnormalities, aberrations, and perversions" in 1885.

8. The following note appeared in the original 1894 article: "We recommend Lacassagne's classification to our readers who want to get a clear idea of the question. For more information, they may also benefit greatly by consulting Chevalier's book."

9. This whole section of acknowledgments does not appear in the 1894 article.

genius as a writer have earned him the trust of many unfortunate individuals. Among the many documents that are scattered throughout the voluminous correspondence of this celebrated writer, *The Novel of an Invert* is one of the most startling. On this subject, all my thanks goes to Émile Zola. I add to this my deepest gratitude for the warm welcome that I always found at his home.

My esteemed adviser, *Professor Lacassagne*, to whom I am again very happy to express my admiration and my respectful friendship.

I am also very grateful to Mr. *Dmitry Stefanowsky*, assistant to the imperial prosecutor at Kharkov; Mr. *Macdonald* of the Department of Education in Washington; Mr. *Patté*, my friend; Mr. *[Adrien] Storck*, my friend and publisher; Mr. *[Georges] Carré*; Mr. *L. Dugas*; Mr. *Mario Pilo*; Mr. *Max Dessoir*; *Baron Schrenck-Notzing*; the eminent philosopher *Tarde*; all of whom contributed to my inquiry.[10] To *Krafft-Ebing* and *Moll*,[11] I express my sincere admiration for their beautiful and solid works, certain passages of which I recommend to readers as particularly important.

But it is Mr. *André Raffalovich*, above all, whom I must acknowledge, not only for the friendly expression of unwavering sympathy, but also for the generosity with which he has placed at my disposition the studies he published in the *Archives d'Anthropologie Criminelle*—studies of a profound and

---

10. Beyond the information that Saint-Paul provided in the text, we have been unable to find information about all these men. However, Adrien Storck was the publisher in Lyon of *Archives d'Anthropologie Criminelle*, where the first version of "The Novel of an Invert" appeared in 1894–1895, and Georges Carré was the publisher in Paris who issued the first edition of Saint-Paul's book in 1896. Mario Pilo (1859–1920) was an Italian expert on art and music whose work on the psychology of art and beauty was translated into several languages. Max Dessoir (1867–1947) was a German philosopher and psychologist who wrote an article on the evolution of the sexual instinct in 1894 that influenced Sigmund Freud and others. Albert Freiherr von Schrenck-Notzing (1862–1929) was a German physician and psychiatrist who wrote a treatise on *Therapeutic Suggestions in Psychopathia Sexualis with Special Reference to Contrary Sexual Instinct*. Gabriel Tarde (1843–1904) served as a magistrate before becoming a professor of philosophy at the Collège de France, specializing in criminology; he was known for his acute observations on the social conditions of crime.

11. The famous Austrian psychiatrist Richard von Krafft-Ebing (1840–1902) was the author of *Psychopathia sexualis*, which was published in several editions and translated in many languages. Albert Moll (1862–1939) was a German psychiatrist, one of the founders of the new field of sexology. The French edition of his work was published in 1893 by Saint-Paul's publisher, Georges Carré.

true philosophy—studies that I reproduce in this work. Among these studies, the one on Wilde is particularly valuable, because of the profound knowledge that Mr. Raffalovich has about life in London.

I must add that my research is far from complete, and that I will gladly and gratefully accept all new responses, all unedited documents, from far and wide, that concern inversion.[12]]

Inquiry Into Sexual Inversion: Responses

The first results of our inquiry, published on January 15, 1894, were not long in coming.[13] Mr. André Raffalovich sent us some curious and interesting observations in response to the first paragraph of the questionnaire;[14] we are also infinitely grateful to Mr. Émile Zola, who has generously provided us with an extremely interesting document.

In addition to this, he has promised to send us other notes and thoughts on the topic. His well-deserved popularity, his sincerity that is not compromised by any false modesty, his boldness, and his genius as a writer have earned him the trust of many unfortunate individuals who are suffering from this terrible deviation, which the uneducated man considers a disgrace and the thinking man a deformity. Sadly, many of these documents are scattered throughout the voluminous correspondence of this celebrated writer. Let us hope that they will be recovered.

In the meantime, I am offering my sincerest thanks for this *Novel of an Invert*, which I will begin to publish today. It is the true story of a man with an illustrious name, a very well-respected name in Italy. As accurate as a scientific observation, as interesting as a novel, as sincere as a confession, it is perhaps the most complete and the most engaging narrative of this genre.

---

12. Note in the 1896 edition: "Please address all psychological documents (especially those dealing with inversion or suicide, which are particularly useful at this moment) to Dr. Laupts, c/o Mr. Carré, publisher, Rue Racine 3, Paris."

13. The text in this section was published in Dr. Laupts [Georges Saint-Paul], "Enquête sur l'inversion sexuelle: Réponses," *Archives d'Anthropologie Criminelle* 9 (1894): 211–12.

14. Raffalovich sent Saint-Paul a long response to the questionnaire, which he later published as "L'Uranisme. Inversion sexuelle Congénitale. Observations et conseils," *Archives d'Anthropologie Criminelle* 10 (1895): 99–127.

Observations: Feminine-Form Born Invert Type

A confession addressed to Émile Zola.[15]—*The Novel of an Invert.*—I. Letter to Émile Zola. Antecedents and infancy.—II. Childhood and first deviations.—III. Adolescence and first acts.—IV. Postscript. Second document. New confessions.—V. Third document, last postscript.—Value of the observation from the scientific point of view: clarification of the types designated in the novel: the feminine-form born invert; the occasional woman-loving invert; the pervert.

[INTRODUCTION]

One of the advantages of a psychological inquiry is to shed light onto certain documents that are enveloped in obscurity. Truthfully, this has not been the case with *The Novel of an Invert*. For a long time, Émile Zola knew its value. As soon as he knew about my research, he offered it to me. I accepted it gladly and published it in *Archives d'Anthropologie Criminelle et de Psychologie Normale et Pathologique / Archives of Criminal Anthropology and Pathological and Normal Psychology*.

This confession is sincere; it is true—derived from a truth that we feel from its emotion and its sadness, which sometimes take the lead in the course of its recital. Sometimes the writer feels almost like a deformity or a monstrosity, a useless and dangerous being, an abnormal being in the midst of human society, judged by the examples that he provides, by the lust that he exhibits. Without a doubt, at certain moments, when the memory of guilty pleasures returns to his imagination, passion becomes the be-all and end-all. However, when encountering most documents of this kind, this confession also contains, from its portrayal of tainted instincts, what is indispensable to know about those instincts in order to have a precise idea about the author, to understand his feelings, his needs, his desires, and his thoughts; in a word, to be able to determine his psychology. He does not misuse vulgar language or licentious images. From a very aristocratic background, having had a privileged upbringing, naturally refined, living in a particularly sensitive milieu, he knows all too well what he owes to the illustrious writer in whom he confides; his objective is none other than to reveal the best and worst of himself, exposing his wounds and delving into them, it is true, but only to make them known

---

15. We are presenting in this section the introductory and concluding remarks to chapter 2 of Saint-Paul's *Tares et poisons* (1896), 46–47, 93–104.

in psychological terms, for the most part, though at times his exposition is disrupted by searing memories of adored and accursed sins.

I thought it necessary to render certain sections in Latin. This was not necessary in a scientific study of inversion, but I did so here for the sake of readers unfamiliar with medical treatises who might come across this document.

[Text of The Novel of an Invert]

[CONCLUSION]

This is the document that was sent to me by Émile Zola.[16] It is very interesting, and the attentive observer can distinguish in it several types of inverts, all very different from each other, and in particular the contrast between them that is depicted so well makes the characters in this story strikingly memorable. If one had wanted to write a case study on the most typical cases of inversion, one could not have succeeded better in presenting them, making them come alive, and setting them in motion, at least in my opinion. And this *Novel of an Invert* has the advantage of being a *true, entirely authentic* story for which we have definite proof. Its cry of pain would be convincing in itself, especially since, at times, interrupting the recollections of evil and perverse joys, a lament bursts forth from the author of these lines, who sees himself to be a defective being, a deformity, an evil thing, an unnatural creature, with no use or benefit to anyone.

Without unduly emphasizing the information this observation provides, I believe that it is useful from the point of view of inversion to say a few words about the characteristics of some of the individuals in this novel, which is especially valuable for the contrasts that it reveals between the

---

16. Original note in the 1896 edition: "There is also a postscript: a postcard addressed to 'Émile Zola, Writer, Paris.' This final document is very interesting because it shows us the preference for the act, so long refrained from for fear of pain, that awaited only the right moment, circumstance, or, let's put it most explicitly, the practical means of achieving it. This preference is innate in the feminine-form born invert: from early youth onward, it existed in him. (See the section on Childhood: 'Furiosa cupiebam ardebam ut aliquid facerem ex hoc inguine quod dextram totam implebat, acriterque cupiebam in corpore meo foramen esse quo in me posset introduce quod tam vehementer apppetebam.'" [English translation: "I had an overwhelming desire to do something with this virile member that filled my whole hand, and I so desperately wanted an orifice in my body to put it in—this thing that was the object of all my desires."])

weak invert and the *strong invert*, between the *feminine form* of inversion and the *pedophilic form* of inversion.

The author of this novel is a born invert in the feminine form; he is the classic type of a defective person, of a sick man. This individual is a woman, both physically and morally. Physically, we are convinced of it by reading the very detailed descriptions in which he repeatedly refers to his feminine attributes that strike everyone who meets him for the first time. He has slender joints, a fine-boned face, and wide hips that at first glance make us uncertain about the sex of this almost beardless youth whose closest relatives and servants have, with great pleasure, treated as a girl and called *Mademoiselle* since he was a child. No doubt his genital organs are male, but all the secondary sexual characteristics are female, and that is what reveals the hesitation, the uncertainty, and the error that are at the origin of his constitution and have guided the development of such a being. One could say that he is "a failed hermaphrodite."

Mentally and morally, even more than through his outward appearance and gestures, he is a woman. Unlike other boys whose earliest point of pride is to put on trousers, his had been not to wear them. His first great sorrow, he declared, was to have been forced to wear boys' clothing. This desire to be a woman, to dress as a woman, persisted throughout his whole life. No doubt, in response to this tendency, to this pressing need for him to identity as a woman, he continues to dress up in women's clothing as often as possible, for himself and for his friends, out of both preference and pleasure. This is a common trait in all feminine-form born inverts.

To this first symptom, to this first indication of his strange and abnormal sexuality, which was evident since his earliest childhood years, was added, since the first stirrings of puberty, another indisputable sign: a lack of interest in girls and an excessive and exaggerated friendship for boys. From an early age, male genitalia attracted him, and thanks to the complicity of servants, he satisfied his overwhelming curiosity, perhaps too strong to be normal.

On this subject, it is necessary, I believe, to make a few remarks. An exaggerated friendship between very young people cannot and does not necessarily lead to a diagnosis of inversion for them. At the onset of puberty—an onset that is earlier in our race than is generally acknowledged—the genital instinct begins to manifest itself in a very powerful way. If at this time the desires of the youth, often still very platonic, cannot be directed toward a young girl, either because of the particular circumstances or because of the confinement or the segregation of these boys in private schools or boarding schools; if too many young men are shielded from all *discrete* feminine influence just when it would be most necessary for them; if puberty is obstructed by one of these abnormal conglomerations of male youths, where it cannot manifest itself according to its natural instincts, or at least according to its normal tendencies, then it often leads, in the overstimulation of aroused desires, to a genuine licentiousness, at least in the imagination, and sometimes it is susceptible to being expressed, if not by acts of genuine inversion, at the very least by all sorts of sexual experimentation either by boys alone or together. One must never have listened to the conversations of these young people, or have seen the obscene caricatures that circulated in their classrooms, or have voluntarily closed one's eyes to these *misdemeanors*[17] in order to believe that the passages in this confession, no matter how revolting, regarding the first acts of curiosity that were satisfied by servants, were really the symptom of a specific perversion. Perhaps only the intensity of desire is an indication of the particular condition of this subject.

This is a point that is overlooked in our morals and customs. In our educational institutions we do not anticipate the onset of puberty with all its disastrous consequences. We still have to establish a system of diversions—physical and intellectual exercises—that build up the muscles, engage the imagination, and tire out the body without exhausting it during this time in life.

If this is not done, you will see secret vices take hold of many young men, not for the vast majority of them, but for some. The onset and development of very passionate friendships that develop between young members of the same sex—very intense, very sincere, more often than not exclusively platonic—something that happens more frequently, perhaps, between young girls—are dangerous because they impede the normal evolution of sexuality and affect future generations' heredity with unnatural tendencies and predispositions.

At this age, curiosity and the need to know are so acute, and they are so thoroughly ignored by teachers and parents who prefer to leave to chance bad companions and poorly understood dictionaries the task of

---

17. "Misdemeanors" is in English in the original text.

informing the child about the facts of pregnancy and procreation. If the child is intelligent, he will seek that knowledge, and despite everything, he will succeed in finding it. He learns about it from older companions who are already perverted; if, like the author of our confession, he is not in a high school but raised carelessly and in isolation—another danger—in close contact with servants who will sometimes enjoy teasing him, occasionally by corrupting him, the most extraordinary beliefs and the most unrealistic and absurd ideas about depravity will take root in the boy's mind, no matter how virginal or naïve he was until then.

How many men—and not the least distinguished of them who have become the most normal adults—would blush—not to say, must blush—at the memory of what they said, heard, or did at that stage in their lives! How many of them would be astonished if they could identify in their memories of puberty the role that the sexual instinct played, often without their realizing it, in the inception and development of their first friendships.

Friendship is, above all, one of the emotions of our earliest years—that is indisputable. It is thus natural in young people to feel it so intensely, but we must beware of all *exaggerated* and *instinctive* friendships between two young adolescent boys. Most of these friendships remain platonic; they are no less dangerous, though; they create habits and bad tendencies, abnormal ones; they reveal a condition we need to keep an eye on, depending on the case, with varying degrees of urgency.

In fact, the danger is quite different when the abnormal tendency is the result of a lack of representatives of the opposite sex who would normally be objects of affection, or when it is a spontaneous, instinctive, and inescapable expression of an innate tendency. Deprived of feminine love, many physically male individuals—who are male in desire as well—transfer to those who resemble females a need for affection that could not be directed to the normal object it would naturally have been directed to. Thus, either they are attracted to normal, feminine-form men—bothering them sometimes with declarations of a very ardent friendship—or they are attracted to feminine-form born inverts, like the one in this novel. In that case, things become much more serious: the born invert, if he enjoys it, will respond to the desire of the adolescent who seeks and loves in him the woman that he really is; he will pervert him, and if circumstances do not extract him from this bad company, he will turn him into a genuine invert; he will give him the taste for the strange, the abnormal, and the pedophilic.

That is what the author of *The Novel of an Invert* reveals to us. Completely a woman because of the delicacy and oddness of his body, because of his fickle, coquettish, vain, and flighty personality, finally and especially because of *his desire for men, his complete lack of sexual desire for women, his contempt, his hatred, and his disgust for women from the sexual point of view*, he does not hesitate to seduce a young man, a very masculine and very handsome one, probably a normal man up to that point, and one who succumbs to an attraction to him as if he were attracted by a woman, yielding to an almost normal love, yielding also, perhaps, as he hints in one of his postscripts,[18] due to certain financial considerations.

Be that as it may, the seduction of this young man seems unjustifiable to us, certainly, but understandable. Just as one is fundamentally and completely inverted, *in the beginning*, the other, by contrast, may necessarily be much less so. What we can say about the person who is the author of this confession is that he is a woman. Consequently, there is almost no inversion in the young petty officer who is well and truly a man; he went with him as he would have gone with one of those women whom he rarely visited because "he had so little money."

I would like to sketch out here the evolution of this acquired inversion, which is, in the beginning, hardly inversion at all, but which ends by becoming a perversity. Let us imagine this young petty officer leaving his village, timid, awkward, without money, almost virginal, all attributes that isolate him from the sex that normally ought to be loved. Let us even assume he has a nobler sentiment: a disgust for venal love and the common prostitutes, the only ones he could afford. One evening, intoxicated with wine, he let himself get drunk by a quasi-feminine being who used all his innate cunning, all the mannerisms of a fine and aristocratic nature, all the cajoleries of a charming child, feigning a complete and exquisite naïveté. He succumbed. By this, I understand that he allowed himself to feel a very tender sentiment for this ephebe and to yield to minor sexual acts. He was guilty, but his actions certainly do not reveal a defect, an innate deformity, a sickness, a *genuine* perversion. It was only familiarity and the sexual activities of his friend, every day a little more daring, that distanced him more and more from normal feelings and inculcated in

---

18. The passage to which Saint-Paul referred is found in the main part of one of the letters, not in one of the postscripts. In this collection, see the subsection of *The Novel of the Invert* titled "Third Document (1888 or 1889)."

him the desire more and more, not just for men, but for young men, which made this individual either indifferent in sexual matters or a genuine invert.

After returning to healthy habits, if this individual should marry, he would probably pass on to his children a troubling predisposition, a tendency toward inversion, which, without the physical signs, will make them the type we could call *predisposed cerebral born–inverts*.

If he lacks the courage to resist debauchery and to become a man once again, if he does not change his milieu, if he does not meet a woman in his life who will rescue him from habits that are becoming ever more entrenched, that have become completely victorious, sometimes even exclusive, then he will become completely inverted and wholly perverted. It seems naïve to repeat, and yet we must not forget, an observation as old as the world that can be traced back to Aristotle, I believe: "Habit is second nature." This is entirely true regarding the sexual instinct as it is in all other things; and it explains perfectly how an individual who is normal can become perverted. Why would the human body not submit to unnatural sexual acts, since it submits, in the context of respiration, circulation, and nutrition, to necessary acts that seem to be a priori much more damaging?

The perverts created in this way, at times entirely manufactured, will become in their turn elements of disorder and debauchery, on the lookout for unnatural tendencies, in search of people whose sexual equilibrium seems less stable; with the greatest of ease, they will find the born inverts, the weak personalities, who are easy to dominate, and to whom they will give their first lessons in debauchery.

Thus it is with the captain in his novel, this real satyr, for whom every part of the body must provide sexual pleasure, this truly perverted being who pursues men and women indiscriminately, but who maintains, no doubt, an especially distinct predilection for young boys. Certainly, we cannot say that it was he who is responsible for corrupting the main character of this novel, but he did introduce him while still very young to evil pleasures. He corrupted him entirely, gave this adolescent, who only wanted to learn, a complete education. He was the first to suggest to him the idea of "pederasty," as properly understood, which the young boy rejected at first, not out of disgust, or out of a lack of desire, but out of the fear of pain.

I do not think I need to delve any further into all the aspects of the psychology of this novel: it is simple and speaks for itself. The extraordinary vanity, the lack of affect, the minimal amount of filial love on the part of the novel's author, the acute pain, neither persistent nor very profound, of feeling abnormal, often the pleasure in being vicious and proud of his vice, and, in the end, the need to tell his story, to reveal himself entirely, as well as a thousand other details, all this must provide, for the acute observer or the doctor who studies inversion, evidence to classify this person among the ones I call *feminine-form born inverts*. The lack of balance in his personality and the special psychology of this person are easily explained, as is the case with all feminine-form born inverts. Sexual appetite is the primary, the most powerful of all the instincts, and the only indispensable one for the survival of our species. It determines male or female psychology in men and women. In a being as complicated as the born invert, it must therefore produce forms that are completely incongruous and strange, dominated by anxiety and the lack of balance; other than in a few rare exceptions, it definitively affects the person in whom the basic drive of life, procreation, is hindered or eliminated. Everything that suppresses, abolishes, or degrades an individual's sexuality instills in him problems with mental health. No doubt, in our day, the incidence of degeneration and manias, which is expressed by a tendency for suicide or phobias, etc., springs from the fact that in our nation, the procreative functions, in most cases, often do not accomplish what they are supposed to do normally. Thus it is incumbent on us, for the vitality and the future of the race, to study the causes of pathology and to identify dangerous and bad elements among those who, in significant numbers, must be classified as persons afflicted by sexual perversion: the pervert and the feminine-form born invert.

In Memoriam: Émile Zola

EDITORIAL COMMENT BY CLIVE THOMSON
AND MICHAEL ROSENFELD

This document was first published in the medical journal *Archives d'Anthropologie Criminelle*, and then as an off-print under the same title.[1] The recently discovered letters exchanged between Saint-Paul, his wife Yvonne, and Zola's wife Alexandrine after the death of Émile Zola on September 29, 1902,[2] allow us to retrace how their friendship evolved. On October 13, 1902, the doctor sent Mme Zola a condolence letter, to which she replied a few days later. Except for a short thank-you note in 1904 from Mme Zola, they did not communicate until February 1907, when Mme Zola learned via a mutual acquaintance that Saint-Paul was stationed in Villefrance-sur-Mer, just fifteen kilometers from Monaco, where she was currently staying as a guest of Prince Albert of Monaco. They met and thus rekindled a friendship between the two families, which lasted until Mme Zola's death in 1925.

As Saint-Paul wrote in his article, Mme Zola revealed how much affection her late husband had for the young doctor who, uninvited, came knocking at his door and impressed him with his curiosity and intellect. Émile Zola's contribution to the doctor's doctoral thesis yielded two newspaper articles in *Le Journal* and *Le Figaro* and was a key document for the theory

---

1. Dr. Laupts [Georges Saint-Paul], "À la mémoire d'Émile Zola," *Archives d'Anthropologie Criminelle* 22, no. 168 (1907): 825–41. The off-print contained the following note: "Professor Lacassagne and the author authorize the reproduction of these pages consecrated to the memory of Émile Zola under the understanding that this article or the portion that is reproduced here is an excerpt from no. 168 of *Archives d'Anthropologie Criminelle, de Medicine Légale, et de Psychologie* (Lyon: A Rey et Cie.; Paris: Masson et Cie.)."

2. Michael Rosenfeld and Clive Thomson, "Lettres inédites."

Saint-Paul developed in his dissertation. A second important issue in this article was the doctor's account of his talks with Zola. It provides a rare glimpse into the novelist's ideas on homosexuality and the history of the Italian's text, which we study in our introduction to this book.

In Memoriam: Émile Zola

Nothing hardens men's hearts more than repeated successes. Perhaps that is because success is accorded not only to decent men. After they become famous, the politician, the man of letters, the doctor, the scientist, the powerful industrialist, and the ultra-rich merchant all forget their beginnings. The habit of being flattered does not make them more wary of the base compliments of flatterers, and the practical ability to take advantage of events—an aptitude worthy of victory—makes famous men prefer those who can be of service to them. The sweet sound of flattery and of self-interest, these are the only tunes that ring in their ears.

Then we must take their *indolence* into account. To make the necessary effort to help an author at the beginning of his career, to peruse a manuscript or to cut open the pages and read the newly published work of an unknown writer, is too much for literary giants, whose senses are dulled by the roar of the crowds. Believing themselves to be above humanity, they think they would be lowering themselves to communicate with anyone other than the high priests of their cult. Many famous men do not work at all; they believe that every single one of their words is made of gold and that, so long as their publisher pays them royally for their nonsense, it does not matter that ordinary people are languishing in a rut or are trying to climb out of a ditch to get back on the road.

In the end, the public's appetite for consumption is not limitless. To the extent that production responds to demand, it may happen that the market is saturated. Is it conceivable that a young man, full of talent, would cut into the profits of literary giants? *Talent*—that is the enemy! That is the motto of some.

When an author has become famous, and if his fame is the result of hard work and the advantages due to a powerful intellect, and when he remains accessible to the *young*, then his worth cannot be overstated.

Perhaps the future will be a happy one for up-and-coming writers. What I mean is that maybe the time will come when it will be a recognized truth that a superior man—a man useful to humanity—must be a man of integrity. While waiting for the hypothetical advent of this blessed era, many of us will have to note that only those who are truly great will be willing to take a few minutes from their leisure time to help, encourage, and advise the unfortunate ones who do not yet have the courage or the willpower.

I was twenty-two years old. I had just finished my studies. I was full of enthusiasm and presumptuousness, as is typical for a young man. I was full of dreams, completely confident in my future worth, but along with that, I was hardworking and determined to dedicate myself to a serious study, to devote all my effort and all my energy to it.

I knew almost nothing about life. I knew nothing about Paris. I arrived from Lyon, ready to challenge myself with a difficult task, with the advice of Lacassagne as my only guide.

The first impression that I had of the simplicity of a great man came from Alphonse Daudet.[3] I went to his house right away, without a second thought and with no inkling that a man like him might refuse to speak with a man like me. I will gladly describe his welcome, but not all his words, because some of them were not meant for the public.

Daudet spoke in the same way he wrote. He was a charming man with the most delicate and most profound talent that could be imagined. He spared no effort to help young men. Sometimes mixing a Provençal dialect with the purest French, he enchanted his attentive and respectful audience. He welcomed me without knowing anything about me. He did so because he knew Lacassagne. He admired the professor from Lyon. "Lacassagne," he said, "isn't a man; he's a world."[4]

We had much to discuss during our long conversations.

Daudet introduced me to his son Léon.[5] He wanted to make sure that I obtained an observation from him for my study on interior language. Léon Daudet was the first example of the existence of the audio-visual, the category based on him that I described for the first time in 1893, and to which

---

3. Alphonse Daudet (1840–1897) was a poet, playwright, and novelist, best known for his *Tartarin de Tarascon* series. He was the father of Edmée, Léon, and Lucien, all of whom, especially the latter two, had important careers in French literature and history.

4. Note in the original: "Daudet was very much interested in the work and theories of Lacassagne about whom he spoke with an enthusiastic warmth."

5. Léon Daudet (1868–1942) became a journalist for the right-wing, Royalist, Roman Catholic, anti-Semitic newspaper *L'Action française*.

I gave his name. Nowadays, it is recognized by all the specialists, both in France and abroad.

Daudet also enabled me to meet one of the Margueritte brothers,[6] and then a young writer, Mr. Léon Riotor,[7] who helped me enormously by trying to explain the nature and the purpose of my research to the readers of *Le Journal*.[8] His article, which caused quite a sensation, resulted in some interesting letters.

My relations with Daudet lasted until the day when that unrelenting illness deprived the world of letters of this unsurpassable storyteller, this exquisite and poignant novelist whose work will endure as long as humanity does. I could only wish that I could attain the level of talent necessary to describe this unfortunate great man, whose myopic eyes had difficulty discerning the letters that his crippled hand traced with so much pain. Sleep—divine sleep—the balm of wounded souls—and, one could add, the balm of sick organs—had long ago abandoned this unfortunate body, stricken by pain. I am only repaying my debt of gratitude by showing how good, how patient, how welcoming he was toward newcomers. . . . He spared no effort for them as long as they were willing.

It was not Daudet, however, who sent me to Zola. I believe at the time I arrived in Paris the two great novelists had already fallen out. I went to Zola's home without any introduction from anyone or anything to recommend me.

I encountered a gentleman with a handsome head and with a powerful intelligence. He was somewhat reserved. He did not talk idly, but once a subject interested him, he would discuss it with elegance and precision, and when he was gripped by enthusiasm, he became quite eloquent.

He thought the subject that concerned me was significant. I gave him one of the questionnaires that I had drawn up in Lacassagne's laboratory.

---

6. Paul Margueritte (1860–1918) was famous for his pantomimes. He collaborated with his brother Victor Margueritte (1866–1942), an army officer, who was a playwright and novelist as well.

7. Léon Riotor (1865–1946) was a poet, novelist, and art and literary critic.

8. Note in the original: "Not only did Mr. Riotor write some articles, but he was the conduit to a certain number of writers, and I owe to him the case studies of Claretie, Coppée, Coquelin the younger, Dubut de Laforest, and others. These documents supplemented—not without contrasts at times—those that I obtained from my teachers: Lacassagne, Renaut, Lépine, Augagueur, and others at the Faculty of Medicine in Lyon."

Its very complicated questions required a lot of attention and a few days' reflection. He read over the document with care, asked me for clarifications, and promised me to think about the subject. Several days later, he invited me back to his house.

He had thought deeply about the subject. At his invitation, I sat at his writing desk and wrote down, almost from his dictation, the observations that the readers of the *Figaro* and Lacassagne's *Archives* were the first to read.

I am not reproducing that study here. It is well known, and Zola was, afterward, examined with the most scrupulous attention by a doctor, Dr. Toulouse, who devoted an entire book to him.[9] I recall only two very interesting passages from the document that I received from Zola: one on the manner in which he worked, and the other on the power of his visualism.

> I collect as many documents as possible; I travel; I have to place myself in my subject's environment; I consult eyewitnesses about the facts that I want to describe; I do not invent anything. The novel makes itself; it evolves out of the materials. Thus, for The Debacle, I went to Sedan; I consulted the best sources of information; the characters appeared spontaneously. Did the novel need a colonel, captain, lieutenant, corporal, men? As soon as a character appears, I make him my own; I live with him; I am satisfied only with what takes root in my imagination. For me, words do not have much importance. . . .
>
> Already, at that time (during my childhood), my memory was what it is today. It took in information quickly and greedily and then released it. It was a sponge that soaked up everything and then emptied it out. It was an all-engulfing river whose flowing waters soon disappear into a sandbank. A very distinct characteristic of my memory is that my retention of memories depends on my desire and my choice to retain them. I have an excellent visual memory, but if I do not look with the intention of retaining it, then nothing remains; if I do not want to remember, then everything is lost. . . .
>
> After the research is done for a novel, I can recall, when I want to see them, all the memories that I need.
>
> My visual memories are powerful, extraordinary in three dimensions. My memory is enormous and prodigious. It troubles me. When I conjure up the objects that

---

9. Édouard Toulouse, *Enquête médico-psychologique sur les rapports de la supériorité intellectuelle avec la névropathie. I. Introduction générale: Émile Zola* (Paris: Sté. d'Éd. Scientifique, 1896).

I have seen, I see them again as they really are in their broad outlines, their shapes, their colors, their smell, and their sounds. It is a materialization to the extreme. The sun that was shining on them nearly blinds me; the smell suffocates me; the details catch hold of me and prevent me from seeing the totality. Also, in order to summon up the memory, I need to wait a certain time. I will not write my novel about Lourdes until next year; I will take up the notes I have collected; my memory will be refreshed; everything will be ready. The main supports and the cross beams of the whole structure will clearly stand out. . . .

This ability to summon up my memories doesn't last very long. The clarity of the image is so precise and so unbelievably intense; then the image fades away and disappears; it is gone. For me, this is a welcome occurrence. I have written many novels; I have accumulated a great deal of material. If all my memories stayed with me, I would crumble under their weight. As the novel progresses, this forgetting is even quicker. When I come to the end of the book that I am writing, I forget the beginning. I need an outline for each planned chapter; for twenty chapters, twenty detailed outlines. Then I start writing in peace. With this simple guide, I am sure not to lose my way. My desk blotter, filled with information, notes, news items, and reminders, is indispensable. I consult it endlessly. . . .

What I do best I do at the start. Fatigue comes quickly; with four or five pages written, I stop; I do not work more than three hours a day. I have the reputation of being a hard worker, but that is an error. I am very regular and very lazy. I work very quickly so as to finish as rapidly as possible and not to do anything more.

This master writer's case study was a gem around which many other treasures eventually came to cluster. I published it in a book that is out-of-print today and that was successful only in the Faculty of Medicine. I mentioned that the articles by Riotor, which were published in Le Figaro and Le Journal, resulted in my receiving some very interesting confessions. This happened only indirectly because readers did not understand the questions asked, and if they revealed their psychology, it was not at all about the topics of the study. The vast majority of the public believed in a kind of phrenology whose goal is to reveal mysterious insights into the minds of men through scientific methods.

Their disappointment was great, once the book was published, when readers realized that it did not reveal anything extraordinary. Neither Zola's document nor the Léon Daudet category seemed to be sensational discoveries. I was not expecting any great success, but I held on to these first documents religiously.

Enriched over the years, the inquiry, which will last as long as I do and to which anyone is free to contribute, led me to study new subjects in psychology and pathology. At Alcan's request, the little volume published in 1892 was succeeded by a more comprehensive work in the study of contemporary psychology in 1904. It was in this book, *Le Langage intérieur et les paraphasies / Interior Language and Paraphasias*,[10] that curious and loyal readers will be able to find Émile Zola's observations, among many others.

However, when this work was published, inexorable destiny had toppled the giant. The proofs had just come out when the cruel event occurred that took away the mentor who had become a friend. And it was only in a simple footnote at the bottom of a page that I could express my sad gratitude and my affection for the Master who had been so good to me. Only there could I express in a few lines everything, all the pious regrets, that his death had aroused in my heart.

Since the day when Zola had listened to my request with so much kindness and had agreed to help me with my research on interior language, I had not stopped keeping in touch with him.[11] There was never a single time when I asked to see him when a note did not come by return mail setting a date. I traveled a lot, I went far away, to Africa, to the Sahara; wherever I was, if I wrote him a letter, a reply would come as soon as possible, more often than not, a simple friendly note, but occasionally a long letter in which he discussed my ideas or advised me.

I have kept these writings. Unfortunately, the longest letters—and the most interesting ones—are lost. Perhaps I ought to accuse some unscrupulous collector of autographs, but I really must blame only myself. Just like Zola, I am afflicted with an unfortunate mania that I inherited from my father, a mania for saving everything I receive, whether printed materials or handwritten ones. Over the years, the papers have piled up, and the

---

10. Note in the original: "*Le Langage intérieur et les paraphasies* (Paris: Alcan, 1904)."
11. Note in the original: "I ought to mention this aspect of tolerance on Zola's part and of youthful clumsiness on mine. It was at the beginning of our relationship. I told him, not without some impertinence which was also absolutely unintentional, that I had read only two of his novels: *L'Assommoir* and another one whose title I had forgotten. 'The one that takes place on the railroad,' I told him ('*La Bête humaine*'). He smiled. A few days later, I received *La Débâcle* with a cordial, hand-written dedication." The copy given by Zola to Saint-Paul is still in the Saint-Paul family archives. It is an 1894 edition with the following dedication: "To Dr. Georges Saint Paul, from his cordial and devoted Émile Zola."

most precious ones have sunk into an ocean of worthless documents. And now when life seems to me to be too short to achieve all I would like to do, I shrink from the idea of sorting and clearing out everything. And I can write these few lines guided only by my own memories.

Zola faithfully kept up with my work. There was nothing that did not interest him, and he enjoyed advising me about a number of subjects.

One day I spoke to him about sexual inverts, several of whom I had examined with Lacassagne in Lyon. Already obsessed by the ideas that inspired *Fécondité / Fecundity*,[12] Zola was, I believe, already interested in studies on sexuality.

Zola knew about the existence of inverts. For a Frenchman, it was not an easy task to study the problem of homosexuality when the translation of Krafft-Ebing's work was unknown to everyone except a few psychologists, or when a publisher was dragged before the courts for having published Moll's work. With the audacity of youth, I did not hesitate to study the dreaded topic. I see now in the letters that Zola addressed to me at that time, in his advice to be careful, an admonition that reveals a great deal of concern. "I believe," he wrote in July 1895, "one must not disregard a publisher's anxieties. . . . Personally, I don't believe one must find a publisher no matter what."

Zola had not read any studies on inversion. He was unfamiliar with Krafft-Ebing, Moll, Chevalier, or Lacassagne, but he had received documents and confessions from unfortunate individuals who painfully described their torment, and since he was immensely kind and had an extraordinarily lucid mind, he understood and was moved.

"Certainly," he wrote to me, "morality and justice are right to intervene because they must uphold the public order. But by what right when one's willpower has been partially eliminated? We don't condemn a hunchback

---

12. Note in the original: "The duty to reproduce was, for Zola, at that time, a real obsession. One day he told me: 'So much seed is wasted in Paris in one night. What a pity that all of it does not engender children.'" (Saint-Paul later included this note in his essay "Zola and Inversion," reproduced in this volume.) "I recalled this statement recently when thinking about the thesis of a work that was just published by Librairie Maloine, *Plus fort que le mal*. And I thought that this book, making the case for marriage for damaged or defective individuals, would have pleased Zola."

because he was born that way. Why despise a man for acting like a woman if he was born half a woman?"[13]

> In another confidential letter that I received around the same time and that I have unfortunately been unable to find again, an unhappy man sent me the most poignant cry of human suffering that I have ever heard. He did not yield to these abominable loves, but he asked: Why, if he felt in the core of his being an aversion to women and a passion for men, was there such universal contempt for it? Why was the justice system ready to punish him? Never has someone possessed by a devil, never has a poor human being subject to the unknown destinies of desire, screamed so horrifically in pain! This letter, I remember, troubled me greatly, and don't we see the same thing in The Novel of an Invert, but with a more felicitous lack of awareness? Are we not witnessing a genuinely physiological phenomenon, a hesitation, a partial error of nature? Nothing is more tragic, in my opinion, and nothing calls out for a cure, if there is one.[14]

The sight of and, above all, contact with inverts were disagreeable to Zola. "I have met them in society," he told me one day, "and I feel an instinctive revulsion when shaking their hands—a revulsion that I have trouble controlling."

The first time we discussed inversion, a very natural question came to my lips: "Why haven't you dealt with inversion? Why haven't you devoted one of your novels to this subject? Isn't it worth the trouble?" Zola never gave me a precise answer. No doubt, he told me he did not dare, and later on, he wrote the same thing to me.[15]

> When I received this very curious document (The Novel of an Invert) several years ago, I was struck by the great physiological and social interest it offered. It touched me with its absolute sincerity, because in it one feels the passion, I will almost say, the eloquence of truth. Just think: the young man who is making this confession is writing in a language that isn't his own; and tell me whether in certain passages he doesn't attain a style marked by feelings that are profoundly felt and expressed. It is a complete confession, naïve, spontaneous, one that very few

---

13. First published in Zola's preface to Saint-Paul's Tares et poisons. See part 1 of this volume.
14. First published in Zola's preface.
15. Later republished in "Zola and Inversion."

men have dared to make, qualities that make it extremely valuable from many points of view. Also, thinking that its publication might be useful, at first I had wanted to use the manuscript, to give it to the public in some form for which I had searched in vain and which caused me to give up the idea.

At that time, I was in the midst of an extremely difficult literary battle. Critics treated me daily as if I were a criminal, capable of all vices and all debaucheries. Do you really see me, at that time, as the principal editor of The Novel of an Invert? First, I would have been accused of inventing the story out of whole cloth, out of my own personal corruption. And then I would have been condemned for having considered the whole business only as a vulgar speculation on the most repugnant instincts. And what an outcry would have been heard if I had said that no subject is more serious or sadder than this one, that there isn't an affliction more common or more profound than this one—one that we pretend not to believe exists—and that the best thing to do to cure these ills is to study them, to expose them, and to treat them!

But, my dear doctor, chance had it that, in chatting together one evening, we began to discuss the human and social disease of sexual perversions. And I entrusted to you this document that had lain dormant in one of my drawers. And that is how it came to see the light of day, in the hands of a doctor, an expert, who would not be accused of trying to cause a scandal.[16]

I don't believe a fear of criticism stopped Zola. The fear of criticism is a poor excuse for a man of such courage and endowed with so much mettle. I believe the real reason was that he came to know the question rather late in his career, I would say, at a time when, since he was already involved in a work whose progress was well organized in his mind, he did not want to interrupt his studies by undertaking new, delicate, and complicated research.[17]

I admit that the thought also crossed my mind briefly that his candidacy for the Académie française might have made him avoid it.

In reality, that was not true. Zola had decided—not without a struggle—that he wanted to be in the Academy, first to satisfy some of his friends, and then because he thought that, since he was the head of a literary school, he deserved it. He was too astute not to realize that he would never be a

---

16. First published in Zola's preface.
17. Later republished in "Zola and Inversion."

member, but he had too much intellectual and moral honesty not to despise the Academy.

It is a rare virtue to look down on the Academy.[18] In a great man, it is a sign of excellent taste and often of a great deal of innate honesty.

Mainly populated by mediocre men, the Academy admits only enough talented men as members to postpone its inevitable downfall. If one were to ask a serious man what purpose the outdated institution served, he would find it difficult to answer; but if one wanted to know what made it so noxious, he would find a multitude of reasons. A famous author—one eligible for membership in the Academy—once told me: "I have reservations about becoming a member; if you only knew how poorly structured it is, I would hesitate to enter." This famous man, however, overcame his aversion; he is an academician, wearing the uniform that impresses gawkers and invariably reminds intelligent men of parrots' feathers. He takes part, like the others, in the public events that provide an ample harvest of trifles for the vulgarizers in all the newspapers.

Zola was not enough of a "*boulevardier*" to be in the Academy.[19] He lacked the cheeky skepticism that reigns at the cocktail hour, pays attention to high society, is impressed by witticisms, and assumes that Pireus is a man.[20] He was not one of those frivolous ignoramuses—that trash of Parisian wit—who are full of conceit, think that they are representative of France, are fluent in writing about the shape of a hat or the color of a tie, impress simpletons, and make the word *French* synonymous with *ridiculous* in the minds of badly informed foreigners. These poor, stupid people—or rather, stupid and malevolent people—whose loud vacuousness cuts short all discussions, and who consider the borders of Paris the frontier of the

---

18. Note in the original: "In speculating on human baseness, in rejecting those who are proud and upright, the Academy demeans itself by looking down on those who do not have support and by too often envying merit; in being useful to cliques, the Academy condemns itself. An Academy composed of conscientious and serious critics—critics whose future would be financially secure, whose role would not be ceremonial but would consist of selecting and publishing the manuscripts of beginners and unknown writers—such an Academy would render useful services. I offer this opinion to its patrons."

19. Saint-Paul used *boulevardier*, figuratively meaning "man about town," to denote a popular, frivolous writer.

20. This expression, meaning to make a glaring mistake and reveal one's ignorance, originated in a fable by La Fontaine.

civilized world, prefer wordplay to thought and a witty remark to actual wit on every subject. As credulous as any fool, they adore everything that the cowardice of some and the self-interest of others offer up as fodder for their need to idolize. No city more than Paris has erected such temples to credulity. The Academy is one of those temples. . . .

Zola brought some splendid provincial qualities to Paris: the ardor of an untarnished republican faith and the inherent heroism of an indomitable courage.

Paris is made better by its provincials: it is the rich blood of the provinces that, enlivened by the lively and spontaneous eloquence of the capital, assures the glory and triumph of the city. She gives them charm; they make her wise and adorn her with virtues.

Buffeted by opposing currents, going from one extreme to the other, supple, refined, passionate, and gullible, the people of Paris sometimes believe in its scientists and its truly great heroes and sometimes praise its charlatans and its buffoons to the skies. They adore talent; they have an instinct for beauty; they boo at lousy actors; they have the best taste in the world; they like their festivals and spectacles; they have incomparable cooks. They are generous but capable of cruelty, extremely intelligent but at times completely stupid, skeptical and yet quick to tolerate the most unrealistic shams, heroic and fearful in the extreme. They are as easily impressed as a child, with the same fickleness and love of flashy things. To please them, artifice and glamor are needed. . . . Zola worked for immortality; he was not enough of a "boulevardier" for the Academy. He was not that, and it was better that he remained that way.

We can easily understand the fact that being interested in inversion—a subject that is becoming more generally known nowadays and is developing into a major topic in Germany[21]—would have doomed even the strongest candidacy for the Academy. But I believe that, far from stopping Zola, this factor motivated him to take on the struggle.

---

21. Note in the original: "See the studies of the eminent scholar Dr. Näcke, the medical officer at Hübertusberg in Saxony, and above all, the results of the inquiries and the extremely large volume of documentation that Dr. Hirschfeld, a doctor at Charlottenburg-bei-Berlin, has collected." Paul Näcke (1851–1913) was a German psychiatrist and criminologist who coined the term "narcissism." He also wrote several articles and books on homosexuality. Magnus Hirschfeld (1868–1935) was a German physician who founded the Scientific Humanitarian Committee, the first gay rights organization in Western Europe.

He followed the beginnings of my work with a great deal of attention. When the book was published, he wrote to me:

> I received a copy of your book; and although I have been able only to glance over it while cutting the pages, I had the distinct impression of a serious and powerful work. You placed the documents in an illuminating context and extracted from them a logical and persuasive analysis. I believe that this volume will be significant for this question of sexuality, which is still so obscure. For my part, I am happy to have helped you a little by giving you a curious document, and I thank you for having used it so well, because the question does interest me.[22]

The help that Zola gave me was not of minor importance. He had written the preface to the book and had given me the intriguing manuscript that I published in chapter 2 under the title The Novel of a Born Invert. A few foreign authors thought that this novel of an invert was really and truly a novel, and even some of them believed that Zola was the inspiration.

I can confirm that this confession, written by a nobleman, is completely authentic. When my book, now published by Masson, was disseminated throughout the world, a copy fell into the hands of the young man who had revealed the secrets of his life so courageously to Zola, and he—the true author of this autobiography—wrote me a very long letter. He sent me a lot of new observations, and what is more, he authorized me to reproduce the new document on the condition that I suppress a few things that could identify who he was. Someday I will publish the complete case study after making the necessary cuts.

Zola had written a page for my first book (Interior Language) that guaranteed its success. This success shattered the belief, so firmly held in the minds of some men of science, that such inquiries in France were definitely doomed to failure. Thanks to the examples given by Daudet and Zola, thanks also, I could say, to a lot of work and patience, the results that I obtained were magnificent and . . . it became fashionable to develop questionnaires.

As if it was not enough for him to put my foot into the stirrup, Zola, as we have seen, contributed significantly to the development of my second book (Sexual Perversion and Perversity), and the help that he gave me

---

22. Later republished in "Zola and Inversion."

brought the work, now a classic, to the attention of other doctors and psychologists.

He no longer had the opportunity to guide me or to collaborate, in a manner of speaking, with me in my research. My studies took me into new territory, not so much in pure medicine as in the invention of medical equipment, and he could not easily guide me. Then I left France and began—periodically—to make notes of impressions that I collected and published later in my *Souvenirs de Tunisie et d'Algérie / Recollections of Tunisia and Algeria*.[23] During each of my stays in France, I went to see him. He was aware of everything that I was doing and enjoyed what I told him about my medical duties.

I often tried to entice him into this misunderstood world, into this world of prodigious, untapped energies that depends on us to be constructive or destructive, the world that is the Islamic world. I would have liked for him to have gone there, to Algiers and Tunis, for him to have crossed the Sahel and the Sahara, for him to have lived in the palaces and the shacks, and then with his prodigious skills as a writer, painter, and moralist, he could have shouted the truth from the rooftops to all of France; he could have publicly revealed what our duties and our true interests are.

Because he was in absolute agreement with this great project of making friends with the Muslims and selecting new citizens from the elites of the native people . . . , he detested the stupid arguments, revolting cruelties, the contempt that debases those who are contemptuous. And he did not want, on the other side of the sea, for France to stop being the France of the Rights of Man in order to revert to the France of the Middle Ages.

However, the program that his ambition chose for him did not allow him to abandon his current battles for new fights. The plan for his work was already irrevocably outlined. He had no time for unplanned skirmishes. . . .

He would have less time than anyone could have imagined. However, an unforeseen struggle was about to engage him. His conscience alone drew him into the arena.

And this was the fight of a giant against a people.

The *Affair*—the affair that engaged the two sides of France—was taking place. It would be absurd for me to retrace Zola's role even in a few words.

---

23. Note in the original edition: "*Souvenirs de Tunisie et d'Algérie*, preface by T. Ribot, published by J. Dauguin, Tunis, 1904."

The entire world followed the progress of this affair with passionate interest, and people admired the fact that an author, who lacked nothing that the most accomplished person would not be proud of, made himself a target of the roughest blows, the vilest insults, and that, because of his love for justice, he stood up against persecution.

I was in Africa, and I remember the shudder that coursed through my entire body when I heard that this man, whose very being represented a praiseworthy loyalty, was accused of the most repugnant acts of treachery. Often, confronting angry looks, I would defend the man who had always been so good to me. Only a few friends offered me the comfort of speaking about him.

He persevered at all costs, even in the face of torture, renewed by this struggle, this struggle of a man against a city, against the City, against Paris. He confronted his opponents with a spark of inextinguishable anger in his eyes, his entire being vibrating with an energy that a pure passion made lively and youthful.

I remember one evening in Paris. I was on leave. I was leaving his house. A long time before then, he had told me: "Come see me. I will always be at home for you." In the midst of those very heated times, he never forgot his promise.

Paris growled with anger. It was the time when the city, in love with Esterhazy,[24] would have lynched Zola. I was in military uniform, and in a contrast that made an impression on me, since I had just left his house, at every step my uniform provoked storms—storms of support or storms of curses. Shouts of "Long live the army" alternated with howls of "Death to Zola"! On the upper deck of streetcars, passengers stood up, hypnotized by the sight of the red trousers of my uniform. And always the loud shouts of "Long live the army" and "Death to Zola" roared from the crowd panting with fury.

The city had seen him, the man it wanted to lynch.

Parisian generosity was worn out, and like all crowds stirred up by evil, this one had the ferocity of cannibals. . . .

I met an artillery officer, a friend of mine. He was an observant and thoughtful man. Sometimes we walked along a boulevard swarming with

---

24. Major Ferdinand Walsin Esterhazy (1847–1923) was the real spy in the French army working for the German Empire, an act of treason for which Captain Alfred Dreyfus (1859–1935) was wrongfully convicted.

people in the throes of madness, both of us astounded at the novelty and the horror of the spectacle.

From time to time, the crowds would calm down, but then the cries would begin again with even more fury. When a gang emerged, making a large breach in the crush of the crowd from whom frightening shouts came, my friend, an ardent anti-Dreyfusard, seized me by the arm and said to me: "All the same, he has a hell of a lot of courage."

Yes, Zola had an awful lot of courage; and this struggle of a man against a city had a nobility and a splendid attraction for both gentle and hardy souls, even those who had feelings different from his own.

The last time I saw Zola, he was still talking to me about the *Affair*. The hour of victory had not yet arrived; he was not to see it. At the very least, the results that he judged essential had been achieved. He praised at length Colonel Picquart, with whom he had lunched the day before. . . .[25]

I will not reveal what he told me. I am a man of science, a scientist, as Augustin Hamon says, not a reporter.[26] I value too greatly the words of the Master to offer them up as fodder for the public, and I think too highly of myself to believe that he would have confided to just anyone what he confided to me. Nor will I reveal the strange prediction that I made to Zola on that day—the last day that I saw him—a prediction that seemed worth no more than an incredulous smile and that later came true.

I remember the last moments that I spent with Zola. In a casual gesture that was not typical of him, he threw his arm around my neck, and, while escorting me to the door of the town house, as he always did, through the marvelous things collected in his home, he said to me: "Work, my friend, work well, work hard, work without stopping. Work, you see, it's everything. The day will come for the harvest."

Those were the last words that I heard from him.

I still have an infinitely grateful and devoted memory of Zola. He made an indelible impression on my way of thinking and acting. Whenever I

---

25. Georges Picquart (1854–1914) was a French army officer, who played a crucial role in the Dreyfus Affair as one of the first senior officers to proclaim Alfred Dreyfus's innocence. Arrested and forced to resign from the army, he was reinstated in 1906, after the exoneration of Dreyfus, with the rank of brigadier general and served as minister of war from October 1906 to July 1909. Alexandrine Zola's letters to Saint-Paul indicate that she remained in contact with Picquart after her husband's death.

26. Augustin Hamon (1862–1945) was a socialist and anarchist and editor of *L'Humanité Nouvelle*.

encounter underhanded wickedness and vile and petty injustices, I remember him.

Years will pass. I do not know what will come of my opinions of some of his scientific beliefs, but his goodness, the example his courage gave me, and my gratitude will last as long as I do.

I know that he took an interest in and demonstrated a kindness toward the stranger that I was then. I know that what he demonstrated to me, he showed to many others as well. Long after his death, I learned that I held a place in his heart, and that he was more attached to me than I had thought.

It is selfish to add that I lost in Zola a friend and an advocate. The fall of a giant oak destroys the forest; the fate of a twig has no history. . . .

People ask themselves what would have become of Zola if he had lived. When it concerns a man of his caliber and his heart, one must not waver. Everyone would have recognized his loyalty, would have respected and loved him, would have admired his courage—the courage of a good and great Frenchman. Those who know how good he was can testify to the fact that he would have bandaged up the wounded after the battle. . . .

I hoped to keep for me alone the sweet and profound feeling of devotion that I have dedicated to his memory, and I had no intention of writing what I was guarding so carefully and so religiously in the bottom of my heart.

But one day, by chance, far from Paris, years after his death, when the affection that he had accorded to the distant disciple that I was was revealed to me, a new and heroic example of courage and goodness in the great name of Zola became clear to me.

And it is in honor of the man from whom I received this affection, moved to tears as much as the vicissitudes of life can provoke in me the ability to be so moved, that I have written these few pages that are so incomplete and so cold, in an attempt to include in them a bit of my soul.

Villa Laupts, October 18, 1907

Second Edition (1910)

EDITORIAL COMMENT BY CLIVE THOMSON
AND MICHAEL ROSENFELD

The second edition was published under the title *L'homosexualité et les types homosexuels / Homosexuality and Types of Homosexuals* in 1910 by Vigot Frères in Paris. It is identical to the first edition in its first five chapters, but in the sixth chapter, Saint-Paul inserted "The Sequel to the Novel of an Invert" and two short texts, "Zola and Inversion" and "Opinion of an Algerian Muslim," as well as a new preface and conclusion, which we are translating in this work. The sixth chapter also contains long analyses of the study of homosexuality in France and Germany, but we have not translated those sections.

 The new preface and conclusion show the evolution in Saint-Paul's theories on same-sex love since 1896. He notably dropped the distinction between perversion and perversity, adopted new definitions of bisexuality, and added a social dimension to homosexuality. His short text on Zola's ideas was very similar to the ones he had already published in his *In Memoriam* text, with subtle differences. The article on the "Opinion of an Algerian Muslim" allowed the doctor to express his opinion on the nefarious influence of colonialism in North Africa and to criticize how women are treated in those societies.

 Saint-Paul's conclusion to this edition is a nationalistic text where he claimed that homosexuality was a "very rare exception" in France as compared to other countries. More interesting perhaps is his view that "every member of a species comprising two sexes is a homosexual in the making," which was his way of admitting that it was a natural phenomenon.

Preface to the Second Edition

I did not suspect in 1893 that the chance to discuss sexual questions with Zola would focus some of my activity for several years on a methodical analysis of the disorders of sexuality. Here are the results of that study, which I have collected and summarized in a new edition that I am submitting to the public today.

Certainly, I do not conceal the naïveté or the offensiveness of a great number of the following pages, and I must warn the reader that, because of typographical difficulties, I have had to give up trying to make a perfectly coherent work out of a number of studies done at different times and to standardize all the materials in order to present a unified theory. Thus, it is that the reader will see that I have abandoned an idea I had previously judged to be crucial—that of a precise distinction between perversion and perversity. Please allow me to recall that at the time when I first approached this subject, one could cite in France only Lacassagne and Chevalier who had discussed it adequately, and also that I was barely older than twenty when I was to come inevitably under the influence of the most remarkable observer of inversion: Krafft-Ebing. Then I considered my research on inversion as little more than a diversion from the studies on interior language and the *maladies of language* that I had undertaken and that I have never stopped pursuing.

However, the work was a great success, and I have the pleasure to state that it has become a classic. It deserves this status because, along with its explanation of certain original concepts, it has the additional benefit of bringing to light documents that, provided occasionally by unknown individuals, it is true, are always of an irrefutable and imperishable truth. One will appreciate the role of new personal testimonies that this new edition brings to the discovery of homosexuality. But the reader ought not to assume that it is possible to add appreciably to the psychological analysis in the first chapters of this book. The psychology of inversion does not have much more to reveal than it has already revealed, and one could not define the homosexual types more exactly than they have already been defined.

Yet interest in the question of homosexuality is no longer solely a psychological one; it has become a social one as well. One of the reasons is the increase in the number of patients that I had described in 1895 in the category of *indifferent* and *intermittent*, and that we now call bisexual or intermediate. Another reason is what we will learn in the last chapter of this book: homosexuals have a tendency to form groups and to exercise a social influence. The phenomenon benefits from the scientific curiosity that naturally attaches itself to the causes and conditions of its production. Personally, I believe that *sexual and para-sexual variations are determined by economic circumstances.* The sexual instinct remains subordinate to the instinct for food.

The literature devoted to homosexuality in the last few years has become quite abundant, but a little uncoordinated. I recommend the following titles:

Havelock Ellis, whose masterpiece, *Studies in the Psychology of Sex* (Philadelphia: Davis), is published in a French translation by Mercure de France.[1]

Professor Näcke of Hübertusburg in Saxony, a prolific and wise writer, one of the most vigorous thinkers in contemporary Europe.

Dr. Hirschfeld, a writer who has brought out a number of works and a journal devoted to homosexuality, published for the most part by Max Spohr in Leipzig.

Dr. Anton Nyström of Stockholm, who analyzed *Sexual Life* in general (see the *French* translation published by Vigot in Paris).[2]

Dr. Éric Simac, a young, vigorous, and talented author (see the *Archives* of Lacassagne and *Annales Medico-Chirurgicales du Centre Tours / Medical and Surgical Annals of the Tours Center*).[3]

And finally, I must point out the *Archives* of Lacassagne, edited by the professor at the medical school in Lyon, which is the only French journal that deals with inversion on a regular basis.

I cannot cite all the new studies on this subject; there are too many of them. The reader must be forewarned that some of them betray the homosexual nature of their authors. As interesting and important as they may be, these works have too often inflated or exaggerated the importance of

---

1. Havelock Ellis (1859–1939) was an English physician who pioneered the study of sexuality in the English-speaking world. His *Studies in the Psychology of Sex* was published in six volumes between 1897 and 1928. The second volume was on "sexual inversion."

2. Anton Nyström (1842–1931) was a Swedish physician involved in sexual reform issues. His book on "the natural laws of sexual life" was first published in Swedish in 1904, translated into French in 1910, and translated into English in 1913.

3. Éric Simac was the pseudonym of Dr. Charles Guichard (1874–1913), who wrote several articles, including an exhaustive bibliography, on homosexuality. See Kevin Dubout, *Éric Simac (1874–1913): Un Oublié du "movement de libération" homosexuel de la Belle Époque* (Paris: Quintes Feuilles, 2014).

homosexuality. In that way, the homosexual writer reveals more than he realizes, more than he would like to reveal about what we still do not know about the psychology of the invert.

Dr. Laupts (G. Saint-Paul), Paris, 1910

Zola and Inversion

Zola was interested in inversion, as he was interested in everything that dealt with sexuality.[4] He followed the genesis of my work *Sexual Perversion and Perversity* with a great deal of attention. When the work finally appeared in bookstores, he wrote to me:

> I received a copy of your book; and although I have been able only to glance over it while cutting the pages, I had the distinct impression of a serious and powerful work. You placed the documents in an illuminating context and exacted from them a logical and persuasive analysis. I believe that this volume will <u>be significant for</u> this question of sexuality, which is still so obscure. For my part, I am happy to have helped you a little by giving you a curious document, and I thank you for having used it so well, because the question does interest me.[5]

The sight of and, above all, contact with inverts were disagreeable to Zola. "I have met them in society," he told me one day, "and I feel an instinctive revulsion when shaking their hands—a revulsion that I have trouble controlling."

The first time we discussed inversion, a very natural question came to my lips: "Why haven't you dealt with inversion? Why haven't you devoted one of your novels to this subject? Isn't it worth the trouble?" Zola never gave me a precise answer. No doubt, he told me he did not dare.

I don't believe the fear of criticism stopped Zola. I believe the real reason was that he came to know the question rather late in his career, I would say, at a time when, since he was already involved in a work whose progress was well organized in his mind, he did not want to interrupt his studies

---

4. This text was published in 1910 in the second edition (p. 431). Parts of it appeared originally in Saint-Paul's eulogy to Zola, "In Memoriam: Émile Zola," first published in *Archives d'Anthropologie Criminelle* 22, no. 168 (1907): 825–841, and reproduced in this volume.

5. This and the subsequent quotes in this section are from Saint-Paul, "In Memoriam: Émile Zola."

by undertaking new, delicate, and complicated research. On the other hand, it may be that this research would have led him at some point in time to deal with inversion. The sexual question was often at the forefront of his preoccupations. To procreate seemed to him to be a primordial duty. He said to me one day, "So much seed is wasted in Paris in one night. What a pity that all of it does not engender children."[6]

Opinion of an Algerian Muslim on Homosexuality

In Algeria and Tunisia, homosexuality is encountered frequently in the Islamic world and also among the Europeans who engage in it with more alacrity than one would believe in France.[7]

One of the results of this contamination is that there is a relative indulgence toward homosexuality in the Algerians' perspective. I would say there is even a kind of tacit respect for the act, and this is because Europeans, known for their energy, are reputed to be homosexuals. In certain indigenous groups, the *Taffar* (the active partner) enjoys a certain status, but the word *Naiec*, which designates the passive partner, is an insult, the frequent use of which testifies to an obvious familiarity with homosexuality. It is clear that in Algeria and Tunisia, the *Naiec* is not unusual. In France, a similar insult would seem nonsensical outside the rarified homosexual circles where such men can be found. One of my friends, an extremely remarkable Arab *couloughi*, one of those truly superior men whom I know, Mr. Ali ben Ahmet G . . . , told me that inversion in the Arab world develops above all in the cities, in the areas where one loves the mind and intellectual things, and that homosexual passions generally begin in platonic friendships engendered by a desire to exchange ideas. The inferiority in the intellectual education of native women is the cause of men's search among other men for an intellectual engagement that leads to pederasty. However, homosexuality does not only exist in cities; it is also rampant in many oases. I indicated this fact in a work that I recommend also to those interested in the condition of Arab women.[8]

---

6. Note in the 1910 edition: "See Laupts, "À la memoire d'Émile Zola" (translated in this volume as "In Memoriam: Émile Zola").

7. The text in this section was included in the 1910 edition (p. 432). Saint-Paul was a medical doctor in Algeria and Tunisia from 1895 to 1901.

8. Note in the original 1910 edition: "See G. Saint-Paul, *Souvenirs de Tunisie et d'Algérie*, 2nd edition. Tunis: Dauguin; Paris: Vigot."

Remarks on The Sequel to the Novel of an Invert

After the publication of *Perversion and Perversity* (1896), I received from the author of the document published in chapter 2 of that work under the title *The Novel of an Invert* a manuscript of about thirty pages, of which I can reproduce here only a few short passages.[9]

[Text of *The Sequel to the Novel of an Invert*]

Some very circumstantial information on the ancestors and the family of the author follows. All of it is very detailed, containing some very curious portraits, and one gets the impression that it is based on reality. It is a portrait of a milieu (not at all homosexual), and this description reveals qualities of observation, psychological intuition, and an upbringing by sophisticated relatives who belong to an aristocratic society, keenly interested in English elegance. Leaving aside what is revealed in this milieu,[10] as well as a number of particularities in regard to the author, I note the following in this document:

[Text of *The Sequel to the Novel of an Invert* (continued)]

"As for me, such as I was born, I will live, and as such, I will die."[11]

Conclusions to the Second Edition

In attempting to distinguish between what I *know* and what I *believe*, here are a few conclusions that I feel confident giving to my research and reflections on homosexuality:[12]

---

9. This short text introduced *The Sequel of the Novel of an Invert*, which had been sent directly to Saint-Paul in September 1896 by the anonymous author.

10. Note in the original 1910 edition: "I include here a few lines written by the author himself: 'She had developed a passion for silver and had collected an enormous quantity of exquisitely engraved silver and gilt silverware. At her death, she left behind some magnificient gems, furs, and gorgeous lacework. In one of the jewelry boxes that belonged to her, I found so many pretty things, including a superb, stunningly crafted coral phallus. It was in a gold setting with a ring on top, indicating that it was meant to be hung on a chain around the neck. Perhaps it was an amulet.'"

11. This sentence ends the text of *The Sequel to the Novel of an Invert* in the 1910 edition. A note in the original edition reads: "A word about an error that I was unable to clarify in the original document: in 'The Novel of an Invert' (chap. II, p. 61), it is necessary to delete the reference to the exaggeration of the man's hips and pelvis. After checking, I discovered that a line was added that was not part of the original manuscript. The error can only be by a copyist or a typesetter."

12. Saint-Paul's conclusions to the 1910 edition are almost identical to his "Lettre au Professeur Lacassagne / Letter to Professor Lacassagne," dated May 20, 1909, which

I. I know that homosexuality exists only as a very rare exception among the total population of the continental territory of France—I mean, the noncolonial territory. I have lived in almost all the regions of France, visiting all the social milieus. One could object that I am a fool and do not know how to observe, but I have compared the results of my case studies with those of a number of other men from the middle class, merchants, industrialists, peasants, workers, aristocrats, hobbyists, priests, soldiers, and officers.

II. I know that homosexuality exists in Paris, in all large cities, and, in a general sense, in all parts of France that are open to cosmopolitanism. I do not know if these social circles are more or less rich in France than in analogous environments abroad. I believe that no one knows anything about that subject or could know at the present time.

III. I know that our studies of psychology generally do not deal with foreigners. Out of one hundred novels published in Paris, ten or so depict French morals and ninety the morals of particular subgroups: foreigners, pimps, adventurers, speculators, or those invented out of whole cloth.

IV. I know that French doctors and experts deny that homosexuality is frequent in France, and for this reason, we are accused of ignorance or naïveté by foreigners. And I know that French doctors and experts are right.

V. I know that homosexuals from the lower class, who are at times the subjects of certain foreign researchers, boast of their relations with well-known and famous men. Prostitutes, whether male or female, whether homosexual or heterosexual, nearly always try, through a natural tendency or a professional interest, to make us believe in their conquests, particularly in their successes with people they consider honorable. If we listen to the trollops, there isn't a virtuous woman anywhere. I know that certain foreign researchers have demonstrated an unbelievable credulity and have accepted without questioning all the information that is favorable to their theses. I believe that many professional prostitutes are not homosexual by inclination but resign themselves to being so for profit.

VI. I believe that homosexuality is contagious and that it is increasing at this time in France and Germany because it is being studied, it is being talked about, and it is being written about. I believe that French inverts have at this moment a certain tendency to stick together.

---

was published in *Archives d'Anthropologie Criminelle* 30 (1909): 693–96.

VII. I believe, above all, that it develops under the influence of economic conditions, that its development is linked to a decrease in the birth rate, to the infrequency of marriage, or to the fact that people are marrying at a later age. I believe that homosexuality is the inevitable manifestation of a kind of unconscious Malthusianism.

VIII. I believe that every member of a species comprising two sexes is a homosexual in the making. I know that there are born homosexuals.

IX. I believe that a key criterion in the diagnosis of homosexuality consists, when one is certain that the subject isn't lying, in the expression of the particular interest that he takes in the question of homosexuality. I believe, in addition, that the homosexual is likely to see homosexuality where it isn't.[13] I have noticed the fact that among known homosexuals there are those who make incorrect observations regarding acts, gestures, or remarks by others in their social milieus, but who are not, in reality, endowed with any kind of sexual implications

X. I believe that homosexuality is difficult to conceal from someone who has, from birth, a certain intuition about human psychology and who knows about the issue. I am convinced that I have known homosexuals who have never confessed their tendency.

XI. I applaud vigorously the work of researchers *quorum pars minima fui.*[14] And yet I know that all researchers are deceiving themselves about new questions, and I believe that the most eminent thinkers have exaggerated just a little the extent of homosexuality in Germany, where it seems to be quite widespread.

XII. I know that the vast majority of my compatriots (noncolonial) have an undisguised, extreme disgust for homosexuality. I know, however, that many of them have committed or submitted to minor homosexual acts during puberty—acts that did not leave any significant trace.[15] I believe in the influence of life circumstances, education, or upbringing, and the heterosexual "initiatives" that I have already noted. In a word, I believe in an on/off switch, especially during puberty.

XIII. All impartial or clear-minded researchers will state that at the present time homosexuality is a rarity in France.

---

13. Note in the original edition of 1910: "Especially when he is chaste."

14. Translation: "in which I played a small part."

15. Note in the original: "That is, if onanism is inevitably tainted with homosexuality."

This I can affirm. And that does not mean that homosexuality does not exist or that it does not proliferate in certain Parisian or French milieus. And these are precisely those who are the first to believe in the superficial observations of a foreigner devoid of a critical method or a critical sense or one who is pressed for time. This does not mean that homosexuality does not occur in all kinds of social environments in France. The future of homosexuality and bisexuality in France as much as in Germany depends on complex elements that it would be risky to discuss.

[I end this work by apologizing to readers for what does not have a sufficient continuity of doctrine and views in all of its parts.[16] The major part of the volume was printed in 1896, and it was not possible for me to make the necessary revisions to the former text in order to bring it into accord with the new theories.

This is a defect that has its good side, since it allows an exact appreciation of the influence that time, experience, and evolution of certain social phenomena have exercised on the concepts of the author, who claims no less a virtue than sincerity—a virtue to which he has never ceased to be anything but entirely faithful.

On the occasion of the publication of *Perversion and Perversity*, I was criticized for having frequently rebelled *against* the subject. I have striven, since then, to ascend to the heights of scientific truth—that is to say, the truth— and to achieve scientific serenity. I find no difficulty in recognizing that I have not always achieved that goal.

Paris, April 1910]

---

16. The parts that follow, in brackets, do not appear in Saint-Paul's letter to Dr. Lacassagne.

Third Edition (1930)

Editorial Comment by Clive Thomson
and Michael Rosenfeld

The third edition was published in 1930 under the title *Invertis et homosexuels / Inverts and Homosexuals*. It appeared in Vigot's series *Thèmes psychologiques / Psychological Themes*, in which Saint-Paul published six other volumes. This edition is substantially revised; it contains the original preface by Émile Zola from the 1896 edition, Saint-Paul's introduction to the second edition, and finally a new preface to the third edition, which we are translating here. Saint-Paul also reproduced his conclusion to the second edition, followed by additional remarks, with an emphasis on a new understanding of same-sex love, which he strove to explain at length as he explored its causes and deplored the fact that no cure existed. He still considered the text written by the Italian as testimony representative of gay men, even though it was over three decades old by then.

Preface to the Third Edition

The first edition of this work, *Sexual Perversion and Perversity* (Paris: Carré, Naud, and Masson), was published in 1896; the second edition, *Homosexuality and Homosexual Types* (Paris: Vigot Frères), was published in 1910. Both of them were signed with a pseudonym (which was also an anagram), Laupts, which I have abandoned because it has frequently caused my works to be classified as German, and I have replaced it with another pseudonym and anagram, G. Espé de Metz, the interpretation of which is a little less easy to decipher, but which leaves no doubt about the culture to which it belongs.

There have been a lot of changes since 1910. Science lost Lacassagne, an unparalleled leader; the German professor Näcke, a conscientious and original thinker, is dead, as well as our young colleague, Éric Simac; Dr. Hirschfeld has been assassinated.[1] The *Annales Médico-Chirurgicales du Centre (Tours) / Medical and Surgical Annals of the Center (Tours)* has ceased publication, and Lacassagne's *Archives d'Anthropologie Criminelle / Archives of Criminal Anthropology* has been replaced by a magnificent publication, *Revue Internationale de Criminalistique / Review of International Criminology*,[2] directed by an innovator, Edmond Locard, director of the Laboratory of Scientific Police Techniques in Lyon, whose gifts, activity, audacity of his concepts, and precision of his methodology have redounded more and more to his credit.[3]

I regret not to be able to spend the time necessary to reproduce in its entirety the large octavo volume of 450 pages of dense text that makes up my previous work. It is completely sold out.

I advise those who study homosexuality to search there for documentation on inversion and homosexuality. Beyond that documentation, they will also find a detailed study on the Oscar Wilde trials, an analysis of his novel *Dorian Gray*, and in the second edition, some thoughts on the Eulenberg case, along with studies on the sexual instinct, morality, education, natural Malthusianism, etc.

I am even more confident in recommending my previous work, since the first two editions, in addition to the original studies that I just mentioned, put on record the opinions of a number of experts, writers, and observers, such as Krafft-Ebing, Moll, Lacassagne, Chevalier, Nyström, Ribot, Lemaître (of Geneva), Dessoir, Legludic, Raffalovich,[4] and the

---

1. Dr. Magnus Hirschfeld died on May 14, 1935 in Nice. It is not clear why Saint-Paul believed that he had been assassinated. In 1920 he was gravely wounded in the head in Munich, and his death had been reported, falsely, in several newspapers at the time. Perhaps this explains Saint-Paul's confusion.

2. Note in the original 1930 edition: "*Revue Internationale de Criminalistique* (Joannès, Desvigues et fils, publishers). Laboratory of Scientific Police Techniques, 35 rue Saint-Jean, Lyon, and for works in German and Scandinavian languages, Stockholm, Vulcanusgatan 9 (Dr. Söderman)."

3. Edmond Locard (1877–1966) was a professor of forensics at the University of Lyon. In 1910 he founded the Laboratory of Scientific Police Techniques.

4. For information on Krafft-Ebing, Moll, Chevalier, Nyström, Dessoir, and Raffalovich, see footnotes in previous sections of this book. Théodule-Armand Ribot (1839–1916) was the first professor of experimental and comparative psychology at the Collège de France in 1889. He was a mentor to Saint-Paul, to whom Saint-Paul dedicated

writers who were willing to make contributions to the study that I undertook under the auspices of the *Archives d'Anthropologie Criminelle* edited by Dr. Lacassagne.

This new edition is, along with the document given to me by Zola, a summary of my essential ideas regarding homosexuality.

For those who deal with certain other foundational problems, I refer them to my *Thèmes psychologiques*:

Fasc.1.a.s.: Spiritualism and Materialism
Fasc.2.a.s.: Intelligence, *function, reflection,* teaching methods
Fasc.3.a.s.: Experimentation with hypnosis on criminals, the question of responsibility, etc.

On the subject of Malthusianism, I would point out my work *J'en appelle au monde civilisé* / *I Appeal to the Civilized World* (Paris: La Renaissance Moderne, [1929]).

In reading the pages that follow, the reader should not be surprised to find repeatedly expressions such as "I believe that," "no doubt," "maybe." . . . He will understand the reason if he is willing to probe the meaning of a phrase that he will encounter as frequently in this work: "We must not be afraid to say: 'I don't know,' 'I believe,' 'it is possible that' . . . ; we must always fear saying: 'I know.'"

Nothing provokes uncertainty, nothing leads to diverse and sometimes opposing interpretations, more than psychological material. *Only the ignorant affirms otherwise.*

But despite all the uncertainties, broader horizons reveal themselves when we reflect deeply on certain subjects. As facts are produced and truths are revealed by our investigations, through observation and research, a beneficial virtue is derived from skepticism: *prudence*.

---

the first edition of his book. He also wrote the preface to Saint-Paul's travelogue on Tunisia and Algeria in 1904. Henri Legludic was a French physician whose work *Notes et observations de médicine légale: Attentats aux mœurs* was published in 1896. It included another autobiography, "Confidences et aveux d'un Parisien: La Comtesse (Paris, 1850–1861)," by Arthur W. . . . [Arthur Belorget], which is more traditional in its narrative techniques. See the English translation, "Secret Confessions of a Parisian: The Countess, 1850–1871" in *Queer Lives: Men's Autobiographies from Nineteenth-Century France*, ed. William A. Peniston and Nancy Erber (Lincoln: University of Nebraska Press, 2007), 7–72. We were unable to find any information about Lemaître of Geneva.

I am persuaded that educators, whether they are secular or religious, who are willing to consider the chapters of this little book less as an exposé of facts and more as themes and subjects to think about and as an invitation to observe, will get a benefit from their reading that will profit those with whom they are charged.

Dr. G. S.-P., October 1929

Acknowledgments

This English-language translation was truly a group effort. Michael Rosenfeld and William Peniston assumed the overall editorial responsibility for this project. William Peniston and Nancy Erber produced the translation: first, for the translation of the published portions of the work for their collection, *Queer Lives: Men's Autobiographies from Nineteenth-Century France* (2007); then, for the unpublished section of the newly discovered manuscript; and finally, for the selections from the writings of Dr. Saint-Paul. Michael reviewed all these translations and made valuable suggestions for improvements. Nancy worked hard with Michael to revise his essay for this English-language edition. Clive Thomson translated his own essay.

Michael wishes to reiterate his gratitude for Clive's unwavering support and for his kindness. "Clive Thomson," he wrote in the French edition of this work, "has always sustained me intellectually and boosted my morale. I wish to thank him for his contribution to this work as well as for his advice and friendship."

Dr. Georges Saint-Paul played a major role in the original publication of this autobiography in serial form in 1894–1895 and in the subsequent editions of 1896, 1910, and 1930. That story is documented by several manuscripts recently found in the Zola family archives and the Saint-Paul family archives that have allowed Michael Rosenfeld to reconstruct the genesis of *The Novel of an Invert* and its *Sequel*. Of particular note is the discovery by Alain Pagès of the original manuscript of the letter the Italian man wrote to the doctor in September 1896. Alain's willingness to share this discovery with Michael and his support for this project are deeply appreciated. Brigitte Émile-Zola, a great-granddaughter of Émile Zola, granted Michael permission to publish the manuscript and the correspondence between her great-grandfather and the doctor. Likewise, the heirs of Dr. Saint-Paul allowed Clive Thomson and Michael Rosenfeld to consult the doctor's archives at their family home. In particular, Marc Stern, Yves Stern, and Patrice de Metz were all very hospitable and enthusiastic about this project. Equally important was the assistance of Kevin Dubout, a scholar on the medicalization of homosexuality in France and Germany, who was the first researcher to discover the existence of the Saint-Paul family archives. It was Mr. Dubout who put Michael and Clive in contact with the descendants of Georges Saint-Paul.

An attempt was made to identify the author of these confessions, including an exhaustive search of portraits and sculptures in various museums in Naples, since the anonymous author described several portraits and sculptures of family members. Unfortunately, this attempt yielded no definitive results. Nevertheless, the following historians helped Michael Rosenfeld in this research: Chiara Beccalossi, Giovanni Dall'Orto, Nicola della Monica, and Roberto Dagnino.

Michael Rosenfeld wishes to acknowledge the hard work of the editorial staff of Les Nouvelles Éditions Place in Paris on the French edition of this text. In particular, he is indebted to its chief editor, Cyrille Zola-Place, and his colleague, Nina Payonne. Mr. Zola-Place was also instrumental in negotiating with the first American publisher, Bill Cohen of Harrington Park Press, on this English translation and adaptation, when we first began to work on this project.

Bill Cohen and William Peniston had many conversations in the course of the work on this project. They discussed content, title, copyright, contracts, and the state of scholarly publications in gay and lesbian studies in the United States in the twenty-first century, among many other topics. Their productive discussions resulted in numerous improvements in the manuscript. Among Bill's team, Steven Rigolosi and especially Ann Twombly were instrumental in editing this manuscript in what we had hoped would be its final production.

Sadly, Bill's sudden death in December 2019 was a shock to all of us involved in this project, as well as to all scholars working in the field of lesbian and gay studies. He was a pioneering publisher, who combined a commitment to social activism with a belief in the importance of advancing knowledge. Many of us are indebted to his work as the publisher of the *Journal of Homosexuality* and the numerous monographs that he worked on throughout the years. He will be sorely missed.

Luckily for us, Caelyn Cobb of Columbia University Press picked up this project, and she found two anonymous reviewers, whose comments allowed us to make some last-minute improvements. We are enormously thankful for her and her team (Marisa Lastres and Monique Briones) at Columbia University Press for making this English-language publication possible. In addition, Anita O'Brien did a splendid job with the copyediting, and Paula C. Durbin-Westby produced the index. We also thank Dr. Margot Irvine, director of the School of Languages and Literatures at the University of Guelph, who provided a grant in support of this publication, in particular, its index.

Established in 2006 by the Cultural Services of the French Embassy, along with the French American Cultural Exchange (FACE) Foundation, the Institut Français, and the Ministry of Foreign Affairs, the French Voices award is designed "to promote French and Francophone literature and to encourage the translation of French fiction and non-fiction." Michael Rosenfeld, William Peniston, Nancy Erber, and Clive Thomson are all thrilled that the fifteen-member committee awarded one of its fifteen awards to the translation of *Confessions d'un homosexuel à Émile Zola* in 2018. This was not an easy choice for them to make. After all, the earliest parts of this book were first published in 1894–1895, not within six years of the publication of the English translation. And they were written by an Italian man, not a Frenchman, although he did write in French. They were written to Émile Zola, one of the most famous writers of the French language, and perhaps that accounts for the committee's interest, but they were published by an obscure military doctor who specialized in psychiatry, not necessary a major selling point. And yet the committee recognized that this is an important story to tell. Without this award, this book would not have been possible, and we are grateful for their decision.

Michael Rosenfeld sincerely thanks Eléonore Reverzy, Damien Zanone, and Elisheva Rosen, who have always pushed him to go further. Daniel Grojnowski, who published a partial edition of the *Roman* and the *Suite* a decade ago, honored him with his wise advice. Colette Becker was kind enough to read and comment on the original study. Wannes Dupont encouraged him to question his premises. Julie Coutu, Sébastien Roldan, Sophie Pelletier, and especially Marion Glaumaud-Carbonnier have always been available to help him with his intellectual work (and grammar!). Their friendship is a permanent source of comfort. Michael's warmest regards go out to several very old friends: Carole, Shirley, Lihi, Gal, Beni, Anne, Gabriella, and Catherine. Finally, he thanks his family for their unfailing support throughout the preparation of this book, and more specifically his mother Harriet for her invaluable help.

Bibliography

FRENCH EDITIONS OF THE NOVEL OF AN INVERT

Laupts, Dr. [Georges Saint-Paul]. "Le Roman d'un inverti." *Archives d'Anthropologie Criminelle* (1894): 211–15, 367–73, 729–31; (1895): 131–38, 228–41, 320–25.
———. "Le Roman d'un inverti-né." In *Tares et poisons. Perversion et perversité sexuelles*, 47–95. Paris: Georges Carré, 1896.
Laupts, Dr. (G. Saint-Paul) [Georges Saint-Paul]. "Le Roman d'un inverti-né" and "La suite du roman d'un inverti-né." In *L'Homosexualité et les types homosexuels*, 47–95, 432–41. Paris: Vigot frères, 1910.
Saint-Paul, Georges. "Portrait d'inverti. Silhouettes de bisexuels." In *Invertis et homosexuels*, 69–128. Paris, Vigot Frères, 1930.
"Le Roman d'un inverti-né." In Pierre Hahn, *Nos ancêtres les pervers: La vie des homosexuels sous le Second Empire*, 231–66. Paris: Olivier Orban, 1979.
Roman d'un inverti-né. Préface d'Émile Zola, extrait de *Perversion et perversité* par le Dr. Laupts. Paris: À Rebours, 2005.
Grojnowski, Daniel, ed. *Confessions d'un inverti-né, suivies de Confidences et aveux d'un Parisien par Arthur W.* Paris: José Corti, 2007.
"Le Roman d'un inverti." In *Bougres de vies. Huit homosexuels du XIXe siècle se racontent*, ed. William A. Peniston and Nancy Erber, 135–204. Paris: ErosOnyx, 2012.
Rosenfeld, Michael, ed. *Confessions d'un homosexuel à Émile Zola: Première édition non censurée du "Roman d'un inverti."* Paris: Nouvelles Éditions Place, 2017.

GERMAN, ENGLISH, AND ITALIAN TRANSLATIONS
OF THE NOVEL OF AN INVERT

Barattin, Debora, ed. *Confessioni di un omosessuale a Émile Zola*. Rome: WoM Edizioni, 2021.
Beulwitz, Rudolf von. "Ein Brief Émile Zola an Dr. Laupts über Frage der Homosexualität." *Jahrbuch für sexuelle Zwischenstufen* 7 (1905): 371–86.

"The Novel of an Invert." In *Queer Lives: Men's Autobiographies from Nineteenth-Century France*, trans. and ed. William A. Peniston and Nancy Erber, 165–247. Lincoln: University of Nebraska Press, 2007.

Il Romanzo di un Invertito Nato. Biblioteca di Progetto Gay, November 2014. http://gayproject.altervista.org/romanzo.pdf.

Setz, Wolfram, ed. *Der Roman eines Kontrarsexuellen. Eine Autobiographie*. Berlin: Verlag Rosa Winkel, 1991.

Thal, Wilhelm. *Romans eines Kontrarsexuellen*. Leipzig: Spohr, 1899.

MODERN ADAPTION OF THE NOVEL OF AN INVERT

Ganes, Samuel. *Penis desiderantis*. Paris: Éditions Gaies et Lesbiennes, 2006.

HISTORICAL, LITERARY, AND CRITICAL WORKS

Annuario della nobiltà italiana, anno 19. Bari: Direzione del Giornale Araldico, 1897.

Apitzsch, Georges. *Lettres d'un inverti allemand au Dr Lacassagne, 1903–1908*, ed. Philippe Artières. Paris: EPEL, 2006.

Archives d'Anthropologie Criminelle, de Criminologie et de Psychologie Normale et Pathologique. Paris: Masson, 1886–1893.

Archives d'Anthropologie Criminelle, de Médecine Légale et de Psychologie Normale et Pathologique. Paris: Masson, 1893–1914.

Ariès, Philippe. "Réflexions sur l'histoire de l'homosexualité." *Communications* 35 (1982): 56–67.

Artières, Philippe. "Lacassagne: Le professeur et l'inverti." *Criminocorpus. Histoire de la criminologie*, January 1, 2005, http://criminocorpus.revues.org/120.

Artières, Philippe, and Gérard Corneloup. *Le Médecin et le criminel: Alexandre Lacassagne, 1843–1924*. Catalog of an exhibition at the Bibliothèque Municipale de Lyon, January 27–May 15, 2004. Lyon, Bibliothèque Municipale de Lyon, 2004.

Artières, Philippe, and Clive Thomson, eds. *Fières archives: documents et images autobiographiques d'homosexuels "fin de siècle."* Paris: Atlande, 2017.

Baguley, David. "L'Indicible de la sexualité dans l'œuvre de Zola." *Nineteenth-Century French Studies* 27 (1998–1999): 108–16.

Benadusi, Lorenzo. *The Enemy of the New Man: Homosexuality in Fascist Italy*. Madison: University of Wisconsin Press, 2012.

Bereni, Laure, Sébastien Chauvin, Alexandre Jaunait, and Anne Revillard, eds. *Introduction aux Gender Studies*. Brussels: De Boeck, 2008.

Berrong, Richard M. "A French Reaction to the Wilde Affair and Increasing Homophobia in Late-Nineteenth-Century France: Pierre Loti's *Judith Renaudin*." *Neophilologus* 95 (2011): 17–189.

Bleys, Rudi. *The Geography of Perversion.* New York: New York University Press, 1995.
Bordas, Éric. "Introduction. Comment en parlait-on?" *Romantisme* 159 (2013): 3–17.
Briki, Malick. *Psychiatrie et homosexualité: Lectures médicales et juridiques de l'homosexualité dans les sociétés occidentales de 1850 à nos jours.* Besançon: Presses Universitaires de Franche Comté, 2009.
Burns, Colin. "Le Voyage de Zola à Londres en 1893: 'Notes sur Londres,' texte inédit d'Émile Zola." *Les Cahiers Naturalistes* 60 (1986): 41–73.
Butler, Judith. *Bodies That Matter: On the Discursive Limits of "Sex."* New York: Routledge, 1993.
———. *Gender Trouble: Feminism and the Subversion of Identity.* New York: Routledge, 1990.
Buvik, Per. "Naturalisme et vitalisme: À propos de la sexualité dans l'œuvre de Zola." *Les Cahiers Naturalistes* 86 (2012): 177–97.
Cabanès, Jean-Louis. [Book review of] *Confessions d'un inverti-né, préface d'Émile Zola, suivies de Confidences et aveux d'un Parisien par Arthur W.,* ed. Daniel Grojnowski. https://serd.hypotheses.org/files/2018/04/CR_20Confessionsinverti.pdf.
Cardon, Patrick. *Discours littéraires et scientifiques fin-de-siècle, autour de Marc-André Raffalovich.* Paris: Éditions Orizons, 2008.
———. "Les Homosexualités d'un prince ou les avatars de la pornographie homosexuelle masculine au tournant des XIXe et XXe siècles." *Romantisme* 159 (2013): 85–97.
Carlston, Erin G. *Double Agents: Espionage, Literature, and Liminal Causes.* New York: Columbia University Press, 2003.
Carroll, Brandon. "'The Insidious Presence That Speaks': The Monster's Confession in the Roman d'un inverti-né (1896)." In *The Unknowable in Literature and Material Culture,* ed. Margot Irvine and Jeremy Worth, 38–53. Newcastle Upon Tyne, UK: Cambridge Scholars, 2019.
Carroy, Jacqueline. "'Comment fonctionne mon cerveau?' Projets d'introspection scientifique au XIXe siècle." In *Écriture de soi, écriture de l'histoire,* ed. J.-F. Chiantaretto, 161–79. Paris: In Press, 1997.
———. "Le Langage intérieur comme miroir du cerveau: Une enquête, ses enjeux et ses limites." *Langue Française,* no. 132 (2001): 48–56.
———. "Zola mise à nu par des psychiatres (1896–1897)." *Les Cahiers Naturalistes* 95 (2021): 15–30.
Chanteloube, Micheline. *L'École du service de santé des armées de Lyon: Album du centenaire.* Lyon: Charles Lavauzelle, 1988.
Chevalier, Julien. *De l'inversion de l'instinct sexuel au point de vue médico-légal.* Paris: Octave Doin, 1885.
———. *Une Maladie de la personnalité: L'Inversion sexuelle.* Lyon: Storck, 1893.
Counter, Andrew J. "One of Them: Homosexuality and Anarchism in Wilde and Zola." *Comparative Literature* 63 (2011): 345–65.

———. "Zola's Fin-de-siècle Reproductive Politics." *French Studies* 68 (2014): 193–208.

Courapied, Romain. "Le Traitement esthétique de l'homosexualité dans les œuvres décadentes face au système médical et legal: Accords et désaccords sur une éthique de la sexualité." Ph.D. thesis, Université de Rennes 2, 2014.

Detemmerman, Jacques. "Le procès d'Escal-Vigor." In *Le Naturalisme et les lettres françaises de Belgique*, ed. Paul Delsemme and Raymond Trousson. *Revue de l'Université de Bruxelles* 4–5 (1984): 141–69.

Dobelbower, Nicholas. "Dérive génétique et déviance génésique." In *Zola: Genèse de l'œuvre*, ed. Jean-Pierre Leduc-Aldine, 225–44. Paris: CNRS Éditions, 2002.

Dubout, Kevin. *Éric Simac (1874–1913). Un oublié du "mouvement de libération" homosexuel de la Belle Époque*. Paris: Quintes-Feuilles, 2014.

Dubuis, Patrick. *Émergence de l'homosexualité dans la littérature française d'André Gide à Jean Genet*. Paris: L'Harmattan, 2011.

Eribon, Didier, ed. *Dictionnaire des cultures gays et lesbiennes*. Paris: Larousse, 2003.

———. *Réflexions sur la question gay*. Paris: Fayard, 1999.

Espé de Metz, G. [Georges Saint-Paul]. *Plus fort que le mal: Essai sur le mal innommable*. Paris: Maloine, 1907.

Féray, Jean-Claude. "Des éclairages nouveaux sur le *Roman d'un inverti* que Zola et Laupts ont rendu célèbre." *Bulletin Mensuel Quintes-Feuilles*, no. 8 (December 2017): 12–14.

Fernandez, Dominique. *Le Rapt de Ganymède*. Paris: Grasset & Fasquelle, 1989.

Finn, Michael. "Naturalisme, sexe et sexologie: Excès catastrophique ou fantaisie médicale?" *Les Cahiers Naturalistes* 85 (2011): 117–33.

Foucault, Michel. *L'Archéologie du savoir*. Paris: Gallimard, 1969. Translated by A. M. Sheridan Smith as *Archaeology of Knowledge*. New York: Pantheon Books, 1972.

———. *Histoire de la sexualité*. Paris: Gallimard, 1976. Translated by Robert Hurley as *The History of Sexuality*. New York: Vintage Books, 1978.

———. *Surveiller et Punir*. Paris: Gallimard, 1975. Translated by Alan Sheridan as *Discipline and Punish: The Birth of the Prison*. New York: Vintage Books, 1979.

Giami, Alain, and Gert Hekma, eds. *Révolutions sexuelles*. Paris: La Musardine, 2015.

Gide, André. *Et nunc manet in te*. Paris: Ides et Calendes, 1947. Translated by Justin O'Brien as *Madeleine (Et nunc manet in te)*. New York: Knopf, 1952; reprint, Chicago: Elephant Paperbacks, 1989.

Gondrand, Pascal. *Le Médecin général Georges Saint-Paul, 1870–1937*. Geneva, 2008.

Gougelmann, Stéphane. "Le Naturaliste, l'homosexuel et 'l'éloquence de la vérité.'" In *Le Réalisme et ses paradoxes (1850–1900)*, ed. Gabrielle Chamarat and Pierre-Jean Dufief, 471–79. Paris: Classiques Garnier, 2014.

Granier, Caroline. *Les Briseurs de formules: Les écrivains anarchistes en France à la fin du XIXe siècle*. Cœuvres-et-Valsery: Ressouvenances, 2008.

Jahrbuch für Sexuelle Zwischenstufen. Leipzig: Verlag Max Spohr, 1902.
Krafft-Ebing, Richard von. *Psychopathia sexualis: Eine klinisch-forensische Studie*. Stuttgart: Ferdinand Enke, 1886. Translated by F. J. Rebman as *Psychopathia sexaulis: With Especial Reference to the Antipathic Sexual Instinct: A Medico-Forensic Study*. Philadelphia: F. A. Davis, 1893. Translated into French as *Psychopathia sexualis. Avec recherches spéciales sur l'inversion sexuelle*. Paris, G. Carré, 1895.
Larivière, Michael, ed. *À poil et à plume: Homosexuels et bisexuels célèbres*. Paris: Éditions Régine Deforges, 1987.
Laupts, Dr. [Georges Saint-Paul]. "Enquête sur inversion sexuelle: Questionnaire-plan. *Archives d'Anthropologie Criminelle* 9 (1894): 105–8.
———. "Enquête sur l'inversion sexuelle: Réponses." *Archives d'Anthropologie Criminelle* 9 (1894): 211–12.
———. "Lettre au Professeur Lacassagne." *Archives d'Anthropologie Criminelle* 24 (1909): 693–96.
Lauretis, Teresa de, ed. *Queer Theory: Lesbian and Gay Sexualities*. Bloomington: Indiana University Press, 1991.
Lauritsen, John, and David Thorstad. *The Early Homosexual Rights Movement (1864–1935)*. New York: Times Change Press, 1974.
Lejeune, Philippe. *L'Autobiographie en France*. Paris: A. Colin, 2003.
———. *Autobiographie et homosexualité en France au XIXe siècle*, ed. Clive Thomson. Paris: Éditions de la Sorbonne, 2017.
———. "Autobiographies et homosexualité en France au XIXe siècle." *Romantisme* 56 (1987): 79–94.
———. *Les Brouillons de soi*. Paris: Seuil, 1998.
———. *On Autobiography*, ed. Paul John Eakin; trans. Katherine Leary. Minneapolis: University of Minnesota Press, 1989.
———. *Le Pacte autobiographique*. Paris: Seuil, 1975.
Leroy-Forgeot, Flora. *Histoire juridique de l'homosexualité en Europe*. Paris: Presses Universitaires de France, 1997.
Maguire, J. Robert. *Ceremonies of Bravery: Oscar Wilde, Carlos Blacker and the Dreyfus Affair*. Oxford: Oxford University Press, 2013.
———. "Chronique dreyfusienne." *Les Cahiers Naturalistes* 67 (1993): 326–34.
Martin, Brian Joseph. *Napoleonic Friendship: Military Fraternity, Intimacy and Sexuality in Nineteenth-Century France*. Durham: University of New Hampshire Press, 2011.
Matte, Nicholas. "International Sexual Reform and Sexology in Europe, 1897–1933." *Canadian Bulletin of Medical History* 22 (2005): 253–70.
Mazaleigue-Labaste, Julie. *Les Déséquilibres de l'amour: La genèse du concept de perversion sexuelle, de la Révolution française à Freud*. Montreuil-sous-Bois: Ithaque, 2014.
Meyer-Plantureux, Chantal. *Antisémitisme et homophobie: clichés en scène et à l'écran*. Paris: CNRS Éditions, 2019.

Mitterand, Henri. *Zola*. 3 vols. Paris: Fayard, 1999–2002.
Moll, Albert. *Les Perversions de l'instinct génital*. Paris: G. Carré, 1893.
Murat, Laure. *La Loi du genre: Une histoire culturelle du "troisième sexe."* Paris: Fayard, 2006.
Nye, Robert. *Masculinity and Male Codes of Honor in Modern France*. New York: Oxford University Press, 1993.
Oosterhuis, Harry. *Stepchildren of Nature: Krafft-Ebing, Psychiatry, and the Making of Sexual Identity*. Chicago: University of Chicago Press, 2000.
Pagès, Alain. *L'Affaire Dreyfus. Une histoire médiatique*. Paris: Les Études du CRIF, no. 61 (October–November 2020).
Pagès, Alain, and Owen Morgan. *Guide Émile Zola*. Paris: Ellipses, 2016.
Pastorello, Thierry. *Sodome à Paris, fin XVIIe—milieu XIXe siècle. L'homosexualité masculine en construction*. Paris: Créaphis Éditions, 2011.
Peniston, William A. *Pederasts and Others: Sexual Identity and Urban Culture in Nineteenth-Century Paris*. New York: Harrington Park Press, 2004.
Raffalovich, Marc-André. *Annales de l'unisexualité*. Paris: Masson, 1897.
———. *Uranisme et unisexualité: Une Étude sur différentes manifestations de l'instinct sexuel*. Paris: Masson, and Lyon: A. Storck, 1896. Translated by Nancy Erber and William A. Peniston as *Marc-André Raffalovich's Uranism and Unisexuality: A Study of Different Manifestations of the Sexual Instinct*, ed. Philip Healy with Frederick S. Roden. New York: Palgrave Macmillan, 2016.
Revenin, Régis, ed. *Hommes et masculinités de 1789 à nos jours*. Paris: Éditions Autrement, 2007.
———. *Homosexualité et prostitution masculine à Paris 1870–1918*. Paris: L'Harmattan, 2005.
Rivers, Christopher. "Improbable Prescience: Émile Zola and the Origins of Homosexuality." *Excavatio* 14 (2001): 41–62.
Rosario, Vernon A. *The Erotic Imagination: French Histories of Perversity*. New York: Oxford University Press, 1997.
———. "Inversion's Histories / History's Inversion: Novelizing Fin-de-Siècle Homosexuality." In *Science and Homosexualities*, ed. Vernon A. Rosario, 89–108. New York: Routledge, 1997.
———. "Pointy Penises, Fashion Crimes and Hysterical Mollies: The Pederast's Inversions." In *Homosexuality in Modern France*, ed. Jeffrey Merrick and Bryant T. Ragan, Jr., 146–76. New York: Oxford University Press, 1996.
Rosen, Karl. "Émile Zola and Homosexuality." *Excavatio* 2 (1993): 111–16.
Rosenfeld, Michael. *Formes et figures de l'amour entre hommes dans le discours social, les écrits personnels et la littérature en France et en Belgique de 1870 à 1905*. Ph.D. thesis, Sorbonne Nouvelle Paris 3 University and Catholic University of Louvain, 2020.

———. "Gay Taboos in 1900 Brussels: The Literary, Journalistic and Private Debate Surrounding Georges Eekhoud's Novel *Escal-Vigor*." *Dix-Neuf* 22, no. 1–2 (2018): 98–114.

———. "Genèse d'une pensée sur l'homosexualité: La préface de Zola au *Roman d'un inverti*." *Genesis* 44 (2017): 213–17.

———. "Scénographie et esthétique de la sexualité dans l'œuvre de Zola." In *Lire Zola au XXIe siècle*, ed. Aurélie Barjonet and Jean-Sébastien Macke, 365–76. Paris: Classiques Garnier, 2018.

———. "La Sexualité hors-normes dans les Rougon-Macquart de Zola." MA thesis, University of Tel Aviv, 2009.

———. "Zola à la pointe des savoirs. Théories scientifiques et personnages de médecins dans *Fécondité*." *Les Cahiers Naturalistes* 95 (2021): 65–80.

———. "Zola et l'homosexualité, un nouveau regard." *Les Cahiers Naturalistes* 89 (2015): 213–28.

Rosenfeld, Michael, and Clive Thomson. "Lettres inédites de 1893 à 1925 entre Émile Zola, Alexandrine Zola, Georges Saint-Paul et Yvonne Saint-Paul." *Les Cahiers Naturalistes* 95 (2021): 97–126.

Sadoun-Édouard, Clara. "Presse, mondanité et saphisme décoratif." *Romantisme* 159 (2013): 59–71.

Saint-Paul, Georges. *Essais sur le langage intérieur*. Lyon: Storck, 1892.

———. *Souvenirs de Tunisie et d'Algérie*. Paris: H. Charles-Lavauzelle, 1904.

Schor, Naomi. "Le Sourire du sphinx: Zola et l'énigme de la féminité." *Romantisme* 13–14 (1976): 183–96.

Szczur, Przemyslaw. *Produire une identité: Le personnage homosexuel dans le roman français de la seconde moitié du XIXe siècle (1859–1899)*. Paris: L'Harmattan, 2014.

Tamagne, Florence. *Histoire de l'homosexualité en Europe: Berlin, Londres, Paris, 1919–1939*. Paris: Seuil, 2000. Translated as *A History of Homosexuality in Europe: Berlin, London, Paris, 1919–1939*. New York: Agora, 2004.

———. *Mauvais genre. Une histoire des représentations de l'homosexualité*. Paris: La Martinière, 2001.

Tardieu, Ambroise. *Étude médico-légale sur les attentats aux mœurs*. Paris: Baillière, 1857.

Ternois, René. "Mélanges—ce que Zola n'avait pas osé dire." *Les Cahiers Naturalistes* 36 (1968): 156–60.

Thompson, Hannah. *Naturalism Redressed: Identity and Clothing in the Novels of Émile Zola*. Oxford: Legenda, 2004.

———. "Questions of Sexuality and Gender." In *The Cambridge Companion to Émile Zola*, ed. Brian Nelson, 53–66. Cambridge: Cambridge University Press, 2007.

———. *Taboo: Corporeal Secrets in Nineteenth-Century France*. London: Legenda, 2013.

Thomson, Clive. "De la pédérastie à l'homosexualité: La perversion comme site d'un nouveau rapport entre médecin et patient (1880–1900)." In *Médecine, sciences de la vie et littérature en France et en Europe de la Révolution à nos jours*, ed. Lise Dumasy-Queffélec and Hélène Spengler, 161–74. Geneva: Droz, 2014.

———. *Georges Hérelle. Archéologue de l'inversion sexuelle fin-de-siècle*. Paris: Le Félin, 2014.

———. " 'Le Sentiment dont nous parlons': La correspondance de Georges Hérelle." *Études Françaises* 55, no. 1 (2019): 17–31.

Tin, Louis-Georges, ed. *Dictionnaire de l'homophobie*. Paris: Presses Universitaires de France, 2003.

———. *L'Invention de la culture hétérosexuelle*. Paris: Éditions Autrement, 2008.

Tin, Louis-Georges, and Geneviève Pastre, eds. *Homosexualités: Expression/ repression*. Paris: Stock, 2000.

White, Nicholas. " 'L'enclume toujours chaude': Émile Zola's Newspaper Trilogy." *Dix-Neuf* 21 (2017): 327–41.

———. "L'homos et l'heteros des Rougon-Macquart. " *Les Cahiers Naturalistes* 91 (2017): 11–24.

———. "Style Wars: The Uniform and the Polymorphous in *La Débâcle*." In *Fashion, Modernity and Materiality in France*, ed. Heidi Brevik-Zender, 157–78. Albany: State University of New York Press, 2018.

———. "Zola's 'champ limité de la réalisation': *La Débâcle* and the Commune." *Nineteenth-Century French Studies* 49 (2021): 477–98.

Younger, John G. "Ten Unpublished Letters by John Addington Symonds at Duke University." *Victorian Newsletter* 95 (1999): 1–10.

Zola, Émile. *Chroniques et Polémiques II*, vol. 12 of *Oeuvres complètes*. Paris: Cercle du Livre précieux, 1968.

———. *Correspondance*, ed. B. H. Bakker. 11 vols. Montréal: Presses de l'Université de Montréal, 1978–1995, 2018.

———. *La Curée*, vol. 2 of *Les Rougon-Macquart*. 1872. Reprint, Paris: Gallimard, 1960. Translated by Brian Nelson as *The Kill (La Curée)*. New York: Oxford University Press, 2004.

———. *La Débâcle*, vol. 19 of *Les Rougon-Macquart*. 1892. Reprint, Paris: Gallimard, 1960. Translated by Leonard Tancock as *The Debacle*. New York: Penguin Books, 1972.

———. *La Fabrique des Rougon-Macquart: Édition des dossiers préparatoires*, 7 vols., ed. Colette Becker and Véronique Lavielle. Paris: Honoré Champion, 2003–2017.

———. *Paris*, vol. 7 of *Œuvres complètes*. Paris: Cercle du Livre précieux, 1968. Translated by Ernest Alfred Vizetelly as *Paris*. Dover, N.H.: Alan Sutton, 1993.

———. *La Terre*, vol. 15 of *Les Rougon-Macquart*. 1887. Reprint, Paris: Gallimard, 1960. Translated by Douglas Parmée as *The Earth*. New York: Penguin Books, 1980.

Contributors

MICHAEL ROSENFELD graduated in June 2020 with two doctorate degrees in French literature and civilization at the Sorbonne Nouvelle–Paris 3 University and in French language and literature at the Catholic University of Louvain in Belgium. The title of his dissertation is "Formes et figures de l'amour entre hommes dans le discours social, les écrits personnels et la littérature en France et en Belgique de 1870 à 1905." He has published numerous articles on Zola, Eekhoud, and queer studies in various academic journals. From 2014 to 2017, he taught Hebrew language and literature in the Department of Jewish and Hebraic Studies at the University of Strasbourg. He started a one-year post-doctoral research fellowship at the Université libre de Bruxelles in Belgium in October 2021.

CLIVE THOMSON is professor of French literature at the University of Guelph in Canada. He is a psychoanalyst and an elected member of the Toronto Society for Contemporary Psychoanalysis. His publications include Dialogues with Bakhtinian Theory (2012), Georges Hérelle, archéologue de l'inversion sexuelle "fin de siècle" (2014), Autobiographie et homosexualité en France au XIXe siècle de Philippe Lejeune (2017), Fières archives: Documents d'homosexuels fin de siècle (2017), and On croit comprendre le monde avec ça: Entretiens mémoriels avec Henri Mitterrand (2021).

NANCY ERBER is professor emerita of modern languages and literature at the City University of New York. She is the coeditor of Disorder in the Court: Trials and Sexual Conflict at the Turn of the Century (1999) and translator of Paul Thorez's Model Children: Inside the Republic of Red Scarves (1991).

WILLIAM A. PENISTON is the retired librarian and archivist at the Newark Museum of Art, as well as a French historian. He is the author of Pederasts and Others: Urban Culture and Sexual Identity in Nineteenth-Century Paris (2004).

Together, Erber and Peniston have previously translated Queer Lives: Men's Autobiographies from Nineteenth-Century France (2007), Marc-André Raffalovich's Uranism and

Unisexuality: A Study of Different Manifestations of the Sexual Instinct (2015), Nicole G. Albert's Lesbian Decadence: Representations in Art and Literature in Fin-de-Siècle France (2015), and White War, Black Soldiers: Two African Accounts of World War I by Bakary Diallo and Lamine Senghor (2021).

Index

Page locators in *italics* indicate figures.

Académie française, 196–98
"active invert," 16, 163, 209
Albert of Monaco, Prince, 187
Alcan (publisher), 193
Alexis (lover in Virgil), 101
Algiers and Tunis, 200, 209
Amenhotep (pharaoh), 128
amitié (friendship), 51–52n10
anal sex ("sodomy"), xxi, 4, 30, 75, 111, 137
Andromache (Greek mythology), 52–53
Angèle (character, *La Curée*), 50
Angevins, 143
Annales Médico-Chirurgicales du Centre (Tours) / *Medical and Surgical Annals of the Center (Tours)*, 216
Antinous, 61, 89n46, 125–26
Apitzsch, Georges, 7
Arbaces (character, *The Last Days of Pompeii*), 91
Archives d'Anthropologie Criminelle / *Archives of Criminal Anthropology*, 154, 207, 216; "Inquiry into Sexual Inversion: Questionnaire" in, 169; *Novel of an Invert* in, xiii–xiv, xviii, xxiii, 2, 39, 95–96n61, 161, 163–65, 169, 178, 187, 212; Raffalovich's works in, xxii, 20, 161, 176–77;

Saint-Paul's work in, 150–51, 217. *See also* "Inquiry into Sexual Inversion: Questionnaire" (Saint-Paul)
archives of Zola and Saint-Paul families, xiv, 2, 5, 39–40, 139n1, 187, 219–20
Astarte, cult of, 130
Athaliah (daughter of Jezebel and Ahab), 120
audio-visual, category of, 189–90
autobiographies by men interested in other men, 6–7

Baal, cult of, 130
Ball, Benjamin, 161
Ballet, Gilbert, 156, 193
Balzac, Honoré de, 47, 84–85, 99
Baptiste (character, *La Curée*), 26, 48, 76
Barry, Madame du (Marie-Jeanne Bécu), 86
Bellini, Vincenzo, 103
Belorget, Arthur, 6, 6–7n13, 216–17n4
Bête humaine, La / *The Beast Within* (Zola), 25, 27n82, 193n11
Bibliothèque Municipale de Lyon, 169–70
Binet, Alfred, 156, 161
Biologica: Revue Scientifique du Médecin, 21
bisexuality, 162, 205–6

234 INDEX

Bjørnson, Bjørnstjerne Martinus, 37
Blacker, Carlos, 35
Bonald, Louis de, 150
Bonnot de Condillac, Étienne, 150
"born invert," xiii–xiv, xviii, xxiii, 2, 39, 95–96n61, 161, 163–65, 169, 170, 187, 212; feminine-form, 21n66, 22, 174, 178–80, 182, 185; "predisposed cerebral born–invert," 184. See also congenitalist model
Bourget, Paul, 150
Brandes, Georg, 37
Brillat-Savarin, Jean-Anthelme, 91
Brouez, Fernand, 19n61
Bruloff, Karl Pavlovich, 91n55

Canova, Antonio, 93
Captain (Italian's lover), xix, 3, 71–77, 81–84, 89, 108, 137, 184
Carpenter, Edward, 19n61
Carré, Georges (publisher), 11–14, 160, 176n10
Cauldwell, David O., xxiii
Charcot, Jean-Martin, 150, 156, 158n18
Charpentier-Fasquelle (publisher), 27–28, 30, 97
Chevalier, Julien, 34n102, 161–62, 171, 173, 175n8, 206, 216
Christina of Savoy, 118
Collège de France, 150
Confessions d'un homosexuel à Émile Zola: première édition non censurée du "Roman d'un Inverti" (ed. Rosenfeld), xi, 40, 66n19
congenitalist model, xix–xxi, 26, 48, 175. See also "born invert"
contagion theory, 170, 211
"contrary sexuals," as term, xviii
Coppée, François, 151
cosmopolitanism, 209, 211

criminalization of homosexuality, xiii, 3–4, 6, 37, 68n21, 175
cross-dressing: Italian's early experiences with, 51, 55; Italian's views of, xix–xx, xxii, 16, 86, 115, 180; "man-girl," xxii, 115
cultural politics of sexuality, xvii
Curée, La / The Kill (Zola), xix, 25–26, 48, 76–77, 90
"cures" for homosexuality, xv, 33, 44, 163, 165–66, 173, 195–96, 215; heterosexual intercourse as, 17, 32, 104; Italian's rejection of, xxi, 3, 24

Daudet, Alphonse, 151, 189–90, 199
Daudet, Léon, 189–90, 192
Death of Cleopatra (Makart), 86
Débâcle, La / The Debacle (Zola), 27–30, 191, 193n11
Dédé (Essebac), 23
Defects and Poisons: Sexual Perversion and Perversity. See Tares et poisons: Perversion et perversité sexuelles / Defects and Poisons: Sexual Perversion and Perversity (first edition of Novel of an Invert, 1896, Saint-Paul)
degenerationist theories, xxii, 19, 27, 134, 145–46, 166, 172, 175, 185
Desbarolles, Adrien-Adolphe, 49
desire, Saint-Paul's view of, 166–67
Dessoir, Max, 176, 216
"Des types sexuels intermédiaires" / "Intermediate Sexual Types" (Simac), 21
Diderot, Denis, 157
Disciple aimé, Le / The Beloved Disciple (Hermant), 23
Dorian Gray (Wilde), 115, 216
Douglas, Alfred, 30
Dreyfus Affair, xv, 13, 34, 36, 145, 200–202

Drumont, Édouard, 123, 145
Dumas, Alexandre, the elder, 64n18, 88
Dumas, Alexandre, the younger, 64n18
Dumas, Dr., 19
Duvillard, Baroness (character, Paris), 31

economic circumstances, as cause of homosexuality, 207, 212
educational institutions, and sexual experimentation, 181
Eekhoud, Georges, 19n61, 36–37
effeminacy: of Italian's father, xxii, 118; Italian's views of, xix, xxii–xxiii, 16, 18, 87, 115; Raffalovich's opposition to, 20–21; Saint-Paul's invented details, 16; Zola's view, 34, 45
Egger, Victor, 158n18
Élisabeth-Philippine-Marie-Hélène (of France), 52
Ellis, Havelock, 207
Escal-Vigor (Eekhoud), 36–37
Espé de Metz, G. *See* Saint-Paul, Georges
Essais de psychologie contemporaine / Essays on Contemporary Psychology (Bourget), 150
"Essays on Interior Language" (doctoral thesis, Saint-Paul), 8, 150–52, 156–60; dedicatory note, 151–52; summary of argument, 157–58n17, 164
Essebac, Achille, 23
Ettinger (correspondent), 23–24
Eulenberg case, 216

Fécondité / Fecundity (Zola), 8, 194
"feminine-form invert," 21n66, 22, 174, 178–80, 182, 185
Ferdinand II (of Two Sicilies), 93, 118, 144
Ferdinand IV (of Naples), 143
Figaro, Le, 33, 151, 187, 191, 192

Fille aux yeux d'or, La / The Girl with the Golden Eyes (La Belle aux yeux d'or) (Balzac), 47
France: birth rate, 33; French Revolution, 52; nationalism, and stances toward homosexuality, 15, 18, 32–33, 185, 205, 209, 211–13; republic, 86
Freud, Sigmund, xviii

"gay," as term, 1
gay men, letters from, to Saint-Paul, 21–25, 170
Gay Pride, xxiii
gender inversion model, xxii
generational transmission theory, 17, 170, 181, 184
Germany, Paragraph 175, 37
Gide, André, 17n56
governess of Italian, 51–52, 58
Gray, John, 105n12
Greek love, 163
Greenway, Kate, 116
Guichard, Charles. *See* Simac, Éric (Guichard, Charles)

habit, 184
Hadrian, 88, 89n46
Hamon, Augustin, 19–20n61, 160, 165–66, 202
Healy, Chris, 36
Hector (Greek hero), 52–53
Hercules Farnese (statue), 126
hereditary theories, xxii, 12n36, 162–64, 175n7; generational transmission theory, 17, 170, 181, 184; in questionnaire about inversion, 171–73; Saint-Paul's views, 145–46, 164, 166, 169; Zola's views, 34, 38
Hérelle, Georges, 24

Hermant, Abel, 23
hermaphrodite, "failed," 180
Hermaphrodite, statue of, 30, 124
hermaphroditism, xx, 34, 45
heterosexual intercourse, thought to be cure for homosexuality, 17, 32, 104
Hirschfeld, Magnus, xxiii, 23, 37, 198n21, 207, 216
history, as source of personality, 130, 145
History of the Girondins (Lamartine), 52
Homogenic Love (Carpenter), 19n61
Homosexualité et les types homosexuels / Homosexuality and Types of Homosexuals (second edition of Novel of an Invert, 1910, Saint-Paul), 14–15, 17, 39, 170, 205–13; preface to, 205–8; "Zola and Inversion," 205, 208–9
homosexuality: as category, xviii; contemporary identity labels, xxiii; criminalization of, xiii, 3, 4, 6, 37, 68n21, 175; "cures" for, xv, 33, 44, 163, 165–66, 173, 195–96, 215; dangers to homosexuals in nineteenth century, 4; lesbians, 22n68, 169, 174–75; nonprocreative sex, 4, 112, 137, 185, 194n12; as potential for all human beings, 162, 211; social groups, 206–7, 211; "uranists," xx, xxii, 34, 166n33. See also "inversion," studies of
Homosexuality and Types of Homosexuals. See Homosexualité et les types homosexuels / Homosexuality and Types of Homosexuals (second edition of Novel of an Invert, 1910, Saint-Paul)
homosexual writers, credibility of questioned, 17, 207–8, 212
Hôpital Sainte-Anne (Paris), 175n7
Hyacinth (Metamorphoses), 80, 101, 124
Hyacinth, statuette of, 30, 124
Hyacinthe (character, Paris), 30–32, 38

Iliad (Homer), 53n13
"indifferent type," 16, 158n17, 174, 184, 206
"In Memoriam: Émile Zola" (Saint-Paul), 8, 12, 187–203, 205
"Inquiry into Sexual Inversion: Questionnaire" (Saint-Paul), 21–22, 144–45, 164–66, 169–85, 199; Acknowledgments, 175–77; duration of study, 193; Guide Intended to Facilitate Answers, 171–73; Initial Signs of Sexuality, Regarding Current Condition, 172–73; Observations About a Specific Subject, 173–75; Responses, 177–85
intellectual engagement, and homosexuality, 209
interior language: main argument of Saint-Paul's thesis, 157–58n17. See also "Essays on Interior Language" (doctoral thesis, Saint-Paul)
"intermediate type," 21, 206
"inversion," studies of, xviii, 8–9, 161–67; "active invert," 16, 163, 209; classification and definition schemas, xviii, 16, 162–64, 179–80; contagion theory, 170, 211; cosmopolitanism as cause, 209, 211; degenerationist theories, xxii, 19, 27, 134, 145–46, 166, 172, 175, 185; economic circumstances as cause, 207, 212; "feminine-form invert," 21n66, 22, 174, 178–80, 182, 185; generational transmission theory, 17, 170, 181, 184; German works, 7, 21, 162n24, 176nn10, 11; "indifferent type," 16, 158n17, 174, 184, 206; intellectual engagement and homosexuality, 209; "intermediate type," 21, 206; "occasional invert,"

163–65; "passive invert," 16, 163–64; "pedophilic form of inversion," 21n66, 174, 180; psychotherapy for "occasional" invert, 165; puberty, 180–84, 212; seduction theories, xxi, 16–17, 170, 183; social environment, focus on, 162, 164, 205–7, 210, 213; "strong invert," 180; "weak invert," 180. *See also* "born invert"; hereditary theories; homosexuality

invert, as term, 47n1. *See also* "born invert"; homosexuality; "inversion," studies of

Invertis et homosexuels / *Inverts and Homosexuals* (third edition of *Novel of an Invert*, 1930, Saint-Paul), 15, 18, 21, 39; preface to, 215–18

Italian, the: arrogance of, 86, 94, 136; arts, interest in, 32, 52, 101; attempts to change himself, 60; authenticity of, xiv, 5, 23–24n71, 170, 178–79; beauty, passion for, 52, 84–87, 125; brothel, visit to, 3, 59; childhood-first deviations, 51–57; as combination of both sexes, xix, xx, 55–56, 77–78, 80, 129, 134; congenitalist view of his sexual nature, xx–xxi; corruption, view of, 69, 71, 130; cross-dressing, abhorrence of, xxii, 16, 115, 180; and cross-dressing, xix–xx, 51, 55, 86, 115; cruelty of, 86–87; death, desire for, 48, 60, 71, 94–95; depression, experience of, 4, 59–60, 70; effeminacy, views of, xix, xxii–xxiii, 16–18, 87, 115; as egotistical, 94, 102, 126; emotions, lability of, 93–94; ephebe, resemblance to, 124, 134, 183; experiences of anal sex, xxi, 4, 30, 75, 82, 111, 137; as "female soul in a male body," xx, xxiii, 59; on friendships, 51–52n10, 56, 64, 67, 69–70, 76, 80, 108, 135, 152; gendered conflict of, xix–xx, xxiii; gender inversion model, rejection of, xxii; hands of, as beautiful, 59, 92–93; handwriting of, 40, 46, 89n48, 90n52, 53, 96n62, 98, 139n1; health of, 94–95, 103–4; on his personality, 80–90; history, interest in, 52, 88–89; Hyacinthe (character, *Paris*) and traits of, 30–32; identity evolution of, xxiii–xxiv, 3–4; imaginary spiritual lovers of, 60; imaginary worlds in childhood, 52–55; influence on Zola's opinions, 2–3, 32–38; on "innate science," xxi, 100; intelligence of, 51–52; internalized homophobia and transphobia, xx, xxii, 48, 56, 59–60, 70–71, 77–78, 84, 94–95, 178; isolation of, 22–23, 54, 60, 67–68, 70, 77, 114; *La Curée*, views of characters in, xix, 26–27, 48, 76–77; letters found in Zola and Saint-Paul family archives, xiv, 2, 5, 39–40, 219–20; letter to Saint-Paul, xx–xxii, 2–4, 7, 15, 98, 99–137, 139–40, 170, 205; literature, interest in, 32, 53, 70, 88, 103; Little Madonna and Mademoiselle as nicknames of, xix, 51, 180; on love, 81; masturbation, experiences with, 3, 58; military service, 62–71; music, passion for, 32, 53, 103; mustache, fears of, xix, 55; mythology, passion for, 52–54; painting, study of, 58–59; Paris, move to, 48, 58–59; physique of, xix–xx, 30–31, 50–51, 61–62, 80, 114, 124–25, 131, 132, 133–34; physique of, as similar to woman's, xx, 61, 86; portrait of, 126;

Italian, the (continued)
reaction to *Tares et poisons*, xxi, xxiii, 2, 5–6, 15–18, 100; reclassifications of, xvii–xviii; resistance to labeling himself, xviii–xix, 16–18; self-acceptance of, 3, 4, 102, 112, 210; servants, sexual experiences with, xix, 56–57, 180, 182; sexuality, description of, 134–36; sexuality, early understandings of, 55–56; ugliness, attraction to, 87–88; vanity of, 20, 21n64, 101–2, 126; women, aversion to, 31–32, 59, 80, 183, 195; women, friendships with, 104–5; youth-first acts, 57–62. *See also* Italian's family; Italian's lovers

Italian's family, 100–101; Anglomania of, 116–17, 119, 143, 210; brother, eldest, 93, 123–24, 127, 144; brother, second, 93, 123–24, 144; brother, third, 50, 53, 93, 123–24, 127, 144; brothers mentioned, 50–53, 60, 78, 127; deaths, 102–4, 106–7; family tree, 142, 143–46; father, xxii, 49–51, 58–60, 86, 94, 104, 118–19; father's grandchildren, 94; grandfather, maternal, 119–20, 127; grandfather, paternal, 50, 93, 116–18; grandmother, maternal, 127, 145, 146; grandmother, paternal, 117–18, 122; great-grandfather, paternal, 116, 143; great-grandmother, maternal ("Jezebel"), 119–22, 128, 143–46; Jewish ancestry, xxii, 3, 31, 48, 50, 119–22, 144–45; marriage of parents, 122–23; mementos, 118; mother, 31, 48–51, 53, 60, 93, 104, 119, 122–23; nephews, 123, 127; as source of his nature, 94, 101, 115–16, 129–30, 144–45; Spanish ancestry, 78, 116; suicides, 120; uncle,

paternal, 119, 127. *See also* Italian, the

Italian's lovers: captain, xix, 3, 71–77, 81–84, 89, 108, 137, 184; diplomat, 106–7, 137; man from Milan at hotel, 18, 95–96n61, 96, 108–13, 137; sergeant, xx, xxi, 3, 16–17, 28–30, 63–70, 81, 107–8, 114, 132, 133–34, 137, 183; Spaniard, 75, 83, 137; ticket controller on train in Belgium, 136

Italy, unification of, 68n21

Ivanhoe (Scott), 72, 88

Jahrbuch für Sexuelle Zwischenstufen / Yearbook of Sexual Intermediates (Hirschfeld), 37

J'en appelle au monde civilisé / I Appeal to the Civilized World (Saint-Paul), 217

Jewish people: in the Italian's ancestry, xxii, 3, 31, 48, 50, 119–22, 144–45; stigmatization of, 145. *See also* Dreyfus Affair

Jezebel (Phoenician princess), 120

Journal, Le, 151, 187, 190, 191

journals, medical, 13, 14, 19, 155. *See also Archives d'Anthropologie Criminelle / Archives of Criminal Anthropology*

Joyce, James, 158n18

Jubilee of Pope Leo XIII, 1, 79

Krafft-Ebing, Richard von, xxi, xxii, 7, 35, 161, 163, 176, 194, 206, 216

Laboratory of Scientific Police Techniques (Lyon), 216

Lacan, Jacques, 167

Lacassagne, Alexandre, 7–9, 27, 149–53, 161, 206, 216; letters to Saint-Paul, 149, 153n7; at School of Military Medicine, 149–50; *Vade*

mecum du médicin légiste / My Guide to Forensic Medicine, 171
Lady Gaga, xvii
Lamartine, Alphonse-Marie-Louis de Prat de, 52
Lamballe, Princess de (Marie-Thérèse-Louise de Savoy-Carignano), 52
Langage intérieur et les diverses formes de l'aphasie, Le (Ballet), 156, 193
Lantier, Jacques (character, La Bête humaine), 27
Last Days of Pompeii, The (Bruloff), 91n55
Last Days of Pompeii, The (Lytton), 91n55
Latin, used for "obscene" parts of text, 11, 30, 57n15, 67n20, 68n22, 74n26, 75n28, 179
Laupts, Dr. See Saint-Paul, Georges
Lauritsen, John, 37n118
Lechmitzky, Athan, 23–24
Legludic, Henri, 216, 217n4
Lejeune, Philippe, 6, 24n73
Lemaître (of Geneva), 216
Le Most, Gabriel, 22–23
lesbians, 22n68, 169, 174–75
Locard, Edmund, 216
lower classes, and homosexuality, 211
Lucien (character, Illusions perdues / Lost Illusions), 84–85

Madeleine Férat (Zola), 90
Mademoiselle de Maupin (Gautier), 95
Magnan, Valentin, xxii, 161, 175
Maison de la vieille, La / The Old Lady's House (Mendès), 23
Maguire, J. Robert, 36
Makart, Hans, 86
"Malthusianism," 212, 216–17
Man from Milan (Italian's lover), 18, 95–96n61, 96, 108–13, 137
"man-girl," xxii, 115
Margueritte brothers, 190

Marie Antoinette, 88
Marie Louise (of Austria), 87
Martin, Brian Joseph, 28n86
Masson (publisher), 14, 199
Maxime (character, La Curée), xix, 25–26, 77
medicalization of sexuality, xvii, 220
Mendès, Catulle, 23
mental health, 185
Mercure de France, Le, 36
Messalina, Valeria, 120
metaphysics, 156–57
Moll, Albert, 11n33, 35, 161, 163, 176, 194, 216
Moloch, cult of, 130
Mozart, Wolfgang Amadeus, 88

Näcke, Paul, 198n21, 207, 216
Naiec (passive partner, Northern Africa), 209
Naples, 89, 143
Napoleon I, 87
narcissism, as term, 198n21
National Alliance for Population Growth, 33
nationalism, and stances toward homosexuality, 15, 18, 32–33, 185, 205, 209, 211–13
Neipperg, Count of (Adam Adalbert), 87
Nineteenth Division (Algerian Division), 12
nonprocreative sex, 4, 112, 137, 185, 194n12
"normal" type, 165
Novel of an Invert, The (the Italian, 1888 or 1889), xiii–xiv, 39, 47–98; as installments in Archives d'Anthropologie Criminelle (1884–1885), xiii–xiv, xviii, xxiii, 2, 39, 95–96n61, 161, 163–65, 169, 178, 187, 212; first document (1888 or 1889), 47–71; second

Novel of an Invert, The (continued)
document (1888 or 1889), 71–79;
second edition (*L'Homosexualité et les types homosexuels*, 1910), 14–15, 17, 39, 170, 205–13; third document (1888 or 1889), 79–95; third edition (*Invertis et homosexuels*, 1930), 15, 18, 21, 39, 215–18; antecedents and first years of childhood, 48–51; censored sections, 2, 4–5, 15–18, 40, 66n19, 78n34, 89n48, 93n57, 58, 100n3, 102n8, 108n21, 140n4, 170; conclusion of, altered, 18; inventory of male partners, 18; Latin used for "obscene" parts, 11, 30, 57n15, 67n20, 68n22, 74n26, 75n28, 179; postcard (1888 or 1889), 97, 179n16; postscripts, 79, 95–96n61, 96; publication history of, 2, 5–15; reactions to, 18–21, 23–24n71, 165, 192. See also *Invertis et homosexuels / Inverts and Homosexuals* (third edition of *Novel of an Invert*, 1930, Saint-Paul); *Homosexualité et les types homosexuels / Homosexuality and Types of Homosexuals* (second edition of *Novel of an Invert*, 1910, Saint-Paul); *Suite d'un roman d'un invert-né / Sequel to the Confessions of a Homosexual* (the Italian, 1896); *Tares et poisons: Perversion et perversité sexuelles / Defects and Poisons: Sexual Perversion and Perversity* (first edition of *Novel of an Invert*, 1896, Saint-Paul)
novels with gay content, 23, 38
Nyström, Anton, 207, 216

"occasional invert," 163–65
"Opinion of an Algerian Muslim" (Saint-Paul), 205, 209

Pagès, Alain, 2, 39
Palermo, 143
Paragraph 175 (Germany), 37
Paris (Zola), 30–32, 38
Paris, Saint-Paul's view of, 197–98, 201–2, 211
Parker, Charles, 101
Par les colons: l'Algérie aux Algériens et par les Algériens / Through the Eyes of the Colonists: Algeria for the Algerians and by the Algerians (Saint-Paul), 160
"passive invert," 16, 163–64
patients: autobiographies of, 6–7; patient-doctor relationship, 152, 164
"pederasty," 184
"pedophilic" form of inversion, 21n66, 174, 180
"perversion," as term, 165, 170, 205, 206
Perversions de l'instinct genital / Perversions of the Sex Instinct (Moll), 11n33
"pervert" ("perversity"), as term, 183–85, 205, 206
Phèdre (Racine), 105n14
physical attributes, applied to moral nature, 95
Picquart, Georges, 202
Pompeii, 91
Ponson du Terrail, Pierre-Alexis-Joseph-Ferdinand, Vicomte de, 88
pornography laws, 36–37
"Portrait d'inverti. Silhouettes de bisexuels" / "Portrait of an Invert. Profiles of Bisexuals" (in *Homosexualité et les types homosexuels*, 1910), 39
"predisposed cerebral born–invert," 184
prostitution, 211
"psychological types," taxonomy of, 157
Psychologie sociale du militaire professionnel, La (Hamon), 19n61
psychology, as field, 150–51

Psychopathia sexualis (Krafft-Ebing), xxi, 7
puberty, 180–84, 212; friendship, "exaggerated," 181–82

questionnaires: on interior language, 151, 154, 158–59, 164. See also "Inquiry into Sexual Inversion: Questionnaire" (Saint-Paul)

"racial purity" theories, xxii, 145
Racine, Jean, 105n14
Raffalovich, Marc-André, 17n56, 19, 104–5n12, 161–63, 216; in Archives d'Anthropologie Criminelle, xxii, 20, 161, 176–77; effeminacy, ideological opposition to, 20–21; Hamon's view of, 165–66; Zola's letter to, 34–35
"rational socialism," 19n61
Revue Internationale de Criminalistique / Review of International Criminology, 216
Revue Philosophique, La, 19
Revue Philosophique de la France et de l'Étranger, 155
Revue Scientifique, La, 13
Ribot, Théodule, 150, 155–56, 161, 216
Riotor, Léon, 8n17, 151, 190, 192
Robertson, William, 21–22
"Roman d'un inverti-né, Le" / "The Novel of a Born Invert," 39. See also Tares et poisons: Perversion et perversité sexuelles / Defects and Poisons: Sexual Perversion and Perversity (first edition of Novel of an Invert, 1896, Saint-Paul)
Rosenfeld, Michael, 2
Rougon-Macquart cycle (Zola), 26–27, 48nn4, 5

Saint Januarius, 106
Saint Mary Magdalene of Pazzi, image of, 53

Saint-Paul, Georges: analysis of Italian's autobiography, xxii–xxiii, 2, 16, 170, 178–85; in Archives d'Anthropologie Criminelle, 150–53; belief in authenticity of Italian, 170, 178, 199; censorship by, 2, 4–5, 15–18, 140n4, 170; colonialism, view of, 205; and degenerationist theories, 27, 145–46, 166, 172, 175, 185; on desire, 166–67; doctoral thesis, 149–52, 156–60; as Espé de Metz, xviii, 215; ethnographic perspective of, 160; family of, 149; friendly nature of, 149, 153–54; interior language, study of, 8, 150–52, 156–60, 164, 206; Italian's letter to, xx–xxii, 2–4, 7, 15, 98, 99–137, 139–40, 170, 205; Lacassagne, relationship with, 149–56; in Légion d'honneur, 155; letters from gay men to, 21–25, 170; letters to Lacassagne, 8–9; as medical student, 149; military career, 12–14, 147–48, 154–55, 160, 187; monograph, idea for, 156; nationalism of, 15, 18, 205, 211–13; neologisms created by, 157n16; network of contacts, 35, 151, 154, 160–61; notebook of, 16, 95–96n61; Paris, view of, 197–98, 201–2, 211; pseudonyms used by, xiii, xv, xvii–xviii, 10–11, 155, 215; psychological perspective abandoned by, 159–60; "psychological types," taxonomy of, 157; questionnaire on interior language, 151, 154, 158–59, 164; research program of, 155; War Cross medal won by, 155; writing style of, 152, 156–58; Zola, friendship with, 2, 8–10, 13, 27, 187, 193, 199–203

Saint-Paul, Georges—Works: "Essays on Interior Language," 8, 150–52, 156–60, 164; "In Memoriam: Émile Zola," 8, 12, 187–203, 205; "Inquiry into Sexual Inversion: Questionnaire," 164–66, 169, 170–85, 199; J'en appelle au monde civilisé / I Appeal to the Civilized World, 217; "Opinion of an Algerian Muslim," 205, 209; Par les colons: l'Algérie aux Algériens et par les Algériens / Through the Eyes of the Colonists: Algeria for the Algerians and by the Algerians, 160; Plus fort que le mal. Essai sur le mal innommable / Stronger than the illness. Essay on the unnamable illness, 14n52; "Portrait d'inverti. Silhouettes de bisexuels / Portrait of an Invert. Profiles of Bisexuals" (in second edition of Novel of an Invert, 1910), 39; Souvenirs de Tunisie et d'Algérie / Recollections of Tunisia and Algeria, 155n12, 160, 200; "Zola and Inversion," 205, 208–9. See also Tares et poisons: Perversion et perversité sexuelles / Defects and Poisons: Sexual Perversion and Perversity (first edition of Novel of an Invert, 1896, Saint-Paul); Homosexualité et les types homosexuels / Homosexuality and Types of Homosexuals (second edition of Novel of an Invert, 1910, Saint-Paul); Invertis et homosexuels / Inverts and Homosexuals (third edition of Novel of an Invert, 1930, Saint-Paul)
Saint-Paul, Yvonne, 187
Sardanapale (Assyrian king), 117, 144
Sarrasine (Balzac), 47n3
Sarrasine, Ernest-Jean (character, Sarrasine), 47n3
School of Military Medicine (Lyon), 149, 150, 151

Schrenck-Notzing, Albert Freiherr von, 176
Schubert, Franz Peter, 88
Scientific Humanitarian Committee, 198n21
secondary sexual characteristics, 172, 180
seduction theories, xxi, 16–17, 114, 170, 183
Sequel to the Confessions of a Homosexual. See Suite d'un roman d'un invert-né / Sequel to the Confessions of a Homosexual (the Italian, 1896)
Sergeant (Italian's first romantic love), xx, xxi, 3, 16–17, 28–30, 63–70, 81, 107–8, 114, 132, 133–34, 137, 183
servants, 126, 180–82; Italian's sexual experiences with, xix, 56–57, 180, 182; in La Curée, 26n79
"sex hormones," xxiii
sexological literature, xviii, 161–64
"sexual inverts," as term, xviii
Sherard, Robert, 35
Simac, Éric (Guichard, Charles), 21, 207, 216
social environment, 162, 164, 205, 206–7, 210, 213
Société Nouvelle, La, 13, 18–19
sodomy, criminalization of, 37, 68n21
Souvenirs de Tunisie et d'Algérie / Recollections of Tunisia and Algeria (Saint-Paul), 155n12, 160, 200
Stonewall, xxiii
Storck, Adrien (publisher), 10–11, 18, 176n10
Strong, Rowland, 36
Suite d'un roman d'un invert-né / Sequel to the Confessions of a Homosexual (the Italian, 1896), xiv, 13–15, 99–137, 205; addendum, 130; as autobiographical text, 7; censored sections, 127–28n51, 131n59, 134,

137n66; discovery of manuscript, 2; other particularities, 139–40; quotes from, xxiii, xxiv, 3–4, 16, 18, 30–31, 143–46; Saint-Paul's conclusions to, 210–13; on Saint-Paul's discretion, 100; Saint-Paul's "remarks" on, 210. See also *The Novel of an Invert* (the Italian, 1888 or 1889)
Symonds, John Addington, 27n82

Taffar (active partner, Northern Africa), 209
Tarde, Gabriel, 176
Tardieu, Ambroise, 6
Tares et poisons: Perversion et perversité sexuelles / *Defects and Poisons: Sexual Perversion and Perversity* (first edition of *Novel of an Invert*, 1896, Saint-Paul), xxi, 9, 12–13, 39, 156, 160–67, 199–200; analysis of Italian's autobiography, xxii–xxiii, 2, 170, 178–85; Italian's reaction to, xxi, xxiii, 2, 5–6, 15–18, 100; methodology of, 166; plan of, 161–65; questionnaire in, 21, 22, 144–45, 169, 170–71n3; survey about homosexuality, 21–22, 144; Zola's preface to, xiii–xv, 2, 9–10, 12, 20–21n64, 25, 32–34, 38, 43–45, 161, 199, 215. *See also* "Inquiry into Sexual Inversion: Questionnaire" (Saint-Paul); *Novel of an Invert, The* (the Italian, 1888 or 1889)
Taylor, Alfred, 101
Ternois, René, 26n81, 27n82
Thèmes psychologiques / *Psychological themes* (Vigot Frères), 14, 215, 217
Thomson, Clive, 30n92
Thorstad, David, 37n118
Three Essays on the Theory of Sexuality (Freud), xviii

Tolstoy, Leo, 37
Toulouse, Édouard, 191
"To Young People" (Zola), 33
Trans Pride parades, xxiii
"transsexual," xx, xxiii
"tribade," as term for female same-sex lover, 22n68
Tribune Médicale, La, 19
"Turk's head," 119, 144

Ulrichs, Karl Heinrich, xx
Uranisme et unisexualité (Raffalovich), 166
"uranists," xx, xxii, 34, 166n33

Vade mecum du médicin légiste / *My Guide to Forensic Medicine* (Lacassagne), 171
Val-de-Grâce School of Applied Medicine and Pharmacology, 154
Vanderbilt, Cornelius, 119
Van Dyck, Anthony, 126
Vautrin (character, *Illusions perdues* / *Lost Illusions*), 85
"verbal type," 157
Verdi, Giuseppe, 88, 103
Verlaine, Paul, 35
vice, premedical model of, xxi
Vigot Frères (publisher), 14, 205, 215
Virgin Mary, 53–54
"visual type," 157

Walsin-Esterhazy, Ferdinand, 36, 201
Wellington, Duke of (Arthur Wellesley), 116, 143–44
Werther (character, *The Sorrows of Young Werther*), 77
White, Nicholas, 28n86
Wilde, Oscar, xxii, 4, 20, 23, 30n91, 101n5, 161, 177; as "occasional invert," 163–64; *Picture of Dorian Gray*, 115, 216; Zola's acquaintance with, 35–36

women: in Islamic world, 209; Italian's aversion to, 31–32, 59, 80, 183, 195; Italian's early feelings toward, 52–54; Italian's friendships with, 25–26, 104–5

World War I, 155

Zambinella (character, *Sarrasine*), 47n3

Zola, Alexandrine, 13, 187

Zola, Émile: as Académie française candidate, 196–98; belief in authenticity of Italian, 5, 179; compassion for homosexuals expressed by, xv, 33–35, 38, 194–95; and Dreyfus Affair, xv, 13, 34, 36, 200–202; effect of Italian's writing on, 2–3, 5, 43, 195–96; gives Italian's letters to Saint-Paul, xiv–xv, 2, 208; homosexuality and plots of novels, 25–28, 48; homosexuals, aversion to, 33n97, 195, 208; influence of Italian on opinions of, 2–3, 32–38; and the Italian's "confessions," 25–32; Italian's view of, 1, 47–48; letters from gay men to, 26–27; letter to Raffalovich, 34–35; medical theories championed by, 34; photograph of, 42; preface to *Tares et poisons*, xiii–xv, 2, 9–10, 12, 20–21n64, 25, 32–34, 38, 43–45, 161, 199, 215; pronatalist views of, 32–33, 34n102, 194n12, 209; reaction to *Tares et poisons*, 12, 199, 208; Saint-Paul, friendship with, 2, 8–10, 13, 27, 187, 193, 199–203; Saint-Paul's "In Memoriam" for, 8, 12, 187–203, 205; Saint-Paul's praise for, 175–77; and Saint-Paul's research on interior language, 151, 156, 159; visual memory and manner of working, 191–92

Zola, Émile—Works: *La Débâcle* / *The Debacle*, 27–30, 191, 193n11; *Fécondité* / *Fecundity*, 8, 194; *La Bête humaine* / *The Beast Within*, 25, 27n82, 193n11; *La Curée* / *The Kill*, xix, 25–26, 48, 76–77, 90, 105n14; *Paris*, 30–32, 38; Rougon-Macquart cycle, 26–27, 48nn4, 5; "To Young People," 33

"Zola and Inversion" (Saint-Paul), 205, 208–9

GPSR Authorized Representative: Easy Access System Europe, Mustamäe tee
50, 10621 Tallinn, Estonia, gpsr.requests@easproject.com

www.ingramcontent.com/pod-product-compliance
Lightning Source LLC
Chambersburg PA
CBHW022045290426
44109CB00014B/984